DIGITAL
BARBARISM

DIGITAL BARBARISM

A Writer's Manifesto

MARK HELPRIN

HARPER

An Imprint of HarperCollins*Publishers*

Parts of this book originally appeared in the *New York Times* (chapter two); *The Claremont Review of Books* (chapter two); and *Forbes ASAP* (chapters one and six).

HarperCollins books may be purchased for educational, business, or sales promotional use. For information, please write: Special Markets Department, HarperCollins Publishers, 10 East 53rd Street, New York, NY 10022.

FIRST EDITION

Designed by Nancy Field

Library of Congress Cataloging-in-Publication Data is available upon request.

ISBN: 978-0-06-173311-6

09 10 11 12 13 OV/RRD 10 9 8 7 6 5 4 3 2 1

I am all for your using machines, but do not let them use you.

Winston Churchill

היום הסורים הולכים ללמוד שהקו בין דמשק לתל-אביב, הולך גם בין תל-אביב לדמשק.

‐ משה דיין

CONTENTS

PREFACE

Even were this book to begin in medias res, which, as an essay-memoir, it does not, a reader might benefit from a brief guide to the terrain it covers. This is especially so because of the chapter titles, which until the chapter is read and despite their subtitles, are for the most part opaque. In a conventional policy book you will not likely find a chapter entitled "Death on a Red Horse," or one, the last, called "Parthian Shot," which refers to an archery maneuver the ancient Parthians accomplished while retiring at full speed on their horses.

But in this book you will. That it is partly a memoir is not least in service of a principle it espouses—that man need not model himself, the way he lives, and by derivation even his arguments, after machines. In its complexity, mystery, intelligence, and beauty, humanity is unexcelled as a masterwork of God and nature. Why then must its qualities be filtered from argument and cleansed from reason as if they were pollutants?

We believe our nature to be, in the literal sense, primitive, lacking in grace and precision, unedifying, something always to be conquered and overcome. But think of the most complex and extraordinary machines mankind has yet devised, take ten of them, and combine their virtues. This tenfold construction—in terms of exactitude, critical timing, coordination, variety, miniaturization, adaptability, calculation, sensory function, integration, and balletic precision down to the atomic level—is neither a billionth as complex nor a billionth as wondrous as the very least among us. The most afflicted, deformed, and unconscious are yet miraculous by virtue of the human nature that, in imitation of the machine, we mistakenly strive to exclude from our deliberations.

It is both strange and unnecessary that we do so, given that the strongest expositions and appeals in history have come from the likes of Dante, Shakespeare, Milton, Montaigne, Lincoln, et al., who made use in them of the astonishments, beauties, and even the imperfections of our mortal nature. Thus, memoir to illustrate argument, so as not to rank the works that we have made above the work that we are.

Necessitated by that, and by a life (my own) spent writing fiction, is an obliqueness uncommon in modern nonfiction, a trust that the reader can, according to Shakespeare's exhortation, "by indirections find directions out." In my view, a reader is not something that pops up in a game of Whack-a-Mole,™ repeatedly to be hit over the head. If you are not Ann Coulter (the love child of two cellophane noodles), or Al Franken (the love child of a bratwurst), you need not be compelled to write like them.

When I was younger I would sometimes write speeches for politicians—except in two cases when the agreement was broken, always from deep anonymity and always without any compensation except a chance to view the horrible workings of government up close in the short space of time between my entry and my dismissal. It was difficult, in fact impossible, to convince most politicians that substance and style, strengthening one another ineffably, are inextricable and organic. With no further addition, the substance of something that is beautifully conveyed magically increases; and something that is conveyed beautifully shines all the more if it is of great substance. Although one always knows when it is there, the superior conjunction of these two elements is invisible. Thus the attraction, other than its encouragement of civilized reticence, of the oblique. And thus its powers.

What follows is an affirmation of human nature versus that of the machine, via a defense of copyright, the rights of authorship, and the indispensability of the individual voice. Of late, these have come under sustained attack. A movement that, whatever its ideological origins, finds its most congenial home and support in the geek city states of

Silicon Valley, has successfully channeled and combined the parochial interests both of giant corporations and legions of resentful adolescents who believe that they have a natural right to whatever they want. It is known informally as the "Creative Commons," and the charitable mask it presents, selfless people contributing their work—software, music, writing—to the common weal, is merely the cover (not much bigger than a postage stamp) for a well organized effort to cut away at intellectual property rights until they disappear.

Its driving force, its Concord and Lexington, was the clash between youth who suddenly found that they could freely obtain all the music by which more than any other group they live, and the record industry, which attempted to stand athwart the flood of new technology and shout stop. The young people and their tools won, and the record industry has been transformed and diminished. In the face of a movement energized by victory in its first battle and enabled by technology that develops almost faster than anyone can assimilate it without altering his mental processes, intellectual property rights do not anymore enjoy the presumption either that they are justified or that they will endure.

That their decline or disappearance would benefit Google, large swaths of the academy, and "content sharers" is without question. But, as in a crowd looting a supermarket, or a junkie taking a hit, the surge of well being would be only temporary, with deprivation following on as the many threatened engines and instruments that supply the things that people would loot began to die. But despite the fact that (as illustrated by price controls or planned economies) when everything is free there is soon precious little or nothing of it, the attack continues apace. In a world turned upside down, indignant violators of copyright, abetted by tax-exempt "public interest" groups, aggressively sue copyright holders. The tide of opinion, driven by the internet, is running now largely against the idea of intellectual property, if only because relentless winds of propaganda state that to defend it is selfish and retrograde. Even at the risk of appearing selfish and retrograde, I defend it here.

The first chapter, "The Acceleration of Tranquility," views without rancor the deeper elements of contention, which at its heart is an argument over different visions of the world. In it, we travel both with a British statesman to Lake Como in 1908, and by the side of a master of the universe in 2028—to illustrate where we are now and where we might choose to be.

The second chapter, "Death on a Red Horse," is trench warfare, blow for blow, involving the foot soldiers and some of the low-ranking officers of the armies drawn up against the rights of authorship and the individual voice. It begins with an incident of childhood and ends with the masterpieces of Brueghel and Bosch. The trench warfare could perhaps have been avoided. To cite Churchill, referring to Count Ciano, Mussolini's foreign minister, why talk to the monkey when the organ grinder is in the room? The answer is that in this case the monkeys are more important than the organ grinders. They are the infantry in which the ideas of their leaders and academic priests are realized. In their numbers, they are beyond the control even of those who work hardest to rile them up. To worry oneself too much with the theories of the professors would be analogous to having fought the Cold War by debating Soviet theoretician Mikhail Suslov in regard to the embarrassing intricacies of Marxist-Leninist thought. Apart from unavoidable forays, it is best to stay out of such thickets. As the manifestation of the theories shows, and as befits the state of the academy at present, the philosophical basis of the war on copyright is crackpot and stillborn. The actual battle is wherever the gnats in their millions crudely make real the musings of the Mad Hatters. We did not win the Cold War by debating Suslov but by making clear our principles, standing by them, and keeping an eye on the Red Army. That is, in a way, what I try to do in this chapter.

In the third chapter, "Notes on Virginia," the battle moves to higher ground and chases the generals of the anti-copyright movement, taking into consideration some of the historical figures they embrace as their own: some accurately, others not. In claiming Macaulay they are quite right—even as he and they are wrong. But they err when they claim Jefferson. I believe that were the third president somehow able to know of this unsolicited association, he would suffer a nausea so immense as to disturb him even in death. That this book was written in sight of Monticello makes honoring Jefferson by separating him from false claimants especially gratifying. The chapter also deals with some of the peculiar "microeconomic" arguments the opponents of copyright present, such as that copyright is a monopoly, a tax, and a gratuitous imposition upon a non-zero-sum game, all of which make it an inhibition to art.

A machine that can print books individually, on demand, quickly, and at little cost is actually at work now. "The Espresso Book Machine," Chapter four, considers the evolution of the technology that has given rise to the movement against copyright, and how the forces and capabilities that ushered-in the battle can almost effortlessly usher it out and make it moot.

But that would not bring an end to the anti-copyright movement, because many of its foot soldiers, its generals, and Macaulay himself, their muse, are exercised less about copyright than about questions of political economy that bear upon their imagined rights and grievances. Not surprisingly, their arguments that are the most current and the least thoughtful rest upon the assumption that a disdain for the right of property confers a species of moral superiority. In the fifth chapter, "Property as a Coefficient of Liberty," I argue that in its effects the right of property transcends the material and is in fact a pillar of ethics and morals. In this chapter, as in others, illustration is not subservient to theory.

Chapter six, "Convergence" (in visiting with my late Oxford tutor, and witnessing the mortally ill Flannery O'Connor besting in a single short story the many erudite volumes of Teilhard de Chardin) is an explanation and refutation of the deeper ideas that animate the electronic culture to its greatest vacancies, although for practical purposes all you really have to know about its philosophical basis is that its adherents believe somewhere deep down that there is such a thing as the free lunch.

The last chapter, "Parthian Shot," is just that, a strike upon departing, a synthesis, reprise, and plea. Then, of course, there are notes, present for accountability in citation, which is as necessary to argument as honesty is to the law, but one needn't dwell on these.

This book is about copyright and a great deal else, because copyright is far more consequential than may be apparent at first blush. But it is hardly the most important thing in life, and I hope my tone and perspective comport with that. Still, copyright is and has been a bulwark of civilization, and as such is a measure of its health, a version of the trite though true example of the canary taken into the coal mine. Arguments about copyright lead quickly to the larger arguments of culture, the habits and degeneration of the mind, property, individuality, rights and responsibilities, and the illusion embraced by modern man that he controls both the world and his fate. The clash over copyright is a perfect armature for a critique of digital barbarism, as it is a case study central not only to the subject but to the passions it engenders and the consequences as they are felt or yet to be felt. Should the foes of copyright prevail, civilization, though it will survive, will, even if they don't know it, change radically and not for the better. And even if as is likely the bulk of them don't know it, their movement—and it is a movement, replete with foundations, interest groups, and funding—is merely part of a much larger offensive of ancient pedigree. It is a perfectly representative and unsurprising manifestation of the collective versus the individual, of central direction versus local decision, of concentrated powers versus dispersed powers, of the large corporation versus the sole proprietor, of the combine versus the artist, of the industrialist versus the smallholder. They may think not, but you cannot claim to protect the little man while simultaneously liquidating the few rights by which he protects himself against the whiplash of the mass. They claim Jefferson because his passions made him a radical, but his passions made him a radical in defense of the yeoman, the small farmer, the individual.

I claim Jefferson because his passions and ultimately his reason were natural and humane—and he wrote like an angel.

Although there is hardly a shortage of anecdote in the pages below, there is a design. We survey the broad prospect ahead, and then enter a bloody and ongoing battle—mole against mole, tooth against tooth, all in darkness and mud—and then rise to float progressively higher and higher, in clear air over a brightly colored landscape, looking out over the forces arrayed in mutual opposition. There we calmly observe, assess, and comment, and then, at the end, descend once again to the fray. For although we may have risen, we are still obligated and responsible to the battle as it is now being fought, for this is our time, and we have no other.

DIGITAL
BARBARISM

CHAPTER 1

THE ACCELERATION
OF TRANQUILITY
Civilization and Velocity

History is in motion as never before, and those moving with it are so caught up that they do not always see its broad outlines. Like soldiers in a rout, they seek objectives that will ruin them rather than the principles that may save them. Who are these soldiers? They are all of us. And what are the principles? If you search the past, hindsight makes them easy to see, but in the brightness of the present they are almost invisible. Still, it is possible to catch a fleeting glimpse of them, even if only as alterations in contrast.

In that spirit, consider the two paradigms that follow, not as you would two debaters, but rather two paintings hanging at opposite ends of a gallery. You are in the middle, bathed in natural light, forced by circumstance to judge their color and attraction.

I.

AUGUST 2028, CALIFORNIA

You are a director of a small firm that supplies algorithms for the detection of damage in and the restoration of molecular memories in organic computation. Previously, you specialized in repairing the cosmic ray degradation of atomic lattices in gallium arsenide nanorobotics, but the greater promise of organic replication and the lure of photon interlinking led you in a new direction.

You raised $2 billion, most of which was devoted to the purchase of computers and laser armature looms for the growth and manipulation of organic compounds. Though your entire company is housed in a single 40,000-square-foot facility and has only ninety employees, it records assets of $9 billion and annual revenues of $32 billion.

All transactions are accomplished through data links—licensing, sales, billing, remittances, collections, investments. A customer can make a purchase, receive your product, and pay you as fast as he can speak orders to his computer. As the algorithms begin immediately to work for him, the money you've earned begins immediately to work for you, in, perhaps, Czech dormitory bonds that compound interest hourly. You go to your headquarters mainly for picnics, and otherwise work at home, as does your wife, who is a partner in a law firm in Chicago, where she has never been. In her study and in yours are floor-to-ceiling screens that produce three-dimensional images so vivid they appear real. Your best friend has grown rich writing the software that serves as your secretary. The preparation of documents is done by voice in another program, and the secretary concentrates instead on planning, accounting, arranging your schedule, and screening what used to be called calls but are now more or less apparitions.

You instruct the secretary to allow your wife's apparition to override all others. She is at a beach in Alaska (it is a bit warmer now), where you will shortly join her. Recently, you and she have quarreled. In virtual sex, in which you both wear corneal lenses that create a perfect illusion of whomever you might want, she discovered that you were entertaining not a commercial prostitutional apparition but an old girlfriend. Hence her early departure for the Aleutians.

But this is August, the season of vacations, and you and she are bound to make up. You will take a twenty-minute suborbital flight to Alaska, where you will spend several days at the beach in a primitive resort with no screens. Still, you have a backup of e-mail despite a recent tightening of your rejection protocols and a new investment in automated-reply software, the chief disadvantage of which is that, when in conversation with other automated-reply software, it tends to get overly enthusiastic. You were dismayed lately when you discovered that it and another ARS were building a golf course in Zimbabwe, but there is software for controlling it, and software for controlling the software that controls this, and so on and so forth.

Though seventy-five messages remain, you must catch your plane, so you instruct your screen to send them to your notebook. You'll take levels one and two coded personal apparitions as well, in the air and even on the winding track that leads to the resort. As you wait in San Francisco International Airport (having floated there in the Chuck Schumer Memorial Gas Blimp) you read in your notebook. There are no bookstores, and there are no books, but in the slim leather-bound portfolio is an uplink that gives you access to everything ever published or logged, and in any format, including the old Google formats prevalent before the government took control of all information during the celebrity crisis. You can call for a dual-language text of Marcus Aurelius, or the latest paper in Malay on particle acceleration. Your reading can be interrupted by the appearance of a friend in your portfolio, a look at the actual weather in Amchitka, a film clip of Lyndon Johnson's inaugural, or, for that matter, anything, summoned by voice, available instantaneously, and billed to your central account.

"Go to my files," you might say as you sit in the airport, "and get everything I've said in the last five years about Descartes. I made a remark with a metaphor about the law, co-ordinates, and virtual prisons. When you get it, put it on the screen in blue. Take a letter to Schultz, and file a copy at home and with the office."

But as you issue, you must also receive, and it never stops. Though the screen of your portfolio is electronically textured to feel like paper and is as buff or white as flax or cotton, you miss the days of your father, when one could hold the paper in one's hands, and things were a little slower. But you can't go back, you can't fall behind, you can't pass up an opportunity, and if you don't respond quickly at all times, someone else will beat you to it, even if you have no idea what *it* is.

The world flows at increasingly faster and faster speeds. You must match them. When you were a child, it was not quite that way. But your father and grandfather did not have the power to make things transparent, to be instantaneously here or there without constraint. Unlike you, they were the prisoners of mundane tasks. They wrote with pens, they did addition, they waited endlessly for things that come to you instantly, they had far less than you do, and they bowed to necessity, as you do not. You love the pace, the giddy, continual acceleration. Though what is new may not be beautiful, it is marvelously compelling. Your life is lived with the kind of excitement that your forbears knew only in battle, and with an ease of which they could only dream.

II.

AUGUST 1908, LAKE COMO, ITALY

You are an English politician, a member of Parliament suffering patiently between cabinet posts, on holiday in Italy. In the two days it has taken to reach your destination you have fallen completely out of touch, although you did manage to pick up a day-old Paris newspaper in Turin. The *Times* will be arriving a week late, as will occasional letters from your colleagues and your business agent. Your answers to most of their queries will arrive in London only slightly before you yourself return at the end of the month.

The letters you receive are in ecru and blue envelopes, with crests, stamps reminiscent of the Italian miniaturists, and, sometimes, varicolored wax seals over ribbon. Even before you read them, the sight of the penmanship gives away the identity of their authors, and may be the cause for comfort, dread, amusement, curiosity, or disgust. And as you read, following the idiosyncratic, expressive, and imprecise swells and dips like a sailor in a small boat on an agitated sea, the hand of your correspondent reinforces his thoughts, as do the caesuras rhythmically arrayed in conjunction with the need to dip the pen.

Some of your younger colleagues use fountain pens, and this you can detect in lines that do not thin, pause, and then fatten with a new load of ink. Occasionally, a typewritten letter will arrive. This you associate with the Telegraph Office, official documents, and things that lean in the direction of function far enough to exclude almost completely the presence of grace—grace not in the religious sense, but in the sense of that which is beautiful and balanced.

You will receive an average of one letter every two days, fifteen or sixteen in all, and will write slightly more than that. You are a very busy man for someone on holiday, and wish that you were not. Half the letters will be related to politics and governance, the other half to family and friendship. An important letter, written by the prime minister eight days before its reception, will elicit from you a one-page response composed over a period of an hour and three-quarters and copied twice before it assumes final form, for revision and so that you may have a record. You will mail it the next morning when you pass the post office during your walk. The prime minister will receive his answer, if he is in London, almost two weeks after his query. He will consider you prompt.

During your holiday you will climb hills, visit chapels, attend half a dozen formal dinners, and read several books, more than a thousand pages all told. If upon reading a classical history you come across a Greek phrase with an unfamiliar word you will have to wait until the library opens, walk there by the lakeside, and consult a Greek lexicon: one and one-half hours. Sitting in your small garden with its view of lake and mountains, you will make notes as you read, and some of these will be incorporated in your letters. Most will languish until your return to London. By the time you look at them in a new season, only a few will seem worthy, and the rest you will gratefully discard.

In August you will hear music seventeen times. Five times it will have been produced by actual musicians, twelve times by a needle tracing the grooves in a cylinder and echoing songs in extremely melancholy imperfection through a flowerlike horn. You will attend the theater once, in Italian, but you will spend hours reading *Henry V* and *The Tempest* (which you read each summer), and several plays by George Bernard Shaw. In your mind's eye you will see the richest scenes and excitements known to man, and your dreams will echo what you've read, in colors like those of gemstones, but diamond-clear, and with accompaniment in sound as if from a symphony orchestra.

Your shoes are entirely of leather, your clothes cotton, silk, linen, and wool. You and your wife hired a rowboat and went to a distant outcropping of granite and pine. No one could be seen, so you stripped down to the cotton and swam in the cold fresh water. Her frock clung to her in a way that awoke in you extremely strong sexual desire (for someone your age), and though you made no mention of it on the bright rock ledge above the lake, later that night your memory of her rising from sparkling water into sparkling sunlight made you lively in a way that was much appreciated.

Indeed, your memory has been trained with lifelong diligence. You know tens of thousands of words in your own language, in Latin, Greek, French, and German. You are haunted by declensions, conjugations, rules, exceptions, and passages that linger many years after the fact. Calculations, too, built your character in that you were forced to work elaborate equations in painstaking and edifying sequences. As in other things, in mathematics you were made to study not only concept but craft. And, yes, in your letter to the prime minister, you repeated—with honorable alteration—a remark you made some time ago regarding Descartes. At first you could not remember it, but then you did, because you had to.

Necessity you find to be your greatest ally, an anchor of stability, a pier off of which, sometimes, you may dive. Discipline and memory are strengths that in their exercise open up worlds. The lack of certain things when you want them makes your desire keener, and you are better rewarded when eventually you get them.

You cannot imagine a life without deprivations, and without the compensatory power of the imagination, moving like a linnet with apparent industry and certain grace, to strengthen the spirit in the face of want. Your son went out to India, and you have neither seen him nor heard his voice for two years. Thus, you have learned once more the perfection of letters, and when you see him again, worlds will have turned, and for the best. It was like that when you were courting your wife. Sometimes you did not see her for weeks or months. It sharpened your desire and deepened your love.

You have learned to enjoy the attribute of patience itself, for it slows time, embraces tranquility, and lets you savor a world in which you are clearly aware that your passage is but a brief candle.

©

I am of course deeply predisposed in favor of the second example, and in my view the vast difference between the two is attributable not to some inexplicable superiority of morals, custom, or culture, but rather to facts and physics, two things that, in judging our happiness, we tend to ignore in favor of an evaporative tangle of abstractions.

Unlike machines, we are confined to an exceedingly narrow range of operations. Though we may marvel at the apparent physical diversity of the human race, it is, given its billions of representatives, astonishingly homogenous. Of these billions, only a handful rise above seven feet. Not a one is or has been over ten feet. And the exceedingly low standard deviation in form is immense compared to that which applies to function. There is no escape from the fact that after a set exposure to radiation; absent a given number of minutes of oxygen; at, above, or below certain temperatures; or subject to a specific G-force, shear, or shock, we will expire. No one will ever run the mile in two minutes, crawl through a Cheerio,™ or memorize the *Encyclopaedia Britannica*.

Because of our physical constraints we require a harmony of the elements that relate to us and of which we are often unaware. The Parthenon is a pleasing building, and Mozart's Fifth Piano Concerto a pleasing work, because each makes use of proportions, relations, and variations that go beyond subjective preference, education, and culture into the realm of universal appeal conditioned by universal human requirements and constraints.

A life lived with these understood, even if vaguely, will have the grace that a life lived unaware of them will lack. When expanding one's powers, as we are in the midst of now doing by many orders of magnitude in the mastery and flow of information, we must always be aware of our natural limitations, mortal requirements, and human preferences. For example, unlike his modern counterpart, the Englishman at Lake Como is graciously limited in time and space. Because the prime minister is in London or at Biarritz, the prime minister cannot sit down with him and discuss. In fact, during his fictional stay, only one of his colleagues visited, and spent several hours on the terrace with him in the bright but cool sunshine. All others were kept away by time and distance.

The man of 2028, on the other hand, is no longer separated from anyone. Any of his acquaintances may step into his study at will—possibly twenty, thirty, forty, or fifty a day. If not constantly interrupted, he is at least continually subject to interruption, and thus the threshold of what is urgent drops commensurately. No matter how urgent or pressing a matter, the prime minister *cannot* sit down with the tranquil politician. No matter how petty a matter, a co-worker *can* appear to the man of 2028. Screening devices or not, the modern paradigm is one of time filled to the brim, of life choked and breathless. Potential has always been the overlord of will, and the man of the first paradigm finds himself distracted and drawn in different directions a hundred times a day, whereas the British statesman is prodded from without only once or twice. And when he wants light at his Italian lake villa he does not throw a switch or speak a command, he lights a candle, and enters into a relation with it—protecting it from a breeze or being overturned, staying within its dim light, alerted by its flickering of changes or movements, aware of its scent, warmed by its flame, conscious of its burning down.

Were we gods, we might be able to live well without rest and contemplation, but we are not and we cannot. Whereas our physical capacities are limited, those of the machine are virtually unlimited by comparison. As the capabilities of the machine are extended, we can use it—we imagine—to supplement our own in ways that will not strain our humanity. Had we no appetite or sin, this might be true, but our desires tend to lead us to excess, and as the digital revolution has quickly progressed we have not had time to develop the protocols, manners, discipline, and ethics adequate for protecting us from our newly augmented powers. In fact, as is the subject of the first half of this book, we often rush mercilessly and barbarically to abolish them.

The history of the last hundred years has been, as much as anything else, the process of encoding information: at first analog, in photographic emulsions, physical and magnetic patterns in needle grooves or on tapes, waves in packets blurted into the atmosphere, or in the action of x-rays recording paths of varying difficulty through tissues of various densities on plates of constant sensitivity. With binary coding, electrons as messengers, and the hard-fought mathematical adaptation necessary for control, we can now do almost everything in regard to information. We may, for example, look through billions of pages in an instant, or process and match data fast enough so that a cruise missile can make a "mental" picture of the terrain it overflies almost as impressive as that of an eagle.

And because potential has always been the overlord of will, and as the new machines hunger for denser floods of data, images have gradually displaced words. The capacious, swelling streams of information have brought little change in quality and vast overflows of quantity. In this they are comparable to the ornamental explosions of the baroque, when a corresponding richness of resource found its outlet mainly in overdecorating the leaner body of a previous age.

All the king's horses and all the king's men of multimedia cannot improve upon a single line of Yeats. One does not need transistors, clean alternating current, spring-loaded keys, and ten-million-hour "programs" for writing a note or a love letter—and yet this is how we now write notes and love letters, going even to the extreme of doing so on complicated electronic pads that though they tediously strain to imitate a sheet of paper fail for want of simplicity.

I am not decrying the digital revolution per se, or recommending for you and your children the cold water, wood fires, and Latin declensions of my brick-and-iron childhood. I have always understood that the heart of Western civilization is not the abdication of powers but rather meeting the challenge of their use. And, of course, it would take a person of less than doltish imagination not to be attracted by the wonders and aware of the benefits of all this new stuff.

The British statesman of the second paradigm might well have lost a son or daughter to a disease that could have been detected early and with precision by the digital diagnostic techniques of modern medicine. The *Titanic*, four years in the future, might not have gone down—with him aboard, perhaps—had real-time thermal maps of the North Atlantic been available to its captain. And so on. You know the litany, because you are bombarded by it daily.

The impossibility of abdication is also due to the necessity of racing the genie after it has exited the bottle. Although antediluvian nuclear protestors have not, apparently, even a clue, they are on the wrong track. Nuclear weapons are now small enough, reliable enough, simulable enough, and widespread enough to be a rather mundane constant in calculations of the military balance (at least in regard to the major powers). The guaranteed action and volatility is in command, control, communications, intelligence, and guidance. Digitally dependent advances will enable submunitions scattered in great number over a future battlefield to hide, wait, seek, fight, and maneuver. For example, rather than a platoon of tank-killing infantry, a flight of submunitions will not long from now be able to land with little detection far behind enemy lines, where it will hide in the treetops or the brush and await patiently for as long as required the approach of an appropriate enemy target, such as a tank, which it will then dutifully pursue, engage, and destroy, its reflexes as fast as light.

No matter what arms agreements come into being, with the passage of each day a first nuclear strike becomes more and more feasible. The possibility of real-time terminal guidance as a gift from satellites to maneuverable reentry vehicles makes any kind of mobile deterrent just a temporary expedient. Even submarines, nuclear stability's ace-in-the-hole, will no longer be secure bastions for nuclear weapons, as thermal and radar imaging from satellites pick up surface perturbations upwelling from their undersea tracks, and as the panoply of antisubmarine warfare is resurrected (as it will be with the rise of China's submarine fleet), refined, empowered, sensitized, and its weaponry mounted on ballistic missiles that will be able to reach any area of ocean within minutes.

It is also possible that in some war of the not-so-distant future a combatant will electronically seize control of enemy command structures and direct his opponent's arsenal onto his opponent. Eventually, all battles will be entirely computational. The "arms competition" of this sort has already begun. To step out of it at this point would be to lose it, and, with it, everything else.

©

The attraction is strong, the need is real, the marvels truly marvelous, and there is no going back. The speed with which all is taking place is almost a self-organizing principle. Like many changes in history, it seems to have its own internal logic, pulling everything after it. Why then do we need an ethos, a set of principles, and an etiquette specifically fashioned for the rest of a revolution that will follow with stunning force the mere prologue through which we are now living?

One always needs such things, but more so now as we leave the age of brick and iron. The age of brick and iron, shock as it may have been to Wordsworth, was friendlier to mankind than is the digital age, more appropriate to the natural pace set by the beating of the human heart, more apprehensible in texture to the hand, better suited in color to the eye, and, in view of human frailty, more forgiving in its inertial stillness.

Put quite simply, the life of the British statesman was superior because he was allowed rest and reflection, his contemplation could seek its own level, and his tranquility was unaccelerated. While he was, in his time, a member of a privileged class unburdened by many practical necessities, today most Americans have similar resources and freedoms, and yet they, like their contemporaries in even the most exalted positions, have chosen a different standard, closer to that of the first paradigm.

The life of the exemplary statesman, then dependent upon a large staff of underpaid servants, and children working in mines and mills (if not in Lancashire, then certainly in India), is now available to almost anyone and without the attendant injustices. Even if in one's working hours one does not sit in the Cabinet Room at No. 10 Downing Street, one can have a quiet refuge, dignified dress, paper, a fountain pen, books, postage, Mozart with astonishing fidelity and ease, an excellent diet, much time to oneself, the opportunity to travel, a few nice pieces of furniture and decoration, medical care far beyond what the British states-man might have dreamed of, and a single-malt scotch in a crystal glass, for less than the average middle-class income. If you think not, then add up the prices and see how it is that people with a strong sense of what they want, need, and do not require can live like kings of a sort if they exhibit the appropriate self-restraint.

Requisite, I believe, for correcting the first paradigm until it approx-imates the second, and bringing to the second (without jeopardizing it) the excitements and benefits of the first, are the discipline, values, and clarity of vision that tend to flourish as we grapple with necessity and austerity, and tend to disappear when by virtue of our ingenuity we float free of them.

The law itself can be mobilized to protect the privacy and dignity of the individual according to the original constitutional standard of the Founders and what they might expect. Even now, that standard has been violated enough to make inroads on enlightened democracy, which depends first and foremost upon the sanctity of individual rights. As if they could foresee the unforeseeable, the Founders laid down principles that have served to prevent the transformation of the individual to a mere manipulable quantity, of citizen to subject. It does not matter what convenience is sacrificed in pursuit of this. Convenience is, finally, noth-ing, even destructive. The standard must be restored, as it is slipping too fast. Bluntly, there are practices and procedures that, except judiciously and carefully maintained in war, legislation must end, and databases now extant that it must destroy, in a deliberate and protective step back. Revolutions and revolutionaries tear down walls. Though some walls are an affront to human dignity, others protect it. I do not want my life history in the hands of either J. Edgar Hoover or Walt Disney, thank you very much.

Quite apart from the reach of the law is the voluntary reformation of education. A substantial proportion of this country's academic ener-gies is swallowed up in the study of off-the-shelf software. Terrified lest their children be computer illiterate, lemming parents have pushed the schools into a computer frenzy in which students spend years learning to use tools that assemble pieces of what others have done, and relieve the students of the necessity of learning anything other than manipulation. You can't teach someone how to cook by showing him how to put a frozen dinner in a microwave oven. The system is much like *Sesame Street*, which, instead of waiting until a child is five and teaching him to count in an afternoon, devotes thousands of hours drumming it into him during his undeveloped infancy. But while numbers will remain, fifth graders will, when they get to graduate school, have no contact with current computer programs and applications. The "teaching" of computer in the schools may be likened to a business academy in the twenties founded for the purpose of teaching the telephone: "When you hear the bell, pick up the receiver, place it thusly near your face, and say 'Hello?'"

Basic computer literacy is a self-taught subject requiring no more than a few days. Ordinary literacy, however, requires twenty years or more, and that is only a beginning. And yet the schools are making of these two—unrelated—things a vast and embarrassing spoonerism. In the schools, computers should be tools for the limited study of other subjects, not (other than in electrical engineering and applied math) a subject in themselves. The masters of the digital world will be not today's students who will have spent their high school years learning various applications but those who will guide the future of computation at the molecular and atomic levels where they will find it when they are adults, having devoted hard study to physics, chemistry, and mathematics.

In the same vein, but with almost biblical implications, is the necessity of making certain distinctions. Most multimedia is appalling for several reasons. It endeavors to do the integrative work that used to be the province of the intellect, and that, if it is not in fact accomplished by the intellect, is of absolutely no value. It fails to distinguish between entertainment and education, image and fact. It integrates promiscuously, blurring in the addled minds that it has addled the differences between things that are different. It removes as far as it possibly can the element of labor from learning, which is comparable, in my view, to making a world without gravity, drinking a milk shake without milk, or living in an iron lung.

Whenever man opens a new window of power he imagines that he can do without the careful separations, distinctions, and determinations mandated by the facts of his existence and his mortal limitations. And whenever he worships at the feet of modernity he suffers a terrible degradation that casts him back even as he imagines himself hurtling forward.

Put simply, I want and will pay for the *OED* on my computer, I want everything in the Library of Congress (and will pay for copyrighted material), I want great search engines, fuzzy logic, and programs that do statistical analysis, but I do not want my contact with my fellow man to proceed mainly through his imagination—no matter how precise—in the fluorescence behind a glass plate. An example I might cite is that if you sail you really need wind and water: the idea and depiction of them are not sufficient. So with human presence: reality and actuality are necessities.

Whereas the Englishman had the exquisite memory of his wife emerging in wet cotton from the cold water of the lake into the Alpine sunshine, and whereas his relations with her must be based on subtlety and restraint, the man of 2028 on his way to the Alaskan beach will be able to graft by virtual reality any image he pleases onto the tactile base of his wife's body. Variants of this have been in the dreams of men at least since Leda, and Pygmalion, and sex is undoubtedly responsible for much of the momentum of virtual reality, as is the apparent joy of pretending to kill large numbers of people in what are called games. In previous eras this would have been considered mental illness.

Many varieties of sensual manipulation will come to pass, and will be promoted as ways to refresh our existence, but they will, if they are embraced, go far in destroying it. The saving graces and the fragile institutions of humanity depend upon our humanity itself, which in turn depends absolutely upon the discipline or rejection of certain appetites. We have many a resolution that separates us from the other animals, many a custom, practice, tradition, and taboo, and if we do away with these in the pursuit of power, the worship of reason, or the imitation of time-and-space-flouting divinity, we will become a portion for foxes.

The revolution quietly about us is, if not good, yet wondrous, powerful, and great, and has hardly begun. But we have not brought to it the discipline, anticipation, or clarity it demands. We have been so enthusiastic in our welcome as to be obsequious—to machines. Some of us have become arrogant and careless, and many at the forefront of revolution lack any guiding principles whatsoever or even the urge to seek them. In this, of course, we are not alone. Nor are we the first. But there is no question that this revolution must be fitted to the needs and limitations of man, with his delicacy, dignity, and mortality always in mind. Tranquility, having been accelerated, must be slowed.

But rather than being slowed, it is rapidly being displaced by an opposite clothed in barbarism. The changes that have come in train with the digital revolution have not been modulated, buffered, and adapted as once they would have been. Instead, their partisans have entered the citadel of culture disruptively. They would change the language, purposefully degrading and mocking its forms. They would evince enormous hostility to books—to paper and ink, really, including even mail—setting them back further than did the burning of the library at Alexandria (if, indeed, that really happened). Anyone who in the last twenty years or so has had children in school must be aware of the incontrovertible desire to replace books with "media," has heard or read of some children's hostility to books and preference for things that jump around and make noise on a computer screen, and has seen the libraries empty of readers, most of whom now congregate around banks of computers and nearby espresso machines.

Barbarism in language consists of more than just the slighting of its forms and traditions with deliberate abandon. Technical computerese is so poorly defined and deliberately obscure (in the manner of secret words that get you admitted to the tree house) as to be infuriating to any-one used to actual syntax. It is as deliberately prolix as academic prose, and a not-so-distant cousin to the financial products that, built high upon nothing, guarantee inevitable collapse. Here the destruction is not financial but intellectual and spiritual. The abandonment of grammar, capitalization, punctuation, spelling, et cetera, and the substitution for these things of either nothing or of idiotic and inexpressive pictograms, jargon, and expletives, is often not a choice but an artifact of a decadent and dysfunctional educational system. The worst violations, however, come not from neglect but from attention—littering the language with revisions that almost always incline away from both the natural world and human nature: that is, a departure from what is real in favor of an artificial construct of some sort, an idea rather than an actuality. We no longer have husbands or wives but "life partners." We no longer fall in love, we have a relationship, and not with a girl or a boy or a man or a woman but with a "significant other." A question pertaining to one sex or another is now an "issue" "relevant" to one "gender" or another. And we do not drink water but, rather, in imitation of laboratory instructions or machine manuals, "hydrate" ourselves. Language, for its beauty, has as its compass the heart. In imitation of machine-speak—as far from the root and magnificence of language as it is possible to get without just grunting—this has been left behind to die.

Why don't the worthy orators come as usual
to make their speeches, to have their say?
Because the barbarians are to arrive today.[1]

In the poem, the barbarians do not arrive, and the people, who have already surrendered, are regretful that they don't.

Even if the digital barbarians don't rape, pillage, and burn cities, and do not dress in skins (God forbid) or bristle with glaring weapons (God forbid), they do often follow a style of dress and comportment that they call "edgy," and that is nothing if not deliberately provocative, aggressive, and nihilistic—a continuous declaration of irony. That they know the world is horrible and purposeless proves that they are wise. The vast bulk of this army may be just a bunch of wacked-out muppets led by little professors in glasses, but they will do more damage to the underpinnings of civilization than half a million Visigoths smashing up the rotted, burning cities of Rome—because there are so many of them; they are so pervasive and penetrant; their powers are amplified by the machines to which they have given themselves; and they go so steadily and quietly about their business, almost unnoticed, like termites in the wood before an apparently solid house collapses into a foamy heap.

Often overlooked is that though the barbarians of ancient times were not cultivated, in almost every case they had fastened upon one or more technical innovations that enabled them to defeat the superior civilizations they then were able to sack. The Huns and Scythians had revolutionary tactics, the Parthians their fleeing shots, the Mongols their special bows and their techniques of mobility. Even Hannibal, not quite a barbarian except perhaps in the Roman view, and ultimately unsuccessful, had his elephants. Small but powerful technologies were sometimes the ruin of older civilizations that failed to recognize them. And now we have, more powerful than any engine, bow, or gun, the digital and all it brings.

We worship, nationwide, worldwide, in front of its hundreds of millions of altars. Even the tiniest of these, that fit in our ears or that we can barely operate with our thumbs, easily exercise their discipline over us. We sit, immobile, staring, waiting for the screen to fill, waiting for responses that channel our own. No longer the curved line, the flowing ink, but each letter in a box of sorts (a key), and always the same on the screen in its consistent font. The machine has its laws, and will accuse us of committing an "illegal operation," arresting our activity until we submit—"OK?"—with no option to disagree. It requires your consent, but you cannot refuse your consent: not exactly an encouraging political model. Over the years, it is gathering and keeping day by day vast amounts of intelligence that mostly we give it without thinking or protest even when we know of the intrusion. Whole generations have become accustomed to such violations and freely compromise their privacy as if there were no such thing. (This is not new. Charles de Gaulle, in 1934:"Machines of precision and speed, all beautifully geared and handled by experts, cannot fail to excite the interest of the young. It will give them, besides, that kind of prestige which machinery confers upon those who serve it."[2]) The machine knows about us even what we ourselves do not—how many lemons we buy a year, what channels we linger on and for how long, the intensity of our language in the letters we write, the patterns of our comings and goings, the clues to our sentiments, how much money we have, our blood chemistry, what we spend, to whom we speak and when.

More and more, the machine chooses among the preprogrammed options it presents to us, correcting our grammar (so often incorrectly) "as we go," informing us when we write *Potemkin* that we really mean *pumpkin*,"reading" our mail, and taking up our time with false promises to save it. The machine has a destination, if not of its choosing then not of ours either, and we are becoming secondary to it, obedient expediters and facilitators. We model ourselves after it, willingly or unconsciously, and in so doing we have left much behind of which we should never have let go, and lost very quickly much of what best defines our culture and even our intrinsic nature. This is the source of the barbarism that comes in a steady, relentless flood.

But there is not an ounce or an iota of it that cannot be made to disappear simply by an act of will—the will to do without, the will to have less, the refusal to model human nature after the mechanical. Does such willingness exist? How shall we educate ourselves? Upon what shall we model ourselves? Who is servant, and who is master?

CHAPTER 2

DEATH ON A RED HORSE

*The First Targets of the Barbarians Are
Copyright and the Individual Voice*

My third-grade classroom was on the second floor of a rustic shingled building within the grounds of what once had been a great estate. In the mid-fifties the school still reverberated with the presence of Woodrow Wilson, Paderewski, Isadora Duncan, and other visiting notables in an age that had been put to rest by the war. Though beset with nuclear anxiety, the nation was at once pre-eminent and at peace, the long chain of proxy wars that would unfold across the century's second half had just begun, and we were eight years old.

Our teacher, who has been described by others, who did not know her quite as well as I did, as a "stern lieutenant," directed frequent outbursts of rage against the uncomprehending children in her charge. I remember the tightly focused thunder in the woman's voice, and her face reddening with the ferocity of a Luther. She was not entirely of one complexion. Sometimes she would take me aside, sit me down, and then put into beautiful primary-school-teacher's longhand pages and pages of stories that she encouraged me to dictate. Though I was terrified of her, she was the only secretary I've ever had. Nonetheless, because of a habit of defiance inconvenient for an eight-year-old, I was anything but her favorite. (I was never anyone's favorite. Had I been, you would not be reading this.) She punished me in ways both traditional and innovative, and I got quite used to her slapping me around and picking me up by the ears: they are still attached to my head because I never failed to grasp the hands that lifted them (and neither would you). My epiphany came when, sick of my recidivist insolence, she picked me up and threw me bodily into the book-storage closet. A pile of new books, shiny and congruent, broke my fall and did not stop falling until the sound, momentous and defining for all who are imprisoned, of a latch falling and a bolt moving into a strike, after which came a silence that in memory seems to have been, above all, clear. There I was, staring up at blue sky and swollen white clouds progressing past a high rectangular window. Much later, she opened the door and asked if I were sorry. As I had nothing to be sorry for and said so, my imprisonment was elongated.

I came to know that closet fairly well, and to read most of the books in it, many of which were obsolescent elementary-school texts from the twenties and thirties. But I could have done without the books entirely, because I took my sustenance from the window, and could stare at it as long as necessary, particularly when it brought the entertainment of clouds. This was not new to me. As a smaller child, I was left in my room on Central Park West for most of the day with nothing but the window. My father spent half his time in London and my mother had a career to which she attended without guilt after her psychoanalyst (as she called him, though he was probably a psychotherapist) told her that the important thing was not the quantity of time spent with me but its quality. He may have been the first person actually to have said this, which would be quite a distinction.

These conditions, among others, may have had something to do with the development of a "literary" sensibility (something of which, though I have never claimed it, I have often been accused). The essence of this is—in listening to one's own heart and defending what one loves—a devotion to things in their truth, which in turn makes it impossible to bend to currents of fashion or opinion. As much as it is joyous and its own reward, it also wears you down. Had things been different I might have become—and I may have been happy being—a dentist, a croupier, or an investment banker, but now the only thing for which I am fit (or, according to some obviously insane critics, not) is to sit alone and write things down on paper. What else might anyone have expected of a seventeen-year-old who chose to stay immobile on the platform of a Swiss railroad station for as many hours as he had years, and there remain happy and content? Or of a college student at twenty, whose idea of seeing Rome was to settle down by a fountain and watch the stream of water for six unbroken hours? The normal sociality that people enjoy, I find to be torture so exquisite that I sometimes imagine my heart will burst. I dug in my heels when I was two, and other than when required to professionally, I have never been to a party—except once when I slipped in the tenth grade, and, finding myself dancing with a girl literally from Pleasantville, was so euphoric that I had to leave lest I become normal.

Except as part of work (or in a crisis such as a battle, earthquake, or fire), in the presence of more than two people who are not members of my immediate family I slowly begin to disintegrate. I don't like that, and what I like even less is when some people put me in such a position despite knowing from experience that I can't tolerate it. Nonetheless, they do it repeatedly and enjoy and condemn my failure, while they are quite willing to make allowance for thieves, murderers, and publishers. They will with weepy compassion forgive someone who beats them silly or kills for cigarettes, but they will not forgive me when all I want is not to be in the room.

When, however, you are compelled by the laws of the state to attend school, enter the army, or do jury duty, you must be in the room. And as you age, stronger compulsions come into play. Unless you are an heir or heiress you have to make a living, and even in the solitary professions times will arise when you must depart from your isolation and deal with people in numbers. When you have children, you must support them.

You cannot shrink from this, or from teacher conferences or birthday parties. If you are a writer, you more or less have to go on book tours. Even Margaret Atwood, a woman who when unharried knows no bounds in the ferocity of conviction, and yet is so shy that she has actually invented a robot through which she speaks at book events, must nonetheless be virtually present and answer questions—"Do you write with a pencil or a pen?" "Who are your favorite authors?" "Will you write my book about the affair between Golda Meir and Frank Sinatra if I give you twenty-five percent?" There is no escaping the world. This is not to be lamented, in that if you escape the world and its friction you escape education. And you can't do that, or at least you shouldn't, because, as much more than half the world is eager to tell you as soon as you manifest the signs of your discomfort, no man is an island. (To which you can reply, "But what about Arnold Taubman? He was Madagascar.")

Why not soldier on as not-an-island for most of your life, and then, at some blessed point after your obligations have been met and duties fulfilled, finally allow the waters to rush in and dissolve the feeble causeways to the mainland that for decades you have maintained at the cost of a broken heart? I had thought that when I reached sixty (years, not miles per hour, although it did take about six seconds to get there) I might be able to make a partial retreat and exit the controversies in which I have been involved (and which, when the heat of battle maneuvered me into positions I would otherwise have rejected, have pulled me at times beyond where I wanted to go) to spend my last years as I had spent my first: alone except for family, and a few friends one or two at a time; writing descriptively and reflectively rather than combatively; with no thought to reception, position, or victory or defeat in struggles that soon will fade. Not retirement, but a shift in focus to that which is gentle, beautiful, and eternal.

Politicians, businessmen, and actresses there are who struggle mightily to hold back the thick curtains of age. They are so close to the falls of oblivion that they can hear the water's white sound, and yet they are all-consumed in a fight for position in a boat that is soon to be launched into a world with neither gravity nor time. They will tell you that they work for a cause higher than themselves, but, depending upon who they are, you can quickly separate this chaff from the wheat and know that the cause they espouse is merely the disposable costume of their lust for power, or a distraction from the emptiness they dare not confront after a life in the absence of reflection.

I thought that by not being a politician or actor, and with a deep hunger for privacy, I would have a chance to steer my life into tranquility. This was fundamentally and particularly a mistake. Fundamentally, because neither nature nor human society is tranquil. They do have, however, improbable moments that give rise to villages in war zones that sow and reap as passing armies leave them untouched; centenarians who have had good lives, a minimum of pain, and children who love and will outlive them; healthy billionaires; statesmen who save the West; women who are beautiful into their nineties; skiers who never have had a fall; speedy tortoises; and people born without envy.

But these are rare. Naturally, most everything alive, and even almost everything that isn't, is subject to change, shock, assault, and cycles of alternation. A rock formation deep within the earth may seem eternally solid, but it was once molten, once a gas, once cosmic dust, and once pure and inexplicable energy, as eventually it will be again. And as for us, the doorbell rings, the snowstorm comes, the package arrives, the crops dry up, children are born, affections arise or are alienated, marauders traipse across horizons more or less distant, and we grow old until no matter what tranquility we have managed to achieve eventually the prospect of lifting a glass to our lips becomes as threatening and difficult as climbing the north face of the Eiger.

There is no escaping into permanent tranquility similar to what pacifists mistakenly imagine to be permanent peace, but only managing the ebb and flow of continually active force. Still, though it is not possible to stop the waves, one can, in riding them masterfully, render them relatively motionless. This is the job of statesmen in ushering their countries through the high waters of history, of parents in bringing up children, and of people in living their lives. You can have tranquility only sometimes and only up to a point: beyond that is the grave. And of course if you are even slightly empathetic you can never be at rest. The pain and suffering of the world is so widespread and exquisite that it makes the peace for which we may long only an illusion.

Nonetheless, and knowing that I would not be able to do what I wanted to do, I wanted to do it, and I tried. It was not just one thing, but many: forgoing various opportunities; not reading from cover to cover every journal that arrives; now and then allowing the grass to grow too high; going to bed early; welcoming silence. In those efforts at management, not surprisingly, I met many forms of resistance.

My relations with the *New York Times*, once excellent and warm, have of late—that is, in the last twenty-five years—been inexcellent and cold, both from differences of opinion and imperfections in conduct, my own included. But as one of the most wonderful things in this life is the lion lying down with the lamb (or, as some small children believe, the lamp), I was pleased when in the spring of 2007 the *Times*, after a long hiatus but in the most friendly manner, asked me to write an op-ed piece. Having resolved to live less combatively in my remaining years, I thought, Why raise fur when it has been rubbed up against me so kindly? At least to begin with, I would ease in without controversy, even if it meant abandoning longstanding habits. The next time, perhaps, I would formulate something that would generate hundreds of bilious letters, but not now.

I searched my memory and notes for something innocuous. I would choose a topic close to my heart but distant from the fire of partisanship, of which I remain thoroughly sick. Copyright! Except for Hollywood lawyers, who are not even human, who thinks about copyrights other than the few who hold them? Who really cares, or knows even the most elemental facts? I worried only about putting my audience to sleep, and thought of my potential readers as stones skipping unconsciously over a lake, my copyright piece being the lake. Still, this was perfectly consonant with my new life, and a step on the inevitable road to oblivion: gradual, tranquil, gentle, and somnolent. Though I regretted that only one or two people might notice, at least I was sure that I could not possibly anger anyone.

And yet it was a subject I could not dismiss if only because it had engaged a passion fueled by the existence of an inequity. Years before, in making my will, I had to accept that the bulk of what I would leave to my children, the product of a lifetime's work, would after not too long a time simply expire and flow from their hands into the hands of others. Had I built a business, a farm, or a law firm instead of a series of copyrights, this would not be so. It seemed, as simply as I can put it, unfair.

"What if," asked the piece, which, in the form that follows, would run also in the *Claremont Review of Books*, "after you had paid the taxes on earnings with which you built a house, sales taxes on the materials, real estate taxes during its life, and inheritance taxes at your death, the state would eventually commandeer it entirely? This does not happen in our society . . . to houses. Or to businesses. Were you to have ushered through the many gates of taxation a flour mill, travel agency, or newspaper, they would not suffer total confiscation."

Here, I was inexact. Nothing is confiscated, but after it is, in fact, commandeered by the government, which moves it from the state of being protected to the state of being without protection, it is thrown open to the use of all. This is not the case with "many classes of assets abstract or concrete, from land to Treasury bills to stocks, paintings, and much else; once the state has dipped its enormous beak into the stream of your wealth and possessions they are allowed to flow from one generation to the next. Though they may be divided and diminished by inflation, imperfect investment, a proliferation of descendants, and the government taking its share, they are not simply expropriated.

"That is, unless you own a copyright. Were I to write the great American novel tomorrow (again?), seventy years from my death the rights to it, though taxed at inheritance, would be stripped from my children and grandchildren. To the objection that this provision strikes malefactors of great wealth, one might ask, first, where the inheritors of Sylvia Plath berth their 200-foot yachts. And, second, why, when such a stiff penalty is not applied to the owners of Rockefeller Center or Wal-Mart, it is brought to bear against legions of harmless drudges who other than a handful of literary plutocrats (manufacturers, really) are destined by the nature of things to be no more financially secure than a seal in the Central Park Zoo."

This was not, however, merely a rhetorical question: "The answer is that the Constitution states unambiguously that Congress shall have the power 'To promote the Progress of Science and useful Arts, by securing *for limited times* to Authors and Inventors the exclusive Right to their respective Writings and Discoveries.' The italics are mine, the capitalization James Madison's.

"It is, then, for the public good. But it might also be for the public good were Congress to allow the enslavement of foreign captives and their descendants (this was tried), the seizure of Bill Gates's bankbook, or the ruthless suppression of Alec Baldwin. You can always make a case for the public interest if you are willing to exclude from common equity those whose rights you seek to abridge. But we don't operate that way, mostly."

I then went on to point out, in some detail, how freeing a work into the public domain offers only a fractional economic advantage to the purchaser and the publisher, while depriving of any interest in it whatsoever both its author and his heirs; and next dealt with the argument that, as the copyright holder is dependent entirely upon the government for his exclusivity of right, does not then the government's giveth support its taketh?

"By that logic, should the classes of property not subject to total confiscation therefore be denied the protection of regulatory agencies, courts, police, and the law itself lest they be subject to expropriation as payment for the considerable and necessary protections they too enjoy? Should automobile manufacturers be nationalized after 70 years because they depend on publicly financed roads? Should Goldman Sachs be impounded because of the existence of the SEC?"

Why would the Framers, whose political genius has never been exceeded, have countenanced such an unfair exception? After all, "Jefferson objected that ideas are, 'like fire, expansible over all space, without lessening their density at any point, and, like the air in which we breathe, move, and have our physical being, incapable of confinement or exclusive appropriation.' But ideas are immaterial to the question of copyright. Mozart and Neil Diamond may have begun with the same idea, but that a work of art is more than an idea is confirmed by the difference between the *"Soave sia il vento"* and "Kentucky Woman." We have different words for art and idea because they are two different things. The flow and proportion of the elements of a work of art, its subtle engineering, even its surface glosses, combine substance and style indistinguishably in a creation for which the right of property is natural and becoming."

In Jefferson's era 95 percent of the population drew its living from the land. "Writers and inventors were largely those who obtained their sustenance from their patrimony or their mills; their writings or improvements to craft were secondary. No one except perhaps Hamilton or Franklin might have imagined that services and intellectual property would become primary fields of endeavor and the chief engines of the economy. Now these are, and it is no more rational to deny them equal status than it would have been to confiscate farms, ropewalks, and other forms of property in the eighteenth century."

Nonetheless, one cannot ignore "the express order of the Constitution, long imprinted without catastrophe upon the fabric of our history. But given the grace of the Constitution it is not surprising to find the remedy within it, in the very words that prohibit the holding of patents or copyrights in perpetuity: *for limited times.*"

Here was the answer, brilliant, anticipatory, and judicious. "Congress is free to extend at will the term of copyright. It last did so in 1998, and should do so again, as far as it can throw. Would it not be just and fair for those who try to extract a living from the uncertain arts of writing and composing to be freed from a form of confiscation not visited upon anyone else? The answer is obvious, and transcends even justice. No good case exists for the inequality of real and intellectual property, because no good case can exist for treating with special disfavor the work of the spirit and the mind."[3]

This was a simple and unambitious argument for the extension of the term of copyright based upon a more equitable, though hardly absolute, reconciliation of diverging treatments of different forms of property. There is obviously a public interest in the expiration of copyright, but there is also a public interest in copyright itself, and thus potentially in its extension. The question is one of degree. Although I did not state it directly (not being in the habit of negotiating with myself), my hope was that Congress, having not long ago extended the term so that in most cases it might benefit the original copyright holder's children throughout most of their lives, would consider grandchildren as well, and perhaps even great-grandchildren, inasmuch as most owners of other forms of property are allowed theoretically to extend their bequests into eternity. Were I to die next week, one of my own children's children born ten years from now would see the inherited copyright pass into the public domain when she reached my age, whereas the hypothetical grandchild of my hypothetical neighbor, whose legacy was not a bunch of copyrights but, for example, a hotel, could be confident that it would remain in her possession. One may quarrel with the idea or effects of inheritance, but whatever the final disposition it is immaterial to the imbalance here addressed.

When the piece was published, it appeared to have been one of those ghostly columns that pass entirely without notice and in which no one even wraps fish. I filed it and went on to the next thing. But as the state of Virginia passed from a Martian-ice-cap spring to a boiling Venusian May, and as I worried about the first cutting of the hay, an electronic storm began to take shape. Because I look at a computer screen as little as possible, I was unaware of the tempest as it mounted. Within ten days or so, the copyright article had generated (as chronicled by Google) what Churchill called "million-tongued propaganda."[4] In this case, three-quarters of a million "hits," not a single one of which, in my wide sampling, was favorable. And to say that they were unfavorable would be like saying that someone had a touch of Ebola fever. Their language was angry, inflammatory, imprecise, and, shall we say—"Screw you, Helprin!"[5]—sometimes immoderate, although to their credit not as violent, obscene, and vengeful as it often is on the internet in regard to purely political questions, in which they so often confirm the observation of the First Earl of Oxford that "hatred, the more groundless and unreasonable it is, the more durable and violent it most times proves."[6] When a million tongues suddenly wag in unison happy with indignation and the joy of attack, the very nature of this tends to impeach whatever cause they espouse. A mob may be right, but, even when it is, it discredits that right.

Unlike the troublesome and annoying classical nudniks of the past, the electronic nudnik is sheltered by anonymity, his acts amplified by an almost inconceivable multiplication and instantaneousness of transmission. This new nudnik is therefore tempted to exchange his previous protective innocence (think Alfred E. Neuman) for a certain sinister, angry, off-the-rails quality (think the Unabomber) which is perhaps to be expected from the kind of person who has spent forty thousand hours reflexively committing video-game mass murder and then encounters an argument with which he finds himself in disagreement.

It is not merely training that has unleashed this keypeck ferocity, but also changes in certain fundamental conditions. In the electronic media's dissolution of barriers—time, space, isolation—and in the vast expansion of received (or, at least, receivable) information, we have become in proportion infinitely smaller. Were you to have lived next door to Ethan Frome in Starkfield, Massachusetts, at the turn of the last century you would have been one of only a few hundred. Every time a ferry sank in the Philippines or a bank was robbed in Kansas or Italy, you would not know, as you do today. Or if you did, the knowledge would come later, briefly, controllably, in a small printed dispatch with neither sound nor color. You would not have felt as if you were merely one in six-and-a-half or seven billion. Now, as mere atoms amidst this mass, the damage we can do is by comparison so much less that rage counts for nothing but a cry to be heard—even if from a protective and cowardly anonymity. Were anyone to have behaved in such a way (like a "Hockey Dad," a "Shock Jock," or a foul-mouthed blogger) on the real commons of a New England village even as it existed in my youth and young-manhood, he would have been immediately brought up short, if not committed or jailed. In the new "commons," brutishness and barbarism are accepted, just as no one dares, as once they would have, to put a pack of high school students in their place as they half-terrorize a subway car or a bus.

I had touched upon a mysterious nerve, and although the style of the response can be explained, who, exactly, would react in such a way to a plea for the extension of the term of copyright? Had I offended a sub-cult amid those modern people who dress like circus clowns or adorn themselves like cannibals? (That is not an exaggeration if you consider the requirement politely to stifle one's reactions in the face of massive tattooing; nose, ear, and other rings; feathered adornments; perpetual three-day beards; orange and blue hair; and even variations of what used to be called war paint; plus degrees of undress that used to be confined to the *Folies-Bergere* or the pages of the *National Geographic*. If Queequeg were dropped on Santa Monica, trying to find him would be like playing *Where's Waldo?*

I don't claim to want to understand a great deal that goes on these days in America, as most of its raging enthusiasms are beyond my comprehension, but I never would have thought that such a reaction was possible anywhere. I would have bet money that it wasn't, and I would have lost. Because there actually is a kind of tribe, a community of interest, united by a shared passion in attacking copyright. They are in spirit the impossible fusion of the tribe of boys in *The Lord of the Flies*, the extras in a Mel Gibson post-nuclear-holocaust movie, and the American Library Association. Their wildness has been denatured into a crusade against copyright, their audacity lies in button-pushing, and their chief barbarism is the use of intemperate language behind a shield of anonymity on the internet. They are sprinkled like confectioners' sugar over all the United States, although no doubt more than 99 percent of them reside within an iPod's throw of a Starbucks. When mobilized, they are able to surge like a mighty ocean through the abstract channels of the internet. I offended them because I wrote a piece calling for the strengthening of copyright when the heart of their cause is to abolish it. What began as an argument about the duration of copyright quickly devolved into a dispute about its legitimacy.

Make no mistake about this. They may protest that they are not against copyright itself but rather its abuses, extensions, and unnecessary inconveniences. This is an unartful dodge. Not only the persistent undercurrents of their logic and commentary, but their unselfconsciously expressed arguments show their true colors. If, as they assert, copyright stifles culture and intellectual advancement, if it is a tax, a monopoly, injurious to the public good, and of marginal legitimate purpose, why would they be for it? If what they argue were true, I wouldn't be for it either.

Some state the case for abolition directly, unashamedly, and even violently, but though not all of them subscribe to the same views, and each of course has his own take on things, the train they are riding is clearly headed toward abolition, and they do not disavow one another, even the most extreme, except perhaps when cornered. The calculation (or, better, reflex) on the part of the mob is, likely, how much to accept the leaders' apparent overcaution in exchange for the benefit of their respectability, and on the part of the leaders it is, likely, how much setback and embarrassment to tolerate in return for passion, numbers, force, and fuel. One thing is clear after reading hundreds of pages of their unshielded conversation on the internet: the more they succeed, the less coy they will be about their aims and predilections, and the more absolutist these will become.

I had stumbled into this encampment as artlessly as some of my former British Merchant Navy shipmates, in Yokohama in 1966 or 1967, who walked up to a group of smoldering Yakuza, pulled the edges of their eyelids back to simulate an Asian visage, and enquired, "Choinese restaurant? Choinese restaurant?" Thirty years later, I received, figuratively, the same reception they did. The attacks were often ad hominem, seeking to discredit all of my views on any subject, and apparently even my whole life—which they cannot possibly know—as well as my abilities such as they are, my honesty, and my integrity. I will leave out an account of such assaults, as they are irrelevant to the dispute.

Because of the very great number of assailants it is tempting to liken them to mosquitoes on the tundra, but that would be a mistake. Taken together, they are a bull. I put out a cape, and they charged. When I was twenty, I was hitchhiking through France in a glorious summer and found myself, with two young Scots, stranded for several days on the (then) little traveled *Autoroute du Sud*. We spent the daylight hours hoping that a car or truck would pass (which, when they did, was usually at about one hundred and ten miles an hour) and at night we would sleep in the organ loft of the little church at Givry. Sometimes cars would go by only every hour or so. Next to us was a field in which a young bull was grazing. The Scotsmen had been doing missionary work in East Africa and were familiar with large herd animals. It was their idea that, using a long-sleeved shirt, we should teach ourselves bullfighting. The reason I am still here and thus able to irritate people who don't like copyright is that the bull was perfectly behaved, he always went for the shirt, he was apparently frightened, perhaps even cooperative, and he seemed to be enjoying the whole thing. I think he liked us. We liked him. As he was young and new to the game, perhaps for him it was a learning experience, with us in the role of his mother and father.

Almost a lifetime later, I had an encounter with a different kind of bull, a huge, fully grown adult in his prime, who had broken down a gate and was wandering around the road near my house, angry moisture clouds coming double-barreled through his nostrils like shotgun blasts. A few people had stopped, and remained in their cars. Remembering my pleasant experience in France, I thought to be a hero and maneuver the bull back through the gate. On my first try, however, he signaled me by lurching forward, head down, and planting both front hooves upon the asphalt. On my second, more tentative try, he charged. There was no compromise or hesitation. All two thousand pounds of him, dense musculature focused, horns pointed, nostrils flaring, eyes wild, came at me with surprising speed. I was well over fifty but have never sprinted faster in my life. Like a bullet, I zinged into a grove of pines to my right, and the two of us, one of us in adrenalized terror, started weaving around the trunks. Then, with a snort of contempt, he decided to go back onto the road.

The anti-copyright bull, a centurion of the electronic culture, is quick, massive, muscular, untiring, and stupid. Although it can't (or doesn't) really read, write, or think, it and others like it are setting the agenda for your future and mine. We are now busy—sometimes against our will as we open an inbox with six hundred e-mails or are summoned from a mountain pool by a cell phone with an abominable ring—applying machine algorithms to our lives, like it or not. And this new regime is anchored not in a great truth or discovery but in a swarm of dullard machines and a great many fatuous assertions.

Before touring the more pertinent arguments, most of which are sufficiently careless and spurious to be a Disneyland of self-impeachment, one should have some idea of their origins. What occult force has brought so many people together into a movement both as agile and dense as a tyrannosaurus running, a movement that, in the time it takes to fill a fountain pen, can deliver three-quarters of a million badly written missives to every corner of the world? Granted, they are much like the poets of Cambridge, Massachusetts, thirty or forty years ago. There seem to have been about five hundred of these. Each one had a poetry magazine that published five hundred poems in each issue. Each magazine had five hundred subscribers. And each poet had subscriptions to five hundred magazines. The traffic was remarkably heavy and mainly borne by the post office, and, as in the inbreeding of Spanish royalty, the effect was peculiar. There was, however, something almost noble about the fuse of this bud, as it was poetry itself that moved them to their complex arrangement of mutually reflecting mirrors.

The primum mobile of the anti-copyright partisans, however, is a lot less noble than that of the five hundred poets of Cambridge. The force that created their movement, and the glue that holds it together—on account of which they suffer no apparent embarrassment—was their epic battle with the record companies. In 1999, the recording industry was (by revenue) three-quarters the size of the book publishing industry, but by 2006 a good deal less than half its size, thanks to an average annual negative growth of 3.5 percent. For some reason, music seems to be the first pillar to fall. When I arrived in Cambridge as a freshman in 1965, more than half of the Harvard Coop's record aisles was devoted to classical music. A few years later, it was no more than a tenth. And once the locusts have exhausted one husk they turn to another. It is not surprising, however, that they would focus next on the printed word even though what really exercises them is software, their metier. Like good jackals, they go for the weak. Software and motion pictures are not only behemoths, but fast-growing behemoths, having annually increased their revenues, from 1999 to 2005, at 8 percent and 7.2 percent respectively, whereas in the same period book publishing grew at approximately half that rate, and from a smaller base. In 2005, book revenues were $24.42 billion. Revenues from software and the motion picture industry were $193 billion.[7]

It is not difficult to see which is the weakest animal in the herd. Not only is it true that publishing as a sector is financially feeble, but it is (as hard to believe as this may be, given the publishing consolidations of recent years) less concentrated than either Hollywood or Microsoft and its vassals, and it has far less spare money with which to fund its defense. Add to that the difference between the motion picture executive, after whom the pit bull, cobra, and tarantula were named, and the typical mouse-burger publisher, and no strategist worth his double Ethiopian nonfat goat milk latte would advise attacking the hard target before knocking out the soft one. Much like Lenin's rope-selling capitalists, publishers, who live by copyright, publish lots of books attacking it and very few in defense. In fact, at least in the realm of general books rather than legal treatises, this may be the only one. That they have fallen into such a pattern is explained, I believe, by the same thing that explains why such an overwhelming proportion of the West's intelligensia believed that resisting communism and the Soviet Empire was to have been (embarrassingly) on the wrong side of history, and why they acted accordingly, and why to this day they cannot see what was at stake, what happened, how it happened, why, and according to what principles.

Is it not somehow revolting that the forceful drive of the copyright abolition movement, its lust aroused by music "sharing," DVD copying, and software piracy, has turned upon the relative backwater of publishing? The spillover of passions and resources to the literary sphere (or what is left of it) seems disproportionate, unnecessary, unjust, and a touch sadistic, like a cat sporting with a mouse. This is not an oblique plea for a separate peace. All a separate peace usually does is move you back to the end of the line so you can wait to be dessert. Rather, I am indignant that a movement begun by people who wanted to avoid paying for music that to me is worse than North Korean water torture, now mortally threatens the stability of a craft and art that was ancient at the time of Jesus, that encompasses the world, and that has evolved by the love and labor of the greatest souls ever to have graced the earth.

When recently Pearson Education moved to stem the piracy of seventy-eight of its texts, it was met by the assertion that it stood on "shaky legal ground." Those who pirated them displayed on their web site the following appeal: "There are very few scanned textbooks in circulation, and that's what we're here to change. . . . So pick up a scanner and start scanning."[8] It is easy to be sympathetic to students (and their parents) who because of the greed, vanity, and corruption of the people who make and assign textbooks must spend inordinate amounts for worthless tomes stuffed full of unnecessary graphics and obeisances to political correctness of one sort or another (showing a woman in the kitchen has long been almost a capital crime, and, apparently, male Caucasians no longer do math problems), but they are not so oppressed that this is yet or can ever be a justification for pulling down the whole temple. It is said that the American Association of Publishers finds 30,000 to 125,000 pirated files every week.[9] And this is just the beginning.

As have others over the course of history, many have now decided that it is impossible not to be entitled to something that is easily and commonly stolen. Partly because my aging and self-indulgent generation has educated those in its wake to believe that the way to confront moral failing is to reclassify it as virtue, this they have done, and with unalloyed certainty. Copyright must be abolished so they won't have to pay for the music and software that sustains them—like oxygen, which, after all, is free—for so vast a proportion of what they may claim to be their waking hours. Never has a human generation been so transformed by and dependent upon such an electronic blood flow. It is as if they are fighting for a quality upon which their existence depends. Thus, the passion, as strange as it may seem and as terribly mistaken as it is, to argue and declare, like Louis XIV, that the fruit of other people's labor should naturally flow to them. It should not.

The advocates of "music sharing" think that, because the Beatles, half of whom are dead, have hundreds of millions, or perhaps even billions of dollars, and the people who would filch a song or two may have to buy their salad one tomato at a time and use milk crates as chairs, these expropriations are somehow mathematically justified. They aren't, and not mainly because their cumulative effect has destroyed the music industry. They aren't, because what has been done is simply wrong, and in contradiction of the rules and morals of civilization. Those who flatter themselves with such loose opinions should think of what the world would be like if everyone behaved as they do. It's almost a matter of aesthetics. It doesn't matter if you steal a lot or a little, or if you get away with it, or not: theft is ugly.

During my unreconstructed twenties, my father once assigned to me the task of eliminating a huge wasps' nest in a woodpile beneath the kitchen window. Rather than use chemicals, and because fire may have been ill advised so close to the house even if a politician might not understand why, I decided to put my reflexes to the test. I took a heavy shovel and smashed the nest, launching at least a hundred wasps in maximal rage, whom I then engaged in a twenty-minute Battle of Britain, swatting with the shovel at implausibly high speed. There was no reason I should not have died that day, and even less reason to have remained unstung, but I did not, and I did. Never before or since had I or have I reacted so fast and with such unthinking efficiency—not even as the father of two-year-olds. With no time to calculate, much less reflect or strategize, I moved like a radar-directed gun, or something in a cartoon.

The response to my article was crafted by the wasps of the internet, who have been educated to move quickly and in synchrony, to cut and paste, to organize, skip, jump, and race from one thing to another in a frenzy of vituperation while treating people's misfortunes as a form of entertainment. Their style of argument is reminiscent of the Red Guard's. If you have ever been the odd man out at a dinner party—say, one of eight people, seven of whom furiously support a position you do not— you have an idea of what it is like to argue with a hundred, two hundred, twenty thousand, or two hundred thousand people at once. If an argument is converted simply to a contest of strength, endurance, or efficiency of reflex, mass can sometimes quite easily overcome accuracy, validity, and justice.

I could not even think to match my opponents in any reflexive game of speed or volume. In their addictive dialogue with their computers, their keystrokes come in rapid machine-gun surges that end in silences filled by flowerings upon the screens into which they stare like Turkish dope addicts, only to be followed by more surges and more silences, one machine talking to almost another. In such a world virtue is the rapidity and agility with which one responds to preprogrammed, modularized, mechanized routines. Close analysis of text, the slow and careful judgment of the delicate structure of a sentence, and sensitivity to the origins and syntactical placement of words, have long been eclipsed by cartoon-like graphics and machine-gun bursts of language meant not to mean anything as much as to move debate in the manner of the riot-control fire hoses against which many of this tribe may find themselves arrayed when they besiege meetings of the Group of Eight.

These are not sensible people. By now I have read far too much of what they have written not to know that though they eschew style, wit, punctuation, proper spelling, capitalization, and accuracy, they are functionally literate. Nonetheless, they cannot read, which may mean also that they do not read, but rather leap from screen to screen in quick Evelyn Wood–like scans which, like mixing nuts or candy into ice cream, they then meld with predigested versions or accounts of whatever they are supposed actually to have read. The material which they work and rework to death is often just as inaccurate as the collective product they hope to form. Taken for fact, misconception builds upon previous misconceptions until what emerges is the result of a high-speed game of telephone among thousands (or tens or hundreds of thousands) of people, in which responsibility to the truth is considered met if one has read something somewhere that says something close to what one will now further distort.

The press has long done this professionally, and now does it even more, goaded by the need to work fast so as to fill the abysses of the Sorcerer's-Apprentice news cycle and to keep floundering newspapers and media conglomerates out of the red. Let us say that you are a re-porter pursuing a pursuable senator. You pull a story from (what used to be) a major newspaper stating that he likes to have sex with Jocko the Goat. That's good enough. You're not God. You're not the FBI or the Warren Commission. If you have a reputable source, you're covered, and you comfortably repeat it, even though, and probably, the senator may lust after goats no more than you lust after ostriches. The essence of it is that you can avoid responsibility for printing anything as long as someone else has printed it first.

In the internet culture, this is writ large. Relying upon error as authority has long been a flaw in almost every discipline, but when it moved at a stately pace its expansion was containable. Now it spreads geometrically and at the speed of light. It is the oxygen of the keyboard gunners, and without it they would lack sufficient speed to survive. As no one has put any brake on it, it has led to a general climate of unprecedented distortion, as one inaccuracy flows into others that flow into others, rapidly eroding the basic mechanisms of intellectual discipline that have favored civilization.

And then there is the effect of the mechanism itself on the quality of its output. How do you attract attention to your "blog"? (I put the word in quotation marks not in an attempt to delegitimatize it—it is perfectly legitimate—but to quarantine it because it is so ugly that other words should be protected from it. Were it a weaker and more vulnerable thing rather than like a brutally triumphant Teuton drunkenly trampling the undergarments of the Vestal Virgins, it might deserve some pity. But it doesn't.) The question remains, how do you attract attention to your "blog" when there are a hundred million others? You can concentrate on quality, fill a niche or a greater need, and invest the time, money, and work to make it stand out, as many have done, although with no guarantee of success. Or, you can make it sensational, appealing to whatever it is that for obvious reasons will immediately turn our attentions from just about anything to violence, threat, insanity, or sex. That is why television's mainstays are dead bodies, teasingly exposed bosoms, and exploding cars. And so, in "blogging," as in much else, begins the mad race to the bottom. Blogging's anonymity makes it the intellectual twin of road rage. But unlike road rage it is not and cannot be subject to law. The only defense against its lowliness is to know it for what it is and call it thus.

In the great scheme of things, the reaction to my article is, of course, as unimportant as the article itself. This is not false humility. I am well aware of the place an op-ed article on copyright occupies in a world of limitless heartbreak and tragedy. But what happened illustrates a not-so-slow-moving phenomenon of crucial importance, for if this is how we have educated our successors to weigh and judge, they will spitefully pull down the walls of the shelter in which they were peacefully born, and which took their and our forbears thousands of years to construct.

Is it that they cannot read, that they do not read, or both? Despite the fact that the article specifically acknowledged and accepted the Constitution's exact and reasonable command that copyright not be perpetual, and despite my taking pains to illustrate that it is not possible to copyright an idea—thus separating my argument from Jefferson's concern primarily about scientific innovation and patents—the *Times* chose the title, "A Great Idea Lives Forever: Shouldn't Its Copyright?" This is not the first time that a title—the editor's sacred prerogative—argues with or wanders from the content it purports to represent, my favorite being the hypothetical story about the discovery of a Renaissance triptych, titled, "Dead Model Sues Racehorse." The severe inapplicability of title to text was as if Jefferson was given the freshly printed broadside of his *Declaration of Submission to King George III.*

It would perhaps have been comforting that the *Times*'s inaccurate choice was the face that launched three-quarters of a million protests, but it wasn't. Certainly, a large number of people read just the title and then proceeded happily to vent their rage, but, in Lewis Carrollian twilight, even those "analysts" who purported to have read the text, and those who actually did read it, read into it what was not there, and based their arguments, rebuttals, and abuse on something that did not exist, as if they didn't really need a text to set them off, which they didn't, although they said they did, because that, anyway, used to be the custom. As an originalist, I accept the language and intent of the Constitution, the one crystal clear and the other evidenced in the historical record, both of which clearly rule out perpetuity. I stated this not just once but twice. "The Constitution states unambiguously that Congress shall have the power 'To promote the progress of Science and useful arts, by securing *for limited times* [my emphasis] to Authors and Inventors the exclusive Right to their respective Writings and Discoveries.'" And, "It is the express order of the Constitution long imprinted without catastrophe upon the fabric of our history."

I don't know how this could have been misunderstood, unless one reads my further comment that "the genius of the Framers in stating this provision is that it allows for infinite adjustment," as calling for an infinite term. Limited and infinite cannot co-exist as one. Infinite adjustment does not mean infinite extension. That your Barcalounger may be infinitely adjustable does not mean that it will take you into other universes. Nor is my wish that Congress extend copyright term "as far as it can throw" a desire for perpetuity, unless we are talking about a different Congress than the one that the last time it extended as far as it could throw exhausted its strength in adding twenty years.

Even their professional gurus, who stand upon the electronic dais of the movement like a cross between Fagin, the Pied Piper of Hamelin, and Benjamin Spock, and who, sporting elegant-sounding titles and holding elegant-sounding chairs, might be expected to comprehend a newspaper article, did not. A basically stupid person with an advanced degree (and of such people there are many) is like poison ivy with a lawyer. "In a recent article in *The New York Times*," a tenured professor wrote, "Mark Helprin . . . argued that intellectual property should become perpetual."[10] *The Chronicle of* [supposedly] *Higher Education* summarized the argument: "If property ownership is permanent . . . then copyright should be too."[11] These were joined by several hundred thousand misapprehensions, their illusory authority unchecked.

Unlike many or perhaps most of my opponents in the matter, I do not think that the Constitution is a "living" document or that one can rightly ignore its commands or find in it auras or penumbras one fears to put to a legislative test. I so revere the Constitution and the Declaration, which is the conscience and fire of the Constitution, that I construct the Constitution strictly and take it literally, for which I and my colleagues at the Claremont Institute for the Study of Statesmanship and Political Philosophy are often criticized and attacked from many quarters, including those of the Visigoths of anti-copyright.

Therefore, because the Constitution unambiguously instructs that the period of copyright protection be limited, and because the record of constitutional deliberations clearly supports this, it would be inconceivable for me to champion copyright perpetuity absent amending the Constitution, something that not only would I not suggest, and have never suggested, but something that has never occurred to me. Nor would I try to foment trick formulations such as ∞ minus one (which nonetheless is infinite), or propose even tongue-in-cheek, as did Mark Twain, a term of a million years. Anyway, the tribe, being mechanical, is literal to the point of exasperation and does not apprehend any form of wit, ancient or modern.

In reacting violently to the notion of perpetual copyright, however, the opponents of copyright invite the consideration of perpetual copyright, if only in theory. Would it be really so terrible? Among other things, extension to any degree would focus attention on benefiting one's heirs in the long term, which is possible only if a work remains in demand, and is thus an incentive to every author to strive for timelessness and greatness rather than to satisfy the transient lusts of fashion. This appears to have been entirely overlooked amid a rain of sometimes startling arguments.

No, all contracts do not expire after a ten-year statute of limitations ("Copyright needs to be brought in line with other civil contracts and reduced to ten years,"[12]), making even copyright as it now exists a special privilege for "content holders" who exploit oppressed "content consumers" by cruelly extracting payment. Some people seem deeply troubled by the fractionalization of rights among the descendants of authors and composers, with one poor soul apparently believing that copyright inheritance would be determined by DNA investigations, thus providing, evidently to his resentment, "guaranteed work" for "those in the DNA related sciences."[13]

Of course, property has been inherited since the beginning of time, and neither fractionalization nor the absence of "the DNA related sciences" ever put a stop to this. If, hypothetically, the rights to the *Iliad* were hopelessly fractionated among Homer's vast numbers of descendants (look in a phone book), I would propose that orphan revenues be shunted into a general fund employed to prosecute the violators of copyright.

I myself will not benefit from the positions I advocate, as I do not write fashionable books. Nor likely will my children or grandchildren benefit, given the present currents in fiction. Nor am I likely to be harmed—except in a general sense, as will everyone and everything—by the destructive proposals in regard to copyright, its abolition, or truncation, now just gaining ground: I'm too old . But underlying my critics' general aversion to heritability is an apparently personal animus, or, as they elegantly posit: "Who cares about some artist's stupid relatives? They didn't think up the idea and we all know how much trust fund kids suck."[14] Lest you think their criticism not uniformly this elegant, consider this from the *Atlantic Online*: "Did anybody else get the impression that Helprin is espousing this policy because he is certain his works will become beloved classics, and if copyright is extended forever, his ancestors will be wealthy aristocrats?"[15] In just a few generations, we have gone from Hazlitt to Betty Boop.

Far more intelligent than this last, as anything could be, was a friend's challenge expressed to me directly and in a civil and constructive spirit. In regard to my plea for the (partial) equity of copyright (it cannot be perpetual) and a flour mill or Victoria's Secret, he asked: "Do you equate what you have written with Victoria's Secret?"

My answer is, first, yes, in that the qualities of the various properties should be largely irrelevant in the blind eyes of the law, unless we want a kind of *Gong-Show* judiciary that metes out legal treatment according to criteria of taste. This might be superficially attractive to some, until a judge's taste proved uncongenial to their own. One man's red lace brassiere could be another man's *Hamlet*, and vice versa. And, second, no, in that I would hope that what I produce is in at least some ways (though perhaps not in utility and certainly not in popularity) superior to what Victoria's Secret produces (or sells), and therefore not deserving of *less* protection than, say, a garter belt. And, third, neither, because a more apt and closely aligned comparison would be with a publishing house or a bookstore. The product is exactly the same, although the writer is stage one, the publisher stage two, and the bookstore stage three. Stage three can be passed on in perpetuity to the heirs of the bookstore owner. Stage two can be passed on in perpetuity to the heirs of the publisher (many people are surprised to learn that Harold Macmillan, protégé of Churchill, prime minister, chancellor of the University of Oxford, was heir to the publisher Macmillan). For stage one, upon which stages two and three utterly depend, not. "Ah," you might say. "The publisher must print and ship, the bookseller open, attend, and sell, whereas when the writer's work is done all he does is collect royalties." But neither the publisher nor the bookstore have to build new buildings every year, or make a new good name, or new goodwill, to benefit from the revenues these generate. And if such an argument—that is, that on your figurative bicycle you are disqualified because although you may have pedaled uphill, you have coasted downhill—is valid in regard to book royalties, it should be valid elsewhere, meaning that all classes of ownership, whether stocks, bonds, partnerships, real estate, et cetera, that generate income passively should therefore be subject to the same limitations, which they most certainly are not.

Even were copyright perpetual, the extent of its heritability would be a separate question entirely, governed by the law as it pertains to property in general. Though the widely expressed general objections to heritability are irrelevant to the question, they demand a riposte. Very often, those who object to property itself (copyright being a particular form of property) do so in the belief that by exhibiting their "unselfishness" they achieve a certain moral superiority. In theory, at least, they are willing to sacrifice for the common good, though more often than not the level at which they would recommend confiscation in whole or in part rests just above the point to which their own assets have risen. Their argument is that society benefits if all infants start from the same position.

But if, for example, your infant has cerebral palsy and needs as much care as money can buy for the rest of his life, and you are willing to work yourself to the bone and do without to provide for him, tough. This is trumped by the belief that the state should take care of all such people—whether it does or not—and that if in fact it does, as it does not necessarily, you have no right to supplement his care if that would mean the affront of dying and leaving behind, if it exceeds a certain amount, the money for which you have labored and sacrificed. These are the workings of statist compassion: the idea as applied to the collective always trumps the individual person. Thus, it is possible, in pursuit of the "principle" that all children should have milk, self-righteously to create conditions in which no children have milk. With collectivism, it's the thought that counts.

What law, in what system, would obstruct the most natural thing in the world—the desire to help one's children, and their children, through the trials and difficulties of life? Only envy could engender the view that one person's good fortune in this regard is another's deprivation. In a city of houses and shacks, justice is not tearing down houses but replacing shacks with houses newly built. Further, if educating and providing for future generations is a worthy and stabilizing goal for the state, why is it not so for an individual, especially when, as the history of the twentieth century has shown, individual action is generally more successful and efficient than state planning?

Then there is the matter of actual justice. Consider the case of two families, one that eats sparingly and cheaply at home, forgoes entertainment and vacations, knows no luxuries, and keeps the family store open eighteen hours a day; and another that drinks, gambles, vacations, borrows, spends beyond its means, works intermittently or not at all, and indulges itself with debt for which, when relieved by bankruptcy, everyone else becomes partially responsible. When the elders of the first family make their final bow, their descendants are left with the wealth they created and for which all of them exercised discipline and self-denial in their lifetimes. The elders of the second family leave nothing but debt. Where is the justice—assumed by the opponents of heritability—in rewarding the second family by confiscating the assets of the first?

And if one insists upon perceiving justice in this, why does it recommend itself only upon death? Why are the assets of the first family not taxed immediately, lest they give advantage to the children—in education and health, for example—before the demise of their parents? For that matter, what about the heritability of things other than money? Why not an equalization tax on height, strength, vigor, appearance, and musical or mathematical talent? If outcomes are to be engineered by evening legacies, what justifies selective enforcement?

Although the question of inheritance is separate from and immaterial to the question of copyright term, even were it not, copyright would by its nature fall into a somewhat different category. Most copyrights aren't worth very much in monetary value, or if they prove to be, it is seldom initially apparent. Value is determined by demand that will undergo changes that cannot be foreseen. Although a few works will generate large royalties, the vast majority will be unproductive. What is at issue is mainly something other than money. In their febrile deliberations, copyright abolitionists focus on economics, but only touch upon the heart of the matter, and then only in reverse, when they protest what they call the author's monopolistic right to control his own work, expressing their horror that, having inherited this control, the heirs to copyright might use it to distort or suppress the works that are their patrimony.

But the heirs are without doubt more apt to guard the integrity of these works than a vast number of people with less or no stake in them, emotional and otherwise, who, in the absence of copyright, can do what they wish. Without copyright at all, the author loses control of his work. Not just its revenues or disposition, but its substance. Better to leave the work in the hands of heirs the author has chosen because they have a connection and an obligation, than to expose it to a million geeks in airless basements who would rewrite *Doctor Zhivago* to make it more like "Dungeons and Dragons." Why not allow any visitor to the National Gallery to tinker with the Raphaels? The opposition's counter to this question is that whereas the Raphaels are unique originals, *Zhivago*, with a nature sufficiently abstract to be reproducible, can be run off in the billions. That's just the point. No particular copy of it is inherently superior to another, which is why the integrity of each deserves protection equally, the very fact that brought copyright into existence in the first place. The copyright abolitionists, however, find this less compelling than the appeal of the false equality they champion.

They are often indistinguishable from the advocates of what both call the "Creative Commons," a new movement with the fundamental premise that the work of the mind is for the most part the fruit of a vast, unchartable, often unconscious, collective progression. *Commons* is one of those words that, embraced by the commentariat, has spread too rapidly for its own good. During the 2006 Lebanon War, two expressions, "robust" and "disproportionate," were repeated again and again as the press corps happily led itself by the nose. As for "commons," a word popular in academia as part of a communal property philosophy given tremendous momentum by the music-sharing "crisis," one can trace an example of its infectiousness by following the thread from, for example, Barry Posen's essay, "Command of the Commons," in the Harvard journal *International Security*,[16] through various military publications, such as the *Proceedings of the United States Naval Institute*—"A recent term of some consequence is the 'strategic commons'"[17]—and even to the secretary of defense, who spoke of space and cyberspace in particular as the "global commons."[18]

Creative Commons is the self-congratulatory name of a self-congratulatory movement. Somewhat like a kibbutz on the internet, the idea is to write programs—"free ware"—and distribute them without charge. While presumably striking a blow at corporate giants like Microsoft, this demonstrates the generosity and selflessness of the programmer, musician, writer, or scholar who donates his work to the common weal. And it becomes in turn a premise that is promiscuously extended to those works the authors of which do not want to give them away, of whom the presumption becomes that they are *not* generous. Therefore, they are selfish. Therefore, they should be brought around, one way or another, to the ideal—for the public good and to save their souls.

What exactly is a *commons*? *Webster's* defines it, inter alia, as "The legal right that arises either from a grant or a contract or from prescription or operation of a statute and that allows the taking of a profit in another's land in common with the owner or in common with other persons."[19] Note "taking . . . another's." The "Creative Commons" is an invention of something that not only has not heretofore existed, but does not now exist and can never exist except as the manufactured justification of a hankering for appropriation. "Art is nothing if not a dream of the commons,"[20] writes a publisher who makes money by publishing works in the public domain. (Not having to pay royalties means more profit either directly or from greater volume and market share as a result of being able to set a somewhat lower price.) But his role is irrelevant to his statement, which has no logically demonstrable meaning, as art is not created by collective dreaming. Not even D'Annunzio would have said such a thing, although Marinetti, a real piece of work, might very well have. Though the quotation is inchoate, it represents a now apparently widespread and deeply rooted notion.

It is an attempt to create a context for a wholly imagined new taking power. Unlike eminent domain, of which it is the crazed wildling, this imagined power is both arbitrary and capricious, and has no readily perceived limitation other than the appetite of whatever legislative regime is operative at the moment. Unlike eminent domain, its scope is disciplined neither by purpose, custom, nor probity. While ostentatiously referring to a public purpose, it would serve primarily private purposes—unless downloading the latest Kate Smith song (granted, this is a bit dated) without paying for it is now deemed a public purpose, like digging the Erie Canal. And a willing contribution to the "Creative Commons" does *not* bestow upon the contributor or observers the moral authority to compel others to do the same.

The "Creative Commons" has in addition to its shallower roots a much deeper one, a taproot of sorts, which, after a little excavation, can be exposed to view. It is well suspected, if ignored, that money at the margin (that is, over the comfortable minimum) is neither necessary nor sufficient for happiness. Beneath the margin, it is often sufficient, though not always and not necessarily, to promote unhappiness. A large part of politics is forging the public consensus in regard to where the margin lies, even if this would be better determined privately. Inscribed by centuries of economic growth, the default position of modern societies is that the margin is a continually receding horizon. Whereas this notion itself, in contrast to the nature of our absolutely limited life span, is a cause of unhappiness, limiting it is as irrelevant to happiness as is keeping it in play of expansion. A BMW,™ an iPhone,™ or a pantry stocked by Dean & DeLuca, and everything else of that nature, ad infinitum, are neither necessary nor sufficient to make you happy.

That people believe otherwise, however, is not surprising. Those who lack any but a materialist approach to life see both acquisition and de-acquisition, fine tuned, as the keys to a blessed state. As everyone knows, the structure of our civilization promotes this. As much as they want things, they also want to do without certain others, and to parade their renunciations. One set gives them succor, the other publicizes their virtue. Life becomes a carefully balanced grocery list. This is hardly enough to fill a human heart, and so they seek more of it, getting and renouncing furiously at the same time, as if to create an equilibrium of survival.

The lust for routinizing life, welding and wedding oneself to electronic machines, entertainment, fashions, and popularities, is balanced by a countervailing "idealistic" wish for freedom, renunciation, existence without property or possessions, and so forth. Open Source, "Creative Commons," and other rejections of or attacks upon intellectual property (the battle over real property was, for these people, lost with the end of the Cold War) are the romanticized counters to a life poisoned by rigid and inescapable materialism. But as the mere flip side of the premise they are supposed to counter, they are ineffective antidotes. When freely given they are not a solution, and when compelled from others they are simply unjust.

But they elide nicely with the dominant pieties. One of the sources of and continual sustenance for their movement is that, by and large, modern education promotes collectivism versus what it perceives as destructive, self-promoting individualism. Collaboration, collective punishment, and group responsibility are now the watchwords of the classroom. As the chairman of the Oxford History Faculty Board, Christopher Haig, recently put it: "Historians used once to work alone, reading in archives and writing in college rooms. History is now a more collaborative exercise."[21] Undoubtedly he is correct. In primary and secondary schools, writing, a naturally individual act, is now taught as such a collaborative exercise. It is often assigned to teams. Students gather and "brainstorm" (a comic-book word) to decide topics and approaches. They submit their work to what are in essence factory-floor soviets, and are bound by every manner of political inhibition and prohibition as if they were composing essays in a luxurious Vietnamese reeducation camp.

Several generations of students have been subjected to this. The preeminence of the collective was drilled into them in their earliest and most impressionable years as surely as they were made to study the same things about Martin Luther King in one grade after another, as if the worst possible fate for a child would be to forget what he had learned about Martin Luther King the year before. Intense "communitarianism" is continued through elementary and secondary education, and then nailed firmly into the wood by experts, ideologues, and lunatics in the university.

As much as civilization depends upon individual rights and freedoms, it depends upon collective action as well. Imagine a farm in a cove on the coast of Normandy in the year 700. Without collective action and community it would have been static unto this day, without—to draw, for example, from some of the "m" words made possible by collaboration—manufactures, medicine, museums, monasteries, movies, machines, and Mont Saint-Michel. A prehistoric stasis would have certain wonderful and humane advantages—a closed world running on the clock of nature, gentle in pace and expectation—as well as uncomfortable and mortally dangerous drawbacks: seaborne raiders, infectious diseases, starvation. One would see the constellations and feel their mystery ever so deeply, but without the slightest understanding of what they really are. It is all a question of balance.

And in that regard, what we tend to forget is that, whatever the equation, collective action should be the servant of individual thought, persons, and needs, and not their master as is so often the case. Having helped to give birth to civilization, community is also capable of smothering it in regimenting the life of the individual rather than in submitting to the direction of its genius; in relieving (though falsely and ineffectively) the individual of responsibility to himself and those immediately around him by creating a demanding obligation to invisible others and the state; in encouraging conformity; in the dehumanization of customs and standards; in saddling mankind with various brutal and destructive abstractions; and in promoting action by decree rather than in voluntary association, as if the greater part of collective action is commanded by the state rather than private and voluntary in nature, made possible not by fiat but by, in fact, the abstraction and deployment of capital.

But in the schools and in polite society the balance between individual and community is ignored in favor of an ever-insistent bias, often on the most maudlin grounds, toward the collective, which is taught not as one element of a complex equilibrium but as an imperative to which even the slightest resistance is suspect as immorality. This is the ethos of the schools. And after college and perhaps graduate school, students go out into the world, where they become, among other things, editors, writers, and publishers.

The book publishing industry now resembles a river town in the Midwest over which the water has risen and then subsided. Houses with long traditions have been shuffled so many times from one conglomerate to another, now absorbed, now spit out, now split, now joined, that what is happening to them resembles the industry's wild juggling of personnel. Everyone in publishing "used to be" somewhere else, or ten somewhere elses. When the MBAs collapse and reorder the structures of the large controlling corporations, people are thrown from them in Dantesque fashion. Some find another publishing boat into which to climb, some go into other fields, some retire, some drink, and some die.

Many swell the ranks of freelancers, doing exactly what they did before—editing, copyediting, designing covers—but as piecework, without benefits, security, stability, or longevity. The more people are fired, the more freelancers there are to lower the price of services, allowing more firings, further deepening the pool of independent contractors.

Thus, everyone clings to an uncertain position, and is even less equipped than he might be for resisting the pressure to seek the lowest common denominator. With exceptions, of course, books are tribally marketed to niche groups (including idiots) with affinities of interests, outlooks, or opinions, or thrown upon the open and general sea, the level of which is now so low that fish are flopping on sand. No one has control of what is happening. It is the result of the hundred million decisions that taken together mark the decline of a culture—the teacher, lacking anything to say about his subject, who promotes an ideology instead; the publisher who cannot resist the payout from sensationalism and whips it into a dollar-frosted frenzy; the intellectually lazy reader who buys a prurient thriller, knowing that its effect is equivalent to a diet of gas-station junk food, "just for the plane ride"; the drug-addled Hollywood solons who have blurred the line between general films and pornography, and have created a new nonsexual pornography of hypnotic, purely sensational images, substituting stimulation and tropism for just about everything else (except popcorn); narrow intellectuals who mock the ethical precepts, religions, and long-held beliefs of civilizations that have evolved over thousands of years, in favor of theories of more or less everything that they have designed over an entire semester; writers who write according to neither their consciences nor their hearts, but to sell.

The list is long. It embraces scores of millions, perhaps hundreds of millions of people. No one is entirely free of responsibility except perhaps the dead. Not least among them are the libertines of novelty, who promiscuously embrace the new in whatever form just to be on top of the wave. Not only have they institutionalized much of what is harmful, they have cast aside much that is good. The sum of these, their two actions, is a gaping negative that threatens in a decade or two to dissolve the accomplishments of millennia, reordering the ways in which we think, write, and communicate. It would be one thing if such a revolution produced Mozarts, Einsteins, or Raphaels, but it doesn't. It produces mouth-breathing morons in backwards baseball caps and pants that fall down; Slurpee-sucking geeks who seldom see daylight; pretentious and earnest hipsters who want you to wear bamboo socks so the world won't end; women who have lizard tattoos winding from the navel to the nape of the neck; beer-drinking dufuses who pay to watch noisy cars driving around in a circle for eight hours at a stretch; and an entire race of females, now entering middle age, that speaks in North American Chipmunk and seldom makes a statement without, like, a question mark at the end? What hath God wrought, and why didn't He stop with the telegraph? One thing is for sure. In all this dissolution, as the word *dissolution* would suggest, many distinctions have been abandoned, many differences subtle and otherwise have gone unperceived, and respect for the individual and recognition for the integrity of his voice have been left by the wayside.

When, in the sixties, I first started writing for *The New Yorker*, everything I turned in was set in a narrow column of type with immense margins as white as glaciers. Not a single comma, much less a word or phrase, was ever changed without my consent. Suggestions would appear in parentheses, or often as just a question mark, implying that something could be made better. Mr. Shawn and my editors, Rachel Mackenzie and Fran Kiernan, would probably have chosen death (for themselves, not me, although of this I was never completely confident) rather than make a change without my knowledge or against my will. I would have done the same. It is a sacred principle. Many times, I have turned down needed money rather than write according to direction or make even a single alteration that I didn't feel was right. Twenty-two years ago, *Time* magazine wanted me to write the cover story for the centennial of the Statue of Liberty. They offered an extraordinary fee and the most liberal expense account in the world outside of Hollywood. Delighted, I began to work. The choreographer of the centennial was Lee Iacocca, who began to construct a cult of personality that would have given Stalin hives. Thus, to *Time's* annoyance and disbelief, I titled my piece, "The Statue of Iacocca."

"You can't write this," they said. But they had engaged the sacred principle, and my answer could only have been, as it was, "Yes, I can."

No story, no money. I was quite fired. Later, when it became the fashion for Hollywood studios to acquire the copyright of a work and then grant back the publishing rights, my insistence upon retaining the copyright allowed me to watch lucrative film deals collapse. Whereas one cannot control the end product of thousands of people making a movie, one can control every word on the page, something that, beyond saving one's soul, as it does, steadies civilization.

In the fact of copyright the power of law is enlisted in this most important principle that otherwise would be subject to violation at will. No corporation or combine, no matter how great, can breach this wall with impunity. Nor hostile individuals or organized groups. One can write parodies at will, and make fair use, but even the president of the United States cannot legitimately change so much as an apostrophe in a work under copyright. This is far more important and consequential than money, and the shield behind which it finds protection is the copyright that some might abolish for the sake of an ill-defined collectivist ideology that is not much more than a poorly wrought and self-indulgent excuse for downloading music and movies without charge.

Given that so many of these people are purposefully ignorant of any but a communal approach, and that they rank individual authorship below collaboration, it is not surprising that they view the rights of authorship, as these have been understood for most of our history, not as encouraging of civilization but as a discouragement, as in the case of a monopoly, a word they often use to describe copyright. My own experience with editors who have been educated to this point of view has taught me that they are at first uncomprehending, then surprised, then puzzled, and then repelled by the insistence of an author that, if something goes out under his name, he should have the final cut. I have been fighting over commas all my life. There are some people who cannot appreciate music in a minor key, who cannot fall in love, who cannot understand beauty, who cannot or dare not travel beyond the very limited realms of human reason. And there are some who cannot understand the almost insensible complexion of a phrase that is capable of transforming history. If we are in fact to sense those great and subtle signals, as individuals and as a people, we must remain always attentive to the particularities of language. Even in recipes. Even in signs scrawled on parking meters. And especially in literature and public discourse.

The use of one word as opposed to another; the truncation or elongation of a sentence; the placement of a comma; a sense of syllables, sound, and elision . . . these elements arranged ineffably are what make a text unique, inimitable, and great, and although they can be possessed by all the world, first privileges must go to the author as their creator and guardian.

In the Summer 2007 issue of the *Claremont Review of Books*, John C. Briggs, professor of English at the University of California, supplies for comparison Seward's proposal for and then Lincoln's own closing of his first inaugural address.

Seward:

I close. We are not [,] we must not be aliens or enemies but fellow countrymen and brethren. Although passion has strained our bonds of affection too hardly they must not, I am sure they will not be broken. The mystic chords which proceeding from so many battlefields and so many patriot graves pass through all our hearts and all the

hearts in this broad continent of ours will yet again harmonize in
their ancient music when breathed upon by the guardian angel of
the nation.

And Lincoln:

I am loath to close. We are not enemies but friends. We must not be
enemies. Though passion may have strained, it must not break our
bonds of affection. The mystic chords of memory stretching from
every battlefield and patriot grave to every living heart and hearth-
stone, all over this broad land, will let swell the chorus of the Union,
when again touched, as surely they will be, by the better angels of our
nature.[22]

While Lincoln's version is partly the result of a collaboration, and,
as a public document, not subject to copyright, it shows the importance
of authorial control, in this case accomplished not by copyright but
by being the president of the United States while leading the nation
through the greatest crisis in its history. Without such authority over
one's works, an ordinary mortal could not have confidence that the second paragraph, a work of genius, would not be transformed into the
first.

The changes made by Lincoln, inconsequential to some, are those
that can carry the weight of nations and comfort grieving souls. They
can last lifelong, their retention in memory assured by their retention
in the heart. They are worth more than great empires, enterprises, and
temporal victories of every sort. That is the value added, even if some
have no capacity to see it.

The principle applies equally to the great and to the prosaic. Much
more prosaically, once, an editor half my age substituted the word *pricey*
for *expensive* (or, perhaps, *costly*: I don't really remember). I changed it
back, and met resistance. I then explained that I don't use the word *pricey*,
that it's the kind of word that may be suitable for Crocodile Dundee but
sticks out of a sentence and stops a reader cold, that it sounds cutesy

even if it isn't, that it reminds me of the phrase *palsy-walsy*, which I also do not use, and that I would give up my odd and always perilous career in journalism and starve to death rather than put it on record as something I had written. "Don't you think you're overreacting?" I was asked. In her world it was an overreaction. In mine, it was not, and for good reason.

Although mankind frequently takes backward steps, as in the rise of triumphant, dictatorial, murderous collectivism in Europe and China in the twentieth century, and the revival of group identity in the United States in the past twenty or thirty years, the maturation of civilization can be measured, more than even by its art and science, by its recognition of individual rights. This evolution can be charted from earliest times as it left behind serfdom, subservience, communal identity, and the expendability of individual persons. Strangely enough, those who now call themselves progressives would substitute the state for the king and once again make the individual a subservient means to an abstract end. For the sake of a usually vague and materialist goal, they would de-emphasize those rights that have come up through history as slowly as the rise of continents, and yoke man, woman, and child to a plan. There is always a plan, the plan is always for the common good, and it always demands the submission of very large numbers of others who, if they do not comply, become the enemy.

The surest counter to such submission, even when the masses have long been subdued, is the individual voice, which shines through the confusion of oppression as nothing else can. It is the master of an authenticity that only an individual voice can convey—one soul in direct appeal to another—and that even the most oppressed can recognize instantly. Despite generations of indoctrination, mankind is able to hear this voice and to be moved by it as if on the world's first day. The speeches of modern politics are generally so numbing and bland because, unlike Jefferson, Lincoln, and Churchill, modern politicians have abandoned its power and appeal. Without this voice, we are only the creatures of others, who are in turn the creatures of others, and so on and so on, because in the end in such a pathetic state there is no author, there is no one, and there is nothing.

The great promise of history as it has come down to us, a promise self-evident except in times of confusion such as these, is that each man has a right to be his own author and to fix and control his own expression rather than fall under the dictates and oppressions of another, whether in the name of cooperation or in the name of the king. As there is more than one person in the world, this right and necessity cannot be absolute. Neither, however, can it be dismissed.

But there will always be those who will be hostile to what has made them free, and they will always offer as a substitute for history's most enlightening and beneficial turn the ethos of collaboration as if for its own sake, though, thankfully, most of their collaboration is simply talk about collaboration. Nevertheless, they persist. One of their objections to copyright is that it prevents others from taking a work and revising, jumping off from, using, and/or adding to it, as their ideal of the "Creative Commons" would allow in what they call "remix." What a bloody nightmare this would be, infinitely worse than being in a hippie commune in which anyone who wants to can use your toothbrush—or your diaphragm. With each maniacal lack of fixedness, all of history would be demoted to a hallucination and subjected to the decrees of whoever had the most power at the moment. Though this may be the natural view of relativists, it is held at bay by the textual solidity that they are now so keen to abolish. Were they successful, they would be able to calibrate the world according to the ever-changing delusions that they themselves suffer, and they would perhaps finally feel at home.

One of the sine qua nons of achieving such a state is to concentrate power on whatever objective needs to be attained, overwhelmed, or removed, and it goes without saying that one of the ways to employ power is to direct mass. For instance, in responding to my twelve-hundred-word article, they organized by the thousand, coordinating, urging and directing one another to create "wikis": that is, a kind of barn-raising in the electronic ether, in which wiki software allows anyone to contribute to or alter the group work to which he has access on the internet. Although the weaker among them were shamelessly directed by those who were dominant, the product nonetheless sank to the lowest common denominator, which fits their anti-elitist outlook perfectly. With no spur of authorship or responsibility, no controlling intelligence, no discipline of form or shape, no urgency of verification, the wiki courts all the vices of anonymity and rash action. Everything comes from without, as vast numbers of people egg each other on with no check.

Though such collective action is especially prone to hastiness and the pressures of conformity, its chief shortcoming is the suspension of individual judgment in exchange for reliance upon the preponderance of opinion not because it is right but because it is powerful. In December and January, 1914–1915, the Turkish Ninth Corps ascended Allah Akbar in the Caucasus to fight Russian troops at Sarikamish. As the many thousands of Turkish infantry moved along, they did not think that in their vast numbers, the size of a city, they might freeze to death. They took confidence from their mass and from their collective judgment when, in fact, the preeminent characteristic of their collective judgment was that again and again individual judgment was suspended or overruled as, in fact, half the division moved blindly toward their deaths, ten thousand or more, freezing in place in sight of the others.

The individual voice can suffer no such false confidence (although of course it can easily fall prey to its own). By definition it cannot rely on the opinions of others. Because it is almost always more imperiled, exposed, and accountable, it is educated in bearing the consequences of its every utterance, whereas the voice of the crowd never has to pay a price: upon the failure of its assumptions it merely dissolves, and its former adherents, anonymous, comfortably forget what once they asserted, and melt into new streams of opinion. Had each Turkish soldier had to decide individually whether or not to make that winter ascent, they all might have thought harder and better about it in the absence of so many others carrying them and their orders along on an utterly worthless wave of quick-set belief.

In the electronic culture, however, the decision has already been made in regard to such things. To quote Jeremy Carroll, chief product architect of Top Quadrant, discussing an aspect of his work: "Semantic Web technology . . ." will make possible "consensus instructions from many different sources, or instructions that other people have already found helpful (rather than back-breaking searches and comparisons)."[23] It is the labor, care, and learning in making such comparisons that bring the benefits of experience, a sharp eye, and good judgment. As anyone who has ever used it knows, the internet is a magnificent (if often unreliable) research tool. But relieving one of the burden and labor of getting to where one is going erodes context and understanding. You can home in on an exact figure or statistic without any knowledge of its place, position, or historical development. You can extract a quote, literally, out of context. You can use the new power of extraction to take you immediately to a single brick, flat up against your face, of a cathedral, without your having apprehended it from afar during a day's walk while, from amid the undulating hills, watching it take different positions, change with perspective, flash differently in colors depending on the light, and seemingly grow in size from something that distance makes less than a thumbnail to a vast mountainous wall looming above you. All this you must earn, and all this you can miss if you need not contribute labor and time, and if you do not devote to your subject the thought that context demands as surely as a rolling sea calls forth the attentive and continually alert operations and adjustments of good seamanship.

Even the Wikipedia, which has controls and rules governing its content, is easy to hijack. Any obsessive with an ax to grind can contribute to the biography of someone he despises. No one in his right mind would commission Lillian Hellman to write the encyclopedia article on Mary McCarthy, but the wiki invites and encourages such things by its very form. Theoretically, there need be little difference between, for example, the Wikipedia and the *Britannica*, were the editors of the Wikipedia responsibly to check and shape everything in it (the more they would, the less like the Wikipedia and the more like the *Britannica* it would be, and in my experience I have found that they appear not to check and often are factually inaccurate). The Wikipedia uses a vastly larger pool of contributors instead of fewer contributors with certain expertise. I prefer the latter approach, as I would in picking a pilot, a neurosurgeon, a lawyer, a mechanic, or a teacher, which, obviously, makes sense pretty much across the board. But with expertise can come deeply ingrained bias, so perhaps some conjunction between the two approaches will sharpen both. Where the wiki concept fails most disturbingly, however, even with the most careful oversight, is in the attribute of fixedness, for no matter what the precautions or purity of motivation, the wikis are like the *Great Soviet Encyclopedia* on speed. Instead of an office in the Kremlin sending out new paragraphs and doctored photographs to be inserted in a row of heavy books, a process that took weeks or months and was detectable as the paste wrinkled the page, it is done seamlessly, instantly, anonymously, and without cease. Revision as used by the Soviets was a tool to disorient and disempower the plasticized masses. Revision in the wikis is an inescapable attribute that eliminates the fixedness of fact. Both the Soviets and the wiki builders imagined and imagine themselves as attempting to reach the truth. But both have in common the great ease of changing what once was firmly set upon a page. It is only a difference of speed and approach. Tyranny of this sort from a central authority is no worse than lack of accountability from a vast number of anonymous contributors (in the case of the response to my article, a cyber mob of unprecedented efficiency) with the power to revise history at will.

The entries in the bloggy-type wikis are often so quick, careless, and primitive that they are analogous to spitting on the street. Their authors write the way Popeye speaks, though with less polish. This is because there is no investment, risk, or accountability, and thus no matching labor or probity. The difference between authorship and the "wiki," at least in the wiki here at issue, is like the difference between a lifelong marriage and a quick sexual encounter at a bacchanal with someone whose name you never know and face you will not remember, if, indeed, you have actually seen it.

The rights of authorship, the most effective guarantor of which is copyright, protect fact from casual manipulation; slow the rush to judgment; fix responsibility; encourage conscience in assertion and deliberation; and protect the authority of the individual voice, without which we are little more than nicely yoked oxen.

Threatened or vanquished nations usually produce sympathizers, traitors, and collaborators drawn to rivals or enemies largely out of fear. As if sensing the greater market value of working from within, seldom do they openly cross the lines, preferring to remain in place. The quislings and the French *collabos* were uncommonly direct. The habit of fear that drives most of those who betray also keeps them from being demonstrative about their betrayal, and renders their movements carefully calibrated and tentative.

In relation to the question at hand, copyright and authorial rights, one can find people who wish to make a show of generosity by publicly sacrificing their interests. How good they are to refute the selfishness of their colleagues and join the common endeavor by working for free. Were there, however, a shrewdness meter attached to such putative Mother Teresas, the needle would whip against its sides as if Ben Hur were flogging his chariot horses. By writing in favor of copyright abolition and then publishing and selling under copyright, one gains fulsome praise from gullible idiots and sacrifices little except consistency. By issuing "free" CDs with attendant fanfare, one increases the gate at concerts that because of the pervasive theft of digital music have become for many musicians the chief source of revenue anyway.

And, then, public actions contrary to one's interests are frequently suspect if only due to variations in scale. Were Warren Buffett to back up his conspicuous public advocacy of the estate tax by donating, let us say, 99 percent of his wealth not to a cause of his choosing but blindly, so that, as it would be with taxation it would be swallowed in the clueless maw of the treasury, his argument might appear to some to be so buttressed as to be unimpeachable. Should we not then follow his example, as we might (but don't) follow the example of Albert Schweitzer or Saint Francis? That is, after all, where the pressure of suggestion lies. But it lies in more ways than one, for the scale of things makes a difference. The giving up of 99 percent of his wealth will leave the young Buffetts with a mere five hundred million dollars with which to battle the vicissitudes of life. (The same would apply to his partner in supporting the estate tax, Bill Gates's father, who may not have to worry excessively about his children's financial condition after he is gone.) Were we to follow such examples proportionately, however, most of our heirs would have only enough to buy a used Volkswagen or perhaps a few delirious nights at Kentucky Fried Chicken. To put it another way, Warren Buffet says, in effect, "For the sake of the public good, I am willing unselfishly to stand out in the rain, and you should join me." Then you look at him, and you see that he's a duck.

My sense is that writers who make a show of embracing the idea of the "Creative Commons" fall into a few gross categories. Either they have made their mark and have so much already that whatever they do in this regard will serve as an exercise of public relations that will generate more revenue; or, despairing of ever publishing a word or collecting a dime, they have nothing to lose; or they are at points in their careers where they need to look "good" or generate attention; or they are simply cowards who succumb to pressure and coercion. Of course, there may be some who actually are convinced, and are willing to sacrifice the structure and stability of American letters, the lives and interests of an admittedly small class of people like themselves, and their own families. I would not deny in people such as the few of this type a purity of motivation powerful enough to overcome fairness and equity. It does exist, and they are like the people near the head of a line who with noblesse oblige allow a straycomer to step in front of them, thus setting back by one place each of several hundred people behind them. But of this they seem unaware, because they are self-centered and so very delighted with what they take to be their own goodness, and because their backs are turned on those whom they do not see.

Blindness can be inborn, or result from a single stroke, or arise due to accumulating obstructions. In the case of the anti-copyright cultists, as in the case of cataracts, it is the accumulated obstructions that are to blame, specifically the many layers of mutually reinforcing error that, while here applied to the question of copyright, have a deep and devastating effect elsewhere. It really is alarming and disconcerting that those involved in what would be, were they not participating, an intellectual debate, are often unable to understand the sense and syntax of their own language.

Once again, the *Chronicle of* [supposedly] *Higher Education*, in reaction to the statement, "To the objection that this provision strikes malefactors of great wealth, one might ask, first, where Sylvia Plath's inheritors berth their 200-foot yachts." Missing the point that copyright protects mainly people of modest means, and that, therefore, Robin Hood-ism is not only unjustifiable but wide of the mark, they write, "A literature professor might also ask whether it's more important for Sylvia Plath's heirs to own yachts or for scholars and students to have unrestricted access to the poet's works."[24]

Of course, the choice is not between yachts for Sylvia Plath's heirs and unrestricted access to her work for scholars and students. The choice is between access and unrestricted access. That is, between unrestricted access and the heirs having anything at all derived from the work. Though it is hard to imagine anyone so self-centered as to think himself entitled to the product of other people's labor, here it is. A huge class of spoiled "intellectuals," in a perfect example of what they call *dependencia*, disparages the bourgeois organs—business, the family, the state—that sustain them. Presumably the librarians and professors who call for the liberation of works from "monopolistic" copyright want to be paid, and would highly resent being carted off to, let us say, Dick Cheney's undisclosed location, to work for nothing—food, shelter, and everything else not included. Would they ask the United Farm Workers to labor without pay so as to provide easier access to grapes? Should aboriginal art be "open access" so it can be more accessible to decorators in Southampton and Mayfair? How can they possibly cleave to such an opinion? I can think of only three explanations.

First, as the twenty-first-century equivalents of *luftmenschen* and café revolutionaries, they are capable of elevating a theory, notion, idea, or dogma above reason, fact, practicality, and experience. Given that they are able to do this even at the cost of their own destruction, when their own interests are unaffected or advanced it becomes especially easy. Fixed on the idea that the good of the people would be served by a White Sea Canal, Stalin ordered its construction, and was apparently forever undisturbed by the corpses of tens of thousands of its laborers buried unmarked on its bottom and in its banks.[25] The power of ideas is not to be underestimated.

Second, as evidenced by their own testimony in their blogs and plaints, many of these people have tried their hand at writing and are perfectly content to be paid a pittance or nothing at all, and think therefore that this should be a universal condition. Were it the universal condition, everyone who wrote would be supported, like them, by a salary from some other source. The art of letters would exit even further the realm of professionalism, and thus no writer would be able to say, like Newton explaining his miraculous work on the laws of motion and the calculus, "I thought of nothing else." And in addition to being relieved of the risk and robbed of the concentration usually associated with great works, writers would be subject to the judgment, discipline, suggestion, restraint, influence, and possibly the command of committees, boards, administrations, and overseers. This would rob them of the freedom and independence they require above all, while at the same time it nourished the mediocrity attendant to bureaucratization of every type.

And third is that which dares not speak its own name—envy. Even as a child, I was intoxicated by the greatness of the written word, and took refuge in its power as the gift and protection of God. Like music, it is a direct route to the truths that lie beyond understanding, taking those who will follow to a height from which it is possible to see something too bright to comprehend. This attitude and belief has been preserved among the Jews since the invention of writing and the advent of revelation. It is so deeply ingrained in Jewish culture and nationality—apart from religion, where it is certainly not absent—that I am controlled by it atavistically and thus can never be a modern man. When I chose my profession, which I was sure would keep me poor all my life, I did so not because I wanted to copy the existence of Hemingway, F. Scott Fitzgerald, or Nabokov, but because I was compelled to follow the lead of the people from which I am descended, in the most rewarding and satisfying exercise I can imagine: something that, when done with great effort and an honest heart, touches upon the holy; that, even in the face of death and destruction, offers warmth, comfort, promise, and a shield.

As such, it so far exceeds envy as to preclude it absolutely. Although as I age I find that my capacity for envy has diminished almost entirely, I cannot pretend always to have been without it anymore than a mirror in Tom Cruise's house can claim not to suffer from exhaustion. But it was never able to exist in the light of great writing, which should engender in even the most threatened soul only love and admiration. A beautiful paragraph, like a prayer or a song, should cleanse any opportunistic vice, even if only momentarily, and a great work should lodge in the heart to give strength and equanimity forever.

And yet I discovered in my naïveté as a student and teacher of literature in more universities than any human being should experience, a persistent undertone of malice and envy vis-à-vis the great works and great writers that literary scholars exist—or so I thought—to uphold. Even before the open hostility of contemporary criticism, deep anger and envy manifested themselves in a variety of ways. I was astounded by the surprisingly common claim that literary criticism is at least equal to the works it exists to illuminate. Logically, how could it be? After reading for years in both, I judged the chances of this to be as likely as a seahorse winning the Kentucky Derby.

Nonetheless, I have, from obligation and assignment, read quite a lot of literary criticism, although given my memory of it I could never prove this. An impression lingers, however, which is that no matter how virtuous or brilliant (or even necessary) it may be, it does not and cannot—except when it is literature itself—transcend the limitations of the anatomical atlas that illuminates one system per drawing; tracing, say, the course of the lymph through its net of vessels and nodes. There are many schools of literary criticism. They come and they go, supplanting each other like the generations of man. None has ever been triumphant, because none can be complete, as is a literary work no matter its deficiencies. Just as an anatomical drawing is a view from one perspective only, and keeps in darkness the fullness of the rest of the body, the complexity of its arrangement, the interrelatedness of its astonishingly choreographed systems, its very life, and the reason for its being—all of which yet can be sensed and apprehended in a glance, a touch, or a kiss—so is literary criticism inadequate to the life of a literary work due to its unavoidable failure to see it in full.

On the other hand, literary criticism, when informed and (as must be said these days especially) sane, can deepen understanding of a work immeasurably. In the case of literature that is ancient, out of or skew to fashion, from an alien culture west of Riverside Drive, or obscure for whatever reason, the work of literary criticism can provide access that would otherwise be barred by ignorance and sloth. And in the rare cases when it becomes literature, it vaults over at least one paradox and becomes an object that illuminates itself. The nature of such works and their authors, however, usually precludes them from the academy, where (were academicians of only a slightly different nature) they would be killed.

Charitably speaking, much of modern literary criticism is far more vicious and insane than most people realize. Deconstructionism, straddling the American university like a spider, stems from the minds and works of Jacques Derrida and Martin Heidegger, and thus comes with much more than just a whiff of Nazism. It, though not it alone, has relegated the great works of literature, and authorship itself, to the common grave of almost every other virtue regarded as noble in the university of not so long ago. A vast number of scholars may have moved beyond envy to hostility, but the cause of their hostility remains envy, and although they may not admit to it, the opponents of copyright, too, want to comfort themselves by flattening the unevenness of human achievement. The movement, or perhaps school, that goes by the name of "Death of the Author" (a phrase I strongly dislike) arises from exactly this fetid premise. Once you dispense with the author, it is easy to dispense with his rights. And what better way to accomplish all this than to rid the field of professionals; rid every author of control over his work; and, by means of an ever-fluid and changing mass of words floating aimlessly and subject to anyone's agency and intervention, eliminate the rewards and distinctions that vex the dark side of any egalitarian movement.

©

But that may be affording too much credit to people who are sometimes unable to understand even their own language, a phenomenon
that may be influential in shaping what passes for their arguments. Of
this there are, unfortunately, many illustrations: the cyber mob is as productive and vast as it is irritable. One could write a Talmud in reaction
to the oceans of material supplied by commentators who either deliberately or otherwise (probably otherwise) cannot grasp the meaning of a
simple sentence, and who therefore must recoil from subtlety as if from
a snake.

For example, "Section 1" of the *Lawrence Lessig Wiki* (the only way to
cite it: maybe it's a robot) concludes from my statement, "Freeing a literary work into the public domain is less a public benefit than a transfer
of wealth from the families of American writers to the executives and
stockholders of various businesses who will continue to profit from, for
example, *The Garden Party*, while the descendants [not the ancestors] of
Katherine Mansfield will not," that "Helprin turns the concept of 'Public Good' on its head by asserting that the 'Public Good' is something
that can only be measured by profit. . . . [He] makes no mention of the
'Public Good' that comes from the content of a work."[26]

Such a reading fails to place the sentence in context, is unable to
reconcile one clause with the context of another in the sentence itself,
and does not apprehend that the constructional ambiguity of the key
phrase, "less a public benefit than a transfer of wealth," is immediately
clarified by what follows. And even were the resulting misinterpretation
somehow correct, there is no suggestion in the passage that profit is
the only measure of the public good, or, further, that it is any measure
at all.

Whatever its other virtues, the wiki has no means of defense against people who, were their mental capacity their physical strength, could not wind their watches. Within a few days of the appearance of my article, one wiki alone had been altered 11,445 times by warrior ants activated by exhortations on the web such as, "To kick Helprin," urging them to "Go make it better,"[27] or to, "Write your own response to Mark Helprin's Perpetual Copyright Op-Ed."[28] According to the *New York Times*, one wiki sprouted almost instantly, with "more than two dozen bullet-pointed categories under the heading 'Other Points Against Helprin.'"[29] The wiki builders were incited by pronouncements that "Helprin needs quite a history and economics lesson," and "Helprin needs some education."

A skein to which scores of thousands of unmindful people bring their casual or angry wool can be fantastically tangled, but by tracing a thread or two it is possible to see how errors are compounded. An early comment read, "In a recent article in *The New York Times*, Mark Helprin—author of *Winter's Tale*—argued that intellectual property should become perpetual."[30] This was followed by "Helprin is best known for his novel 'Winter's Tale,' which is loosely based on a Shakespearean work of the same name. This raises the question as to whether Helprin intends to pay royalties to Shakespeare's descendants."[31] *Winter's Tale* is not based, loosely or otherwise, on *The Winter's Tale*, and even had it been, and had *The Winter's Tale* been protected by copyright originally and after four hundred years, I would no more have to pay such royalties than, say, the author of one novel about a hard-boiled private detective fighting corruption in prewar Los Angeles would have to pay royalties to the thousands of other authors of previous novels about hard-boiled private detectives fighting corruption in prewar Los Angeles—assuming that the means of expression did not coincide. Nonetheless, this was followed by, "So then Halpron's the guy who did the 'West Side Story' Job for Shakespeare's *The Winter's Tale*,"[32] which was followed by, "The idea of a guy who has the nerve and swank to steal 'Winter's Tale,'"[33] and then by my promotion to "Someone who admits he probably will never create anything of lasting value in the first place."[34]

When hundreds of thousands of off-the-cuff, unchecked remarks are put instantly into wide circulation, the vapors that arise quickly become absurd. As a case study of a style and technique of disputation that is already highly influential in American life and letters and will become more so in the future as the generations educated in and addicted to this fashion rise to take their place, the following capsule tour is illustrative in showing how faulted process alone can divert a potentially productive argument into a nightmarish swamp of fractional thoughts.

"If Mark Twain's copyrights were still valid," we are told on *nytimes. com*, "his works could not be taught in schools because of the prohibitive cost."[35] This carefully considered assertion is decisively proved by the fact that at present and since the founding of the republic no copyrighted works are now or have been taught in schools, and explains why today's students cannot read Maya Angelou and Salman Rushdie, whose works are copyrighted, and are burdened instead with Melville and Emily Dickinson, whose works are not. It is a tyrannical cultural imbalance, a holocaust of sorts, perpetuated by the twisted logic of copyright. Not only that, but the same injustice that forces copyrighted works into oblivion is also responsible for "forcing works by Shakespeare and Mozart out of print to make room for new work . . . a culturally shortsighted strategy at best."[36]

The reason that the economic consequences of copyright both discourage and encourage out-of-copyright works while at the same time they discourage and encourage copyrighted works, and the reason the effect of such a process is so clearly damaging is not because of some failing by the enthusiastic authors of these statements, but because, obviously, the universe is confused. Were the universe, like them, aware of certain prime economic relations, such as, "If you sell it, its [sic] no longer art,"[37] and, "'Property' is a relationship between freely-conversing individuals,"[38] presumably it would no longer be so addled. Admittedly, it might find great difficulty in wrapping its galaxies around the idea of property as a relationship between freely conversing individuals, but with infinite time it might come to understand.

Even if many of these people may have suffered terrible traumas or be regular users of hallucinogenic drugs, their ringleaders are ensconced in prestigious universities, and these eminences (who are sometimes referred to reverentially and without irony as "himself," as if the person so impressed had touched the hand of Obama) are intelligent, qualified, and well-schooled—it is presumed. Here is "himself" in his "blog": "On the Helprin reply: Wow. So I posted the entry calling on people to write a reply to the Helprin piece, and then got on a plane in Boston. When I landed in Frankfurt, I got an e-mail: 'Wow! Pretty amazing wiki article.' And indeed it was (and is). . . . I would have focused the attack in much the same way."[39] Why does this remind me of Idi Amin? I shall send people like this a bouquet in the next chapter, but since they approach this argument with the broad scope of the French encyclopedists, bringing in almost anything and everything in support of their cause, they have made themselves game in more respects than one.

A certain Professor Boyle, in either a tired technique of opprobrium or an intemperate fit of pique, mentioned my name eleven times in a very short article. I don't believe in ad hominem attacks unless—and sometimes not even then—the target is the holder of collective or coercive power so great that his efforts are magnified and his hide made so thick that the only way to pierce it is with an oversharp arrow. In this case, however, various options remain open, although one must be civil even to crapulous professors. I don't know how thick is his professorial hide, but something is thick enough so that a foray into the economics of publishing has led him to state that, "over 90% of works are no longer commercially available 20 years after their publication," and that my proposal in the *New York Times* (which he did not accurately perceive) would "extend this cultural disaster to infinity."[40]

Under current law, copyright continues for seventy years beyond the death of the author. Were I to die tomorrow, my first copyright would at its expiration have existed for 109 years. If I somehow live to a hundred (which, given the annoyance to which I have lately been subjected, I doubt) it will have continued for 149 years. I don't know the actuarial averages for writers or the median ages at which they produce their works, but in this particular refutation one can afford to tie one's hands behind one's back a little. Let us say for the professor's sake that the typical author dies the day after producing his only work, which we may hypothetically and appropriately call *Hapax Legomenon*. Thus, we have seventy years of protection by copyright.

If indeed it is true that nine of ten works "are no longer commercially available 20 years after their publication" (not even in used bookstores? not even on Amazon?), by which he may mean "out of print," something quite different, how can this possibly be an effect of a copyright that, at a minimum, provides half a century more of protection? Is the argument that books that go into print while copyrighted and stay in print for twenty years while copyrighted go out of print because they are copyrighted? What magic influence comes into play to convert a condition that does not hinder publication or however many years of commercial availability into a condition that then has the opposite effect? The fact of books "disappearing" is not caused by the existence of copyright—as the vigorous sale of copyrighted books might suggest. That is, it must be something other than copyright that causes books to go out of print. Such as, Professor Boyle, absence of demand?

The fact that books go out of print is advanced as a reason for restricting or ending copyright. Saying that if something goes out of print it should move into the public domain is equivalent to saying that if a business has a loss in one of its divisions, the assets of that division should be distributed to the public. This is especially mad given that the stated purpose of removing copyright protection from a work for which there is no demand will somehow be sufficient—by eliminating the author's share and saving all of 7.5 percent or less on the list price—to resurrect it. That is, reducing the price of a $15.00 book to $13.88 will reverse its natural death. If more than one publisher issues it, a competition will arise that may reduce the price further. But this kind of competition already exists among bookstores, which are now the overlords of 50 to 80 percent of the list price. What would be left to the publishers in terms of price reduction will remain marginal because, in essence, it (the author's 7.5 percent royalty on paperback editions) is marginal. And of all ways to lower the price of books, excluding only their authors or the authors' heirs from any financial benefit is surely the least justifiable and the most depraved.

Almost unbelievably, a common misconception among the copyright abolitionists is that the value of a book or article is primarily physical. This view contradicts their stress on the (literally) insubstantial nature of a work—and thus, in their conception, the imperative of removing from it all forms of exclusive control—but, then, they often hold tenaciously to opposing positions. Accordingly, if one of their exemplars copies verbatim someone else's book, buys the paper and the ink, prints and carts around the books, advertises them, he's just as much entitled to the proceeds of, for example, *Gravity's Rainbow*, as is Thomas Pynchon. As one of them puts it, in ignorance of grammar and the difference between handwriting and type, "I did all the work of typing in the manuscript just like he did."[41]

Today, while driving into town to get a haircut at a barbershop where the calendar is open to January, 1952, I listened to Alfred Brendel playing Mozart cadenzas. I paid for the CD, as I would rather honor Alfred Brendel than steal from him. How often I have dreamt that I might play like that, and sadly reminded myself that, even if I had the pure musical talent, twelve hours of practice every day for the next twenty years would not do it. I have a wonderful piano, can play the first fifty-two bars of "Für Elise," my rendition of which drives away rats and snakes. Given a few hundred years, I might eventually hit every note, in order, of a transcription of Brendel's cadenzas. But everything else would be lacking, and where the value lies is precisely in everything else. Needless to say, the value added in a novel has little to do with the paper, ink, printing, binding, distribution, or sale of a book. These, as copyright opponents so often point out, are not even necessary conditions for the existence of a work, as anyone who has spent years writing a book is well aware. Depending upon numerous variables such as length, materials, print run, scheduling, and other parametric costs, a physical hardcover book is worth two or three 2008 dollars, more or less. Overhead, shipping, and selling add more. But the buyer judges the real value to be in the content, or he would buy books by the pound, blank books, or whatever book came blindly to hand.

Nor is the unique value in the plot, the themes, or the ideas, as these are, as copyright opponents also repeatedly point out, the common property of mankind and freely available from countless millions of sources. As much as Alfred Brendel cannot claim to own the individual sounds of the notes he plays, neither I nor anyone else can claim ownership of the words in books. What can be claimed, however, the value added, is their unique arrangement, skillful or otherwise. Perhaps there are people who do not have the ability to distinguish one work from another except in a programmatic comparison of plot, idea, or theme, and thus do not understand the essence of what they read. In regard to music, they would lack the ability to distinguish between Alfred Brendel and Vladimir Horowitz, or perhaps even between Alfred Brendel and me. Thus, not surprisingly, what explains the belief that typing a novel into a computer entitles the typist to many of the same privileges as its author, is nothing more notable than a coarse sensibility .

Closely related to the material fallacy is yet another misapprehension, advanced as a debunking of fallacy. Addressing the example of a house as a form of property that, unlike a copyrighted work, is protected indefinitely, a petitioner states, "The fallacy of this argument is that the building owner had to put money into the project before receiving any return."[42]

So, there was no investment in, for example, the writing of *Moby Dick*, or of *Appalachian Spring*. Perhaps such a notion should not be surprising in light of the belief that pushing a button to download something confers rights equal to those of its author. But it is exemplary of something I myself have observed since childhood, for instance, in the philistine mistreatment of John Cheever.

People would demean him behind his back and to his face, often under the flimsy cover of a half joke, and their premise more often than not was that what he did was not real work. When he struggled they intimated that he deserved it, and when he triumphed they intimated that he did not. If the work of your life can be compassed on a foot or two of bookshelf, what can you have put in it, and are you not by definition one of a species of cunning sloth? In John Betjeman's "Reproof Deserved, or, After the Lecture," come the lines:

> "Betjeman, I bet your racket brings you in a pretty packet
> Raising the old lecture curtain, writing titbits here and
> there.
> But, by Jove, your hair is thinner, since you came to us in
> Pinner,
> And you're fatter now, I'm certain. What you need is
> country air."[43]

Where is the investment indeed? A brief against this view has been made searingly well in the lives of writers, poets, and composers, from Samuel Johnson through Melville and Dos Passos; from Blake through Emily Dickinson and Randall Jarrell; from Mozart through Schumann and Erik Satie. Anyone who has read a biography of such a person knows the categories of investment by heart, but rather than approach them historically, consider the hypothetical example of what these days would be considered a wildly successful writer, who has just sold his book for a million dollars. Just imagine; for making up a story and tossing a ream of typing paper in a box at an editor in a cubicle in a skyscraper, you get a check for a million dollars. Why would such a creature need sympathy from, for example, his college classmate, a lawyer for the EPA, who pulls in a hundred thousand dollars a year?

But look closely. It took the creature ten years to write the book. That means they're even. But not quite, because, if they live in, let us say, New York, the creature is going to pay the top federal, state, and city tax rates on his earnings (income averaging having vanished long ago), in addition to the unincorporated business tax and both his and the employer's share of the Social Security tax. Without a steady income the creature (who writes as a profession, not a hobby) cannot possibly get or keep a mortgage, so in addition to forgoing a long-term escalator ride on equity, he forgoes a mortgage deduction as well. Nor can he build equity in claiming more than one year's maximum retirement plan deductions—if he is able, absent an income stream, to have a retirement plan at all. All things considered, he will be left with an average, over a comparable decade (during which he completely depleted his savings), of about forty-five thousand a year, whereas his friend the lawyer, including what he may earn from money invested over the same period, will be left with an average of approximately seventy-five thousand (a lower adjusted gross income as a result of his deductions, a much lower tax rate from all jurisdictions, and no unincorporated business tax or employer's share of Social Security).

When it comes time for the creature to send his children to college (if he can afford to have children) the college will look at the assets off of which he attempts to live—at 5 percent, the $450,000 he has put away, for example, will yield $22,500 before taxes annually—and declare that the family is too wealthy for a scholarship. By the same token, unless he is a screenwriter or holds another job, he will never be eligible for unemployment, and the assets that are his life preserver will bar him from welfare until he depletes them entirely. And this not exactly glorious profile is that of someone who has been able to collect a million dollars for his book, something that has always been rare and is even much less likely these days after the economic rationalization (relatively speaking) of publishing. The writers who make up the vast majority of those devoted to the profession will have no such luck with advances, and all the figures above are in their regard, I am afraid, almost purely hypothetical.

The investment is real. It often consists of years of work without compensation, living in or near poverty, ineligibility for aid, an unstable family life, and then going public with one's deepest beliefs and fragile emotions only to have them savaged by critics who practice a blood sport for the entertainment of commuters on the 5:06 or someone relaxing on a beach. The investment is in sacrificing the ability to get a mortgage or sometimes even an apartment: try telling a renting agent that you're a writer. A half a lifetime ago, my oldest friend, even then a leading photographer, went with me to a comida on the Upper West Side, where, at the end of a meal I was able to pay my share and retain two dollars for my wallet. "How much money do you carry?" he asked, amazed. I told him—this was in the late seventies—that I usually had five to seven dollars on me, which I thought was plenty. (Really, five was the goal, and the extra two dollars made me feel like John Paul Getty.) "How much do *you* carry?" I asked in return. His answer was, "A couple of hundred." He had an American Express card, too, something that I looked upon like the chimps in *2001* gazing upon their mysterious plinth. And for a thirty-year-old writer, I was doing quite well.

Add to these elemental conditions the fervor of those who would abolish copyright, and the effect would be to reduce drastically what a publisher would pay an author because the publisher would be subject to immediate competing editions or downloads of any even vaguely successful book. (The truncation of copyright term, rather than pure abolition, would have commensurate effects, as would—in reverse— its extension.) Thus, the result of copyright abolition (or, by degrees, further limitation) would be to emphasize secrecy and speed in bringing out an edition, the power of marketing and promotion, and the means of distribution—the emphasis upon which, except for the first, has been a growing problem in publishing if only for its detrimental influence on the quality and integrity of manuscripts and their preparation, the corrosion of subject matter into the rust of nonsense or gossip, and the elevation of topicality and marketing. Even now in publishing, "celebrity" trumps everything.

But these problems would go nuclear in the absence of copyright. The world of letters would be vastly diminished, and what remained would become fairly unrecognizable. One of the many consequences would be the virtual disappearance of the profession of writing other than its migration into the academy, think tanks, or various other corporate bodies, where the cadre of writers would find themselves beholden to various types of department heads. With the disappearance of copyright, the sacrifice of the individual voice would be accompanied by the subjugation of the independent voice. Perhaps not coincidentally, at least the leaders of the anti-copyright movement (and likely many of their followers) are in this situation already, an advance guard the performance and temperament of which do not recommend well for the future. (In anticipation of the criticism that I myself am affiliated with a think tank, I should point out that I am not an employee, cannot by law receive direction, and derive only a small part of my income from such association.)

Most real writers have or have had other professions, at the outset of their careers anyway, having been forced to this by the nature of the informal apprenticeship they undergo. This is salutary and instructive, for it gives them knowledge of life and the world that one cannot get from writing school, the essential premise of which is unsustainable. Virtually no writers have not done something else, or a number of things. But when they began to get traction, however, it was possible to make the transition into writing as their sole activity, which, without the structure of copyright, would not have been feasible.

To the challenge that no one should have the right to expect to earn his keep as a writer or composer, and that holding down another job is hardly a tragedy, my answer is that just as a successful dentist, computer programmer, or dry cleaner has the right to expect a living if he can sell his services or his wares, certainly in the richest, most specialized economy the world has ever known, so should a writer if he can sell what he produces. It would be very easy to destabilize or abolish any profession simply by removing the essential laws or protections that make it possible. Such a great affection for a cause that would lead to the abolition of whole vocations at a stroke, especially ones so longstanding and so important to civilization, is frighteningly arrogant. In its essence it is similar to what Burke called the homicidal philanthropy of the French Revolution. But because those who recommend it are so often what I believe are called "dorks," it seems not quite as threatening, like a My-Little-Pony™ version of the Khmer Rouge. People who fall in love with their own radical decrees tend to become thoughtless and cruel.

The oft-cited champion of the anti-copyrightists is Macaulay. That is, Thomas Babington Macaulay, one of the great though cracked pillars of English historiography, a genius of style and a learned and experienced statesman, who, with Carlisle, and various Trevelyans who were Macaulay's relatives all, shaped the understanding of English history for more than a century. Despite his many faults, Macaulay was first among those and his influence has never been surpassed by any single practitioner of his craft, even if Churchill continues to threaten his displacement. In my education it was assumed that one would read Macaulay and study Latin, in much the same way that today it is assumed that a student will know about Harriet Tubman and collect aluminum cans.

Macaulay's oddities are perhaps best expressed by this subtle and arresting line from the Reverend Michael David Knowles's short biographical essay: "In 1835 his sister Hannah left him to marry a promising young servant of the East India Company."[44] And he had very strange views, of which more later, about copyright. Just as today, boundless leaps in the technology of distributing information (which then made possible mass circulation periodicals and enormous print runs for books) shocked and rearranged the field, necessitating changes that in turn brought bitter debate. But in regard to the point here in question, even Macaulay deserts those of our contemporaries who regard his views as the seminal text for their own.

"You cannot depend," he says, "for literary instruction and amusement on the leisure of men occupied in the pursuits of active life. Such men may occasionally produce compositions of great merit. But you must not look to such men for works that require deep meditation and long research. Works of that kind you can expect only from persons who make literature the business of their lives. . . . It is then on men whose profession is literature, and whose private means are not ample, that you must rely for a supply of valuable books."[45]

Without a single fact, this is beautifully stated merely as an assertion. Of course, that is Macaulay's great talent. He could make an argument so gracefully that those incapable of independent judgment would simply be carried along as if on fumes of ether. It is why he has so many disciples among the anti-copyright partisans, and why I have included this quotation that runs against their grain and yet is from someone they mercilessly revere. That they would imperil other than amateur concentration on writing or composing may be explained by a blindness to the potential of both as exemplified in the great texts or models to which one may aspire only if one is willing to shape one's whole life accordingly. Or are they saying that the lines of work in which one finds Bach and Yeats are insufficiently demanding to justify full-time employment?

Then there is the following: "They are aggrandizing the rights of the content holder by stealing the existing rights of the content users."[46] I can best respond to this statement with the following story. Thirty-five years ago, my parents' house was burglarized. The sound of a primitive alarm I had rigged up, muffled as it came from the attic, was interpreted by the burglar as an approaching police siren. He grabbed his loot, jumped in his car, and sped off at panic speed over the lawn and down an ever-narrowing dead-end road that eventually wedged his vehicle between two trees and elevated its front wheels. He then fled on foot, leaving a chunk of himself on a barbed-wire fence. The police had his car, wallet, burglar tools, rubber gloves, and stolen property in the trunk. In my naïveté, I thought we had nailed him. But he then showed up with his lawyer and accused us of stealing his car. Obviously, he fathered descendants.

From the same source, although not the same person: "One theory that supporters of 'intellectual property' have not considered. If this is property as they claim then it has value, and, more importantly, it can be taxed."[47] Of course, its earnings *are* taxed (and what kind of nonproperty is capable of generating a return?), as it itself is taxed upon the death of whoever owns it. But what we have here is, I believe, a call for a wealth tax on what the proponent believes is not actually property. Real estate is taxed this way, as are boats, cars, and other such things in various states and localities as a result of specific legislation, but most property—stocks, bonds, furniture, savings accounts, et al.—is not. Therefore, the fact that it is not taxed does not prove that it is not property, and the fact that it is property does not require that it be taxed. The comment above is an end run, like trying to put Al Capone away for nonpayment of taxes. But there is no Al Capone here, and the end run is simply mean-spirited flailing, a sign that whoever proposed it is ready to use whatever weapons are at hand without compunction but with obvious pride in his supposed cleverness and deliberate ruthlessness.

And if one is to be critical of semantics, the errors here cited flow as if from an inexhaustible well. For example, "Realistically, it's Helprin asking for welfare. He is asking the government to give him a greater subsidy."[48] Based apparently on the belief that all property and labor are held in common, and that wealth is something distributed by the government rather than created by those the government taxes—a notion that, though widely credited, is logically impossible—the author of this judgment does not know the meaning of the word subsidy and thinks someone is a beggar and a freeloader for objecting to a proposal to command the product of other people's labor without charge. But, why not? I'm just "a mouthpiece for the corporate copyright machines,"[49] who wants "to muddy the waters so completely that the issue can't be debated in good faith,"[50] so as "to give politicians backing for their initiatives that lobbyists pay them for."[51] And, "it certainly is interesting that just as a new 'copyright alliance' [that is, the effort on the part of corporations with an interest in copyright to push against the tide, with lawyers and lobbyists attempting to fight a battle that will not be decided by lawyers and lobbyists but by public opinion] has formed to push for stronger copyright laws, we start seeing articles like this one. . . . A conspiracy-minded person might suggest that this is no coincidence."[52]

And I also shot Lincoln. Although I had never heard of the "copyright alliance" and have always been the natural adversary of the corporations to whom circumstances force me to license my copyrights at what, due to their superior weight and resources, are sometimes for me disadvantageous terms, after this I would be delighted to ally with them in defense of copyright in any legal, ethical, and transparent fashion. And people who make accusations of conspiracy must have a lot of rough bark on them to do so given that they themselves have longstanding organizations and programs with enormous numbers of fuzzy adherents, and I, whatever my failings, am entirely alone in this except that Joseph Tartakovsky of the Claremont Institute was kind enough to have the wikis printed out for me because my dial-up connection works at only 20 kbps, which is true but only an excuse, because I much prefer paper and ink.

In fact, I love it, and when I have ink on my pants or shirt, people sometimes ask how I have stained my clothes and I, having in mind Johnson's "ink-stained wretch," reply that my clothes are not stained at all.

For these marks are the badges of the profession, over thousands of years, and, contrary to what a carelessly thinking advocate of the electronic culture might assume, my preference is well educated and of long standing. I have been using paper and ink for more than sixty years, and computers for almost thirty. In our household, we have seven, running on several operating systems. There is not so much in this new world—in fact, of substance there is virtually nothing—so that experience such as I have had would be insufficient to judge it, and I judge it to be wanting. There is a dignity and tranquility to the fixedness of the penned or printed page. It has the solidity of hand work. A marked-up manuscript, with interlinear and marginal notes in various colors and handwritings, lines, shapes, commands, cross-outs is as unique as a fingerprint and as surprising as an abstract painting. And when you're working with it you know that it is there. You can feel it, and see it. It is not constrained to appear in only one page or less at a time. It does not need either fragile bearings, electronically vulnerable semiconductors, or a supply of electricity. It can be dropped, or soaked in water, and survive. It does not blink and flee. It lets you in. The difference is similar to that between holding a baby in your arms or looking at it from without, through the glass of an incubator. "Honest inkwell, sacred to the poet, / from whose ink a world emerges—."[53] Paper and ink. Stick with it.

©

These few examples represent a vast reservoir of hostile inanity. One could fill a "laptop" with them. This is, after all, the era in which students think we fought Germany in the Civil War, electricity was invented by John Travolta, and Frank Perdue was the seventy-sixth president of the United States. But what exactly is going on in a broader sense? The question transcends this particular dispute, in that it implicates underlying forces more general in effect.

As a college student in the sixties, well before what is inaccurately called the "gender" integration of dorms made the traditional difficulties college students have always had in showing up on time a matter of sex, race, and class, I was a student of the late William Alfred, professor of English at Harvard and author of the successful play, *Hogan's Goat*, in which the female lead was played by the young Faye Dunaway. At that time, Harvard had a number of professors whose fame in the real world was greater than that of Professor Alfred, but his extraordinary abilities as a raconteur—and the fact that Faye Dunaway often stayed at his house—gave him status equal or superior to that of Henry Kissinger, Pat Moynihan, Timothy Leary, Arthur Schlesinger, Robert Lowell, and others. To enter his tutorial, one on one, was a prize for which an unreasonable number of students competed, many of them simply dunces who wanted to meet Faye Dunaway. Somehow, I was chosen, to the professor's eventual regret, as I was simply a Faye Dunaway–seeking dunce who had talked my way in on a mixture of bravado, unjustified self-confidence, and pure passion.

I believe he quickly came to the conclusion that this was so, and yet he kept me on, not out of pity or inertia as one might expect, but because one day, upon seeing his glazed expression as I committed literary criticism, I stopped in midsentence and said, more or less, "Look, I don't claim to be intelligent; it's not my strength."

Given that I was a Harvard student whom he was tutoring for an honor's degree, he was quite taken with this confession (other than Richard Bissell, I may be the only person ever associated with Harvard to have made such an appraisal of himself, although there are many who could). Now completely awake, he asked, "What *is* your strength?"

"I'm loyal to what I love, at any cost," I said. "And sometimes I can put together a decent sentence."

Subsequently, there was less analysis of literary texts and more general discussion. I never encountered Faye Dunaway, and although I remember nothing from his lecture courses whatsoever, I remember our conversations, and two things above all. The first was that during the war the army sent him to the Rockies to learn Bulgarian, and that, desperately lonely and forlorn there, he made friends with a pig, with whom, perhaps echoing the circumstances in which he related this to me, he had long conversations. "Pigs," he said, "are very intelligent," and then he turned scarlet.

The second point was something deceptively simple. He told me that, in this time of great political upheaval, he was depressed and despondent. This was no surprise. Weren't all intellectuals? No, he said. Politics can go one way or another and one is seldom satisfied even by one's own party. He was saddened because of a fundamental change he had observed in recent years among his students. Unlike those who had passed through in previous decades, these were different, tragically and alarmingly so. What he went on to say was unquantifiable, or at least unquantified. It was probably unverifiable as well, and yet it was wise and true, and he said it in only five words, but with import that not even Laurence Olivier could have matched. "Now," he said, "they run in packs." He was a playwright, and he could speak in such a way that even something pedestrian and austere was rendered beautifully.

I agreed. It was clear. But, being young, I was not as disturbed as he, though over the intervening forty years I've seen his meaning fleshed out relentlessly, and now share his view, including all that was unspoken— even if I cannot replicate the depth of his understanding. "Now they run in packs." Now indeed they do, and they are either oblivious of the fact (along with much else) or, if not, proud of it in the manner of the possessed, like the invalid who professes love for the illness about to carry him off, or the alcoholic who praises the magnificence of drink.

Only an angel could write even a semi-memoir without imparting to it at least a whiff of confession. I don't like the confessional form, which so often is only prurience masquerading as sincerity, but still I must admit that twenty-five or thirty years ago I was to some extent like the people I have been criticizing, in that I was borne along on an ineluctable current and enjoyed being the advocate of an irresistible change that I saw wreaking havoc among good people who were in the process of being put out to pasture, or, perhaps better, who were like old Eskimos set out on the ice. These good people of whom I speak would have a high position that they had held since F. Scott Fitzgerald was healthy, and then suddenly they would disappear, not because they would die but because of the changes coarsing [sic] through the publishing industry. People would lament their passing and the passing of what they believed, but I would justify and praise the powers that had cut them down.

In the seventies particularly, publishing was rationalized, consolidated, and transformed. Although I was hardly the cause of this and could not have stopped it, I was conspicuous in acceptance of it and have regretted it ever since. Much like my opponents today, I was on the side of the newly dominant power and insufficiently critical of it. What I did was comparable—if not in enormity and scale—to the French collaborating with the Germans after the fall of France. So many French intellectuals, their histories now scrubbed, obfuscated, and faked, made excuses for their conquerors, of which the worst was that because there was no stopping them (which, in fact, there was), one had to find a way to accommodate. Which is what I did with the corporatization of the industry.

To someone who had died in 1965, the industry would now be unrecognizable. The editors and publishers I knew then (some of them, anyway) had fireplaces in their offices. You rode in caged, open elevators from floor to floor, in stone buildings (sometimes). These people, many of whom had been born in the nineteenth century, were not that good at making money, but in the main they were devoted to literature. The financial apparatus was subsidiary to their standards and their calling.

Once, I walked across Boston Common and went up to an office over-looking the Granary Burial Ground. I was so young that in the lobby they thought I was the child of someone who worked there, come to meet his parent after school. The editor I went to see was recovering from a very long and high-proof lunch. Her assistant brought a coffee service and cakes, on china. You could hear the clock ticking. "We won't make any money on this," she said of my first book, "but it's so beautiful that I cannot see failing to publish it."

The Nobel Prize could not have lifted anyone over the Common as buoyantly as I was floated back on my way home, and I had a wonder-ful week thereafter. But then I returned. It seemed as if she had just been exiled—as indeed she had been—and she told me that she was going to give me some bad news. But as she was not the cause of it, she would summon the cause of it, or, as I now know, merely the agent, to tell me himself. Down he came in the elevator cage, courtly and of the old school, a nuclear-grade preppy, her superior, responsible to the laws of economics and the welfare of his many employees. They would not publish the book, they were sorry, but times were changing, the model was different, the pressures overwhelming.

Nonetheless, in the following decades, in New York, as the compa-nies were rationalized, I looked upon the people of the old school, as they were picked off like coyotes shot from a helicopter, with a rather cold eye. Their ideals had been unable to protect either them or the literature they loved. They knew nothing about economics, systems analysis and integration, marketing, or finance. They hadn't a clue about the use of the newly emerging small computers. They were inefficient, uneducated in the hard things of the world. My point was that the machine and the machine-like routines, the iron laws, had conquered. To survive, we had to learn to live with them as our elders had not. We would look toward the benefits of rationalization and efficiency, because the hardness of these things could be turned to the good.

The first editor I ever visited, in the early sixties, had a fire going in the fireplace, and wrote with a fountain pen. She received me patiently and gave me an hour. I was sixteen. The last editor that I visited (not my own) received me hurriedly in a tiny cubicle with a window that did not open. I had the impression that she was forced to look for books that, above all, would be able to run the gauntlet and stay on the shelves long enough to keep her alive in her job. She was very irritated that her work had been disrupted that day as her computer was seized by hundreds of pop-up ads for penis enlargement. As she pointed out with justified irritation, "I don't even have a penis." Sic transit gloria mundi.

My confession is not that I stood on the wrong—though winning—side back then, and not that I was unmoved by the destruction, and that I rationalized it away. Rather, my real sin was that as I formed, confirmed, and spoke my opinions I heard an inner voice that told me I was wrong. I knew all the time, as if I were watching myself in a dream, that even if I had to ride the wave that I was riding, and could not resist, I must not speak out for it, I must not embrace and enjoy its inevitability, I must not look away from those it had overwhelmed and those things for the sake of which they had sunk beneath the surface of the sea, for these were the things that I believed in, too. My confession is that I heard that voice, faintly but incessantly, and I was able to ignore it. I went along, as they do now, with an immoral pride in force.

Obviously, mob action, the surrender to collective suggestion or force, is not new to civilization, and, taking into account its raw and elemental nature, it surely predated civilization and may outlast it. Hominids stoning a mammoth will find each other's enthusiasm a practical necessity of bloodlust (although, strangely, the lust increases as the mammoth succumbs and the task eases). Hard-wired or not, this impulse and ability has come down through the ages intact. I used to believe that it was stronger in the male than in the female, until my daughters got to seventh grade, and often would return home wounded by the invisible feminine swordsmanship of which I had been unaware—and occasionally a casualty—all my life. There are more ways than one to drop a mammoth.

And I used to believe that, as in lynchings or a crowd turning on a supposedly transgressive outsider, the impulse was isolated: suppressed by law and custom, and naturally limited in that it was hard to kindle. My first encounter with it was in second grade, where a friend and I were ostracized by the other boys because he was poor and I was strange. We did quite well under our sentence of rejection, until one day when we were making a city in the sand and were so taken up in the construction of bridges, houses, and palisades built with twigs, that we didn't notice an army of our classmates forming on a hill nearby. They swept down en masse, trampled our city, and beat us with sticks. My friend was bloodied and almost lost his eye, because the little boys in this army were already running on a fuel that had bypassed their souls and taken charge of their bodies.

My next experience of such things was in the thousand athletic contests in which I played in school. Although in baseball the blood lust was well contained by the languid pace of the game and the spacing of the players, it arose quite frequently in hockey and lacrosse, and even in soccer. But all these sports worked in accordance with a system of constraint analogous to the grid baffling of an oil tanker. In the nineteenth century, when petroleum was first transported by sea, an inordinate number of tankers mysteriously disappeared in transit. Their hulls being caulked into a single vessel for the oil, the roll and pitch imparted by the waves would make of the shifting cargo the equivalent of what is known as a "water hammer," and after some resonance in rough weather, this could burst the hull like a bomb, sinking the ship in seconds beneath waters that then ironically were calmed. The solution, quickly determined, was to cage the momentum of the fluid by building crosshatched walls within the hull. No longer could force build upon force unchecked until the breaking point. The effect of this kind of containment is visible both in the divisions of an ice tray and the structure of American government.

In sports, the dampening passion was accomplished by numerous such interlocking walls: the rules of the game, the traditions of sportsmanship, the consequences of the civil law outside this structure, referees, delineated spaces and zones, an audience of people (parents, teachers, girlfriends, trustees, their order of importance determined by the luck or delinquency of each player) to whom one was responsible in various ways and who were influential and able to chastise and withhold. The events themselves, in my experience, took place on fields surrounded by palisades of trees both in the wild and domesticated in orchards. Nature was ever present as an exemplar of stillness, symmetry, balance, and dignity. The structure of all this—spectators on the sidelines, tall trees backing them, teams facing off within a rectangle, the contest timed to the second—provided yet more direction and restraint. And there was no anonymity. We knew each other, and even had we not, we had numbers on our jerseys, like license plates, assuring constant accountability. The impulse was there, and the fire, descended from the stoning and piercing of mammoths, but it was shaped by the civilizing action of many thousands of years.

Other than on the political battlefield, where soldiering for those who, win or lose, usually went on to disappoint, the last time I felt the impulse of coordinated aggression was marching in a column of two thousand heavily armed infantrymen, or, on occasion, in small-unit operations when cohesion was high and everyone was uncharacteristically well rested. Even then, there were the general laws from without and military regulations from within, orders, designs, schedules, and the rigidity of technique imparted by training, most of which was devoted to teaching the preservation of habit and control under stress. Many forms of discipline, day by day, were required and enforced, from strict schedules through codes of dress, salutation, sanitation, equipment maintenance, fire discipline, and by-the-book procedure for everything from patrol to how to tuck your pant legs into your boots. And above all was the hierarchy of command, to which each soldier was bound on pain of prison and, in extreme cases, death. The entire military way of life, it seemed, was a proportional response to the great potential for unwanted destruction possessed by large groups of men primed and trained for war.

More important in vitiating and directing the power of mass actions even than civilizing controls from without, has been the individuality of the person; that is, his separation from others in a semi-autonomy created by fact, accident, and the demands of culture in its various and broad forms. Perhaps the deepest American political expectation is of independent judgment on the part of each citizen, neither rushed, nor coerced, nor coordinated. Ideally, action requires consent, consent requires deliberation, and deliberation requires independence of thought. From the earliest days of the republic this species of independence was sustained by the vast amounts of space and time in which one could come to one's own conclusions and hold fast to them.

The polity was so intensely divided and cross-divided—not so much philosophically as by region, state, area, custom, dialect, law, and distance—that today we would consider its fastest reflexes glacial in speed. The citizenry was different then, educated differently in school, church, and by the landscape itself. It may not have been taught a mass of things, but the quality imparted in the study of classical languages, the Bible, and great works of literature (including the documents of the Founding) enlarged autonomy of thought. For, contrary to modern educational theories, discipline fosters not subservience but independence, as independence requires great strength to uphold. The differences in the quality and depth of political discourse between earlier and the most recent presidents is due to many factors, but not least that the earlier citizenry was primed to deliberate rather than merely to react. It came prepared to receive intelligently something of the nature of Lincoln's First Inaugural, or Washington's Farewell. It expected virtually nothing on the instant, it took time, and it looked hard. That is not to say that all Americans were models of dignity and concentration, but by and large they were quite different from what we are now. In the year of my father's birth, the murder rate, absent any gun laws, was one-eighth of what the last few decades have taught us to accept as normal. Human nature was no different, but the forms of culture that channeled it and the means of understanding it were. Rather than a massive comparison, suffice it to say that although today not everyone is like Paris Hilton, and in the nineteenth century not everyone was like Emily Dickinson, each of these is far more characteristic of her age than would be the other, and that this is self-evident along with all that it implies.

Winslow Homer's beautiful and moving painting, "The Veteran Returns to His Fields," is emblematic of the difference. The veteran has left the long rank and file of blue, or possibly gray, and now stands in informal homespun, a scythe rather than a rifle in his hands. With his back to us, he confronts a field and the horizon above it. The wheat is golden and the sky a deepening blue. Though death is behind him, it is also ahead, and he will reconcile the two, alone, with much time in which to reflect. Having survived the convulsion of the mass, he is now protected on all sides by silence, color, and palisades of light. He will not parade his suffering or present what he has learned to an anonymous audience that would devour it in seconds and then skip forward to something else, and something else, and something else again, which would have left him more alone than had he remained alone in the first place. And he will not submit his conclusions to that impatient mass, but rather to those he loves and to the judgment of God expressed nowhere perhaps but in his heart, where it will be infinitely satisfying and indifferent to the passage of time.

The ethos then, and not that long ago, was of a life of one's own, of privacy, constancy, and tranquility. Sins and virtues were the same, but the arena in which they contested was different and would differently direct the outcome of the battle. Henry Adams thought that at the beginning of the twentieth century the world had begun to move at an unsustainable pace. Little did he know, and perhaps in light of the future little do we, but now the rhythm of life is not that of the dynamo, with its gleaming copper windings, or the steam engine dripping water like a draft animal in the heat, but the silent, invisible, unapproachable electron, incomprehensibly fast and indifferent, to which, as we accommodate, we sacrifice much of what is in us by nature. All for fear of not following in the wake of its speed and power, for fear of missing out, of not having, and of being left behind. The character of the machine is that of speed, power, compression, instantaneousness, immense capacity, indifference, and automaticity.

These are what were apparent above all else in the mass of arguments that came like a flash in response to my simple and rather unambitious newspaper column. The substance was disturbing if only for its implicit comment on the state of contemporary education. The form, however, was most distressing, in that it was so thoughtless, imitative, lacking in custom and civility, and stimulated—as if in a feedback loop or feeding frenzy—by the power it brought to bear not by means of any quality but only as a variant of mass and speed.

In my mind's eye I saw again and again the paintings of Brueghel and Bosch, both the more and less calamitous ones—those of torture and hell, and those depicting the relatively minor sins and difficulties of ordinary life. What did this have in common with a wave of reaction washing over the internet? In perhaps the most nightmarish of all paintings, Brueghel's "The Triumph of Death," one can see absolute horror, hopelessness, terror, and despair. The artist has depicted the kind of holocaust that in an instant can blast away the will and ability to resist. Death is a skeleton riding a horse that is red because it has been flayed and it lacks its skin. And yet the horse serves its rider energetically, carrying him and his immense scythe across a paralyzing landscape to harvest with boundless energy a crop of suffering mortals. Death himself is a human skeleton impressed into service and pressing others to follow. Though the horrors of the painting are many, the one most pertinent is that man has been enlisted into the cause of his own demise, and embraces it with lust. All the characters in the masterful paintings of Bosch and Brueghel, which document a time of dissolution and "paradigm shift" so faithfully that motion appears magically even in the illustration of sloth, are creatures of unconscious impulse and automaticity. They are driven to the quick and the reflexive, and behave as if they are entranced. Even those who may be relatively contemplative are pushed away from the habit of contemplation, in favor of action for its own sake and as the legitimizing principle of life. They cross the landscape in mobs, extending their paroxysms of self-destruction to everything in their path. Thoughtless and overquick, they move and strike like the living dead, their only sustenance being momentum.

In 1947, the critic Howard Daniel wrote that, "The schizoid nature of our modern civilization accents motion (no matter the direction), violence, and sensation. The opportunism of its commercialized culture points up the instability of its ideas and its ideologies; these are [as] subject to rapid change as fashions in dress."[54] (Compared to present change, however, fashions of dress move as slowly as redwoods grow.) This was the beginning of an intense acceleration far greater than the cumulative change and instabilities in the chaotic era of Bosch and Brueghel. Our era is potentially (though not yet) just as dangerous to the person, gentler and more insidious, faster almost beyond comprehension, and far more ruinous to the soul.

The apostles of the machine and what it has wrought have rushed to embrace it without critical regard. In perhaps unconscious service of instantaneity, automaticity, and collectivity, they have taken to the field to war against stability and tradition. And although they may not be aware enough to know, they are certainly keen enough to sense that in this war their chief enemy, irritant, and obstacle is the individual voice. For it is the individual voice that is most threatening to every form of tyranny, every attempted mechanization of the soul, every great challenge to civilization, and every assault upon human nature. Copyright is important because it is one of the guarantors of the rights of authorship, and the rights of authorship are important because without them the individual voice would be subsumed in an indistinguishable and instantly malleable mass. Those who have been taken irreparably into the roiling heart of this mass have a missionary zeal for pulling after them anyone and everyone. The red horse upon which they make their progress is immensely powerful, and it does not tire.

CHAPTER 3

NOTES ON VIRGINIA

Reclaiming Jefferson and
Taking Care of Macaulay

The Charlottesville-Albemarle Airport is on a flat plain of the Virginia Piedmont, looking out at a long majestic line of the Blue Ridge. When I used to live in Brooklyn Heights, I would notice upon my return from Manhattan that, coming off the bridge or out of the subway onto quiet streets of nineteenth-century houses bedecked with flower boxes, my blood pressure would drop and pulse slow. Upon returning to Charlottesville from Manhattan, blood pressure and pulse seem to decline so precipitously as to suggest that one is dead. It is that beautiful, that tranquil, and it has an ineffable quality that promotes happiness. Perhaps this is a combination of climate, terrain, cultivation, and architecture. It may have been this way (minus architecture and cultivation) long before human settlement. Certainly if we are to believe Thomas Jefferson, it was like this in his time.

If a traveler, or a resident returning to Albemarle County, pauses when exiting the airport terminal and glances up into the rotunda, he will see a Jefferson testament inscribed around the lower rim. It conveys the same longing for tranquility of a Marlborough letter of 1703 (of which Jefferson could not have been aware) in which the English captain-general wrote, "I have no other thoughts of happiness but after all is over . . . to end my days quietly with my Lady Marlborough."[55] Later, Jefferson: "I am happy nowhere else, and in no other society, and all my wishes end, where I hope my days will end, at Monticello. Too many scenes of happiness mingle themselves with all the recollections of my native woods and fields to suffer them to be supplanted in my affection by any other."

From my house I can see Monticello. That is no accident. More than half a century ago, my father and mother brought me there on a day late in winter. My school's vacation schedule was misaligned with that of most others, and my father was anyway used to taking me from class at will if he thought it justified—something that I now realize has shaped my view of formal education. Monticello was not the vast enterprise it is today, with long lines, trolleys, shops, and places to eat. Before the interstates and the internet, it was sufficiently isolated so that in part of that morning, askew of school vacations, we were the only visitors.

We found ourselves more or less alone, wandering around the house and grounds. I was able, no doubt illicitly, to touch things that you cannot touch today. I remember my mother's brown suede coat in the pale winter sunshine. Though she has been dead a long time, she was then not much more than half my age now. I felt that we were guests in this great man's house, and it seemed as if at any moment he might appear. Just a child, I had not read the Declaration of Independence and I knew hardly anything about Jefferson, but his spirit was so strongly imprinted there—in inventions, views, decoration, the very layout of the rooms—that, later, upon reading what he wrote (or at least a small portion of it) I was not surprised.

When John F. Kennedy welcomed Nobel laureates with the remark that never had the White House seen such a concentration of genius except possibly when Thomas Jefferson dined alone, he was, *pace* Lincoln, quite right. But for many reasons it is important to note that Jefferson's genius could not have existed in the absence of its tension with his imperfections. That is, it was a product, above all, of his humanity. His genius was not cold but rather reliably passionate. Who else could have written the first lines of the Declaration, the bedrock upon which this country rests, a document that in form and content is transcendent and unsurpassed?

Leaving out for a moment the issue of slavery, it can be said that he was so engaged with life itself and the world in many of its aspects that he had little time for the hierarchy among men, even if he had to live within it and at times near or at its summit. I believe that the virtue of putting such hierarchy in its place stems from a perspicacious understanding of mortality, which Jefferson surely had. Probably in light of this he did not value the regard of others in the way lesser men do, even those of great or supposedly great achievement. The substance of his life and work makes it clear that he would consider as worthless dross the worship that some people devote their lives to obtaining. He wanted to be seen in full, for it is only the man in full, with all his imperfections, who is truly remembered and who can truly be loved.

We know many of these imperfections. Though we may never know for certain the nature—biological or otherwise—of his personal relations with Sally Hemings, and therefore, despite political wishes and temptations, cannot judge them, we do know that the man who wrote the most powerful and effective declaration of human equality that history has ever known owned slaves throughout his life, and, unlike George Washington, did not free them upon his death. We do know that he did not always control his appetites, curiosities, or lusts, that he lived beyond his means, and that he courted another man's wife. We know that in his enthusiasm for equality he was blind to the nature and terrors of the French Revolution, the seeds of which proved more destructive than even he would have been capable of imagining.

Partly because of his knowledge of his own failings, partly due to his obvious convictions, and partly because of the nature of his character and the needs and demands of his agile mind, it seems clear that he would not have wanted to have been frozen into immobile certainty. He could not have wanted his descendants—that is, all Americans—to cite and run, using his opinions as an inflexible whip, as if he could think for those who followed him. To do so would be to betray his achievement and denigrate his spirit. And, like a good father, he would have wanted his descendants not to caste themselves beneath him but rather to engage him as equals as far as they could. Although there are fathers of contemptible character who do not want their children to equal or surpass them, most pray that at the very least their children will try.

I am a writer of fiction, and as such—in a field in which it used to be anyway that character, faith, truth, and beauty outrank intelligence—I value with special regard a man who could write both the Declaration of Independence and the lines inscribed on the interior rim of the airport rotunda, as quoted above. I was therefore bemused when the aforementioned crapulous professor, who is out of North Carolina (which is below Virginia), wrote to taunt me on the grounds that I thought myself smarter than Jefferson (Jefferson was "smart?" What was Hitler, a "bad dude?"); that I had no understanding of him; and that I dared disagree with him.

In regard to the first accusation, what distinguished Thomas Jefferson was not that he was smart, and anyone who might imagine so is simply displaying his own limitations. But, were I somehow pitted against Jefferson in a contest measuring intelligence I do suspect that he would come out considerably ahead. For the record, Einstein, too.

As for the second point, my understanding of Jefferson, Jefferson was nothing if not straightforward. Not being self-consciously an intellectual, and certainly not an academic, he was almost always magnificently clear and in no need of decoding. Understanding Jefferson is really not an issue.

And as for disagreeing, and therefore violating some sort of authority postulated in support of an argument, I would assume that the professor referring so confidently to Jefferson's views would nonetheless censure him in regard to the keeping of slaves. Perhaps even in regard to the expansion of the United States across the vast Indian lands acquired in the Louisiana Purchase. Perhaps even in regard to many other points upon which Jefferson wrote and acted in his eventful life (such as his opposition to federal roads, which have proved indispensable to the economic development of the nation, even as recently as the Interstate Highway System). And so, likely disagreeing on various points, how could he position a selected Jeffersonian opinion as infallible and its contradiction as placing whoever might disagree into a posture of supposed rebellion and inferiority? To love and respect Jefferson does not require that one agree with him uniformly, as Jefferson would no doubt forcefully assert.

But before reclaiming Jefferson from the anti-copyright partisans, we are forced, due to a frequent association made by opponents of copyright, to consider Macaulay. Though Macaulay came after Jefferson, because he was English he may seem to Americans to have come before (we do that), and although not as relevant to the American debate, he is often cited along with Jefferson as an unimpeachable authority. In his article, Professor Boyle attempts to use Macaulay to deliver a coup de grace. Almost everyone requires a fundamental text of some sort. Jews have the Bible and half a dozen others, Christians the New Testament, Muslims the Quran, conservatives the Declaration and the Constitution, Marxists *Das Kapital*, and environmentalists *Silent Spring*. If you look at the progression of these cardinal texts, authorship blurs the further back you go, and sharpens as they advance toward or into our era.

Every system of belief must have its seminal document even if, as in the case of *Das Kapital*, very few people may actually have read it. Priests and professors of all types take it upon themselves actually to read such things, and everyone else mainly discusses snippets, excerpts, digests, and reports. Courtesy of the book reviews, the Manhattan cocktail party or East Hampton (actually, the big money has forced even the rich intellectuals out to Springs) book discussion, particularly if it is heated, takes place usually among people who have not actually read the books they are discussing. I first observed this absurdity after the newspaper strike of 1963, when the *New York Review of Books* emerged from the darkness of Elizabeth Hardwick. Watching those debates—so often between largely bald men with very big beards—was like watching an intense tennis match played entirely without a ball.

For the anti-copyright set, raised on downloads and quarter-second video cuts, there are various professional interpreters to smooth over their followers' many mental crevasses and provide summaries of that which would take more than five minutes to read before eliciting a blizzard of bad grammar. The fundamental text is Macaulay's speech on copyright, to the House of Commons, in February of 1841, opposing a bill to extend the term of copyright to cover a period of sixty years after the author's death. The bill was voted down, only to rise in more modest form not too long after. Macaulay spoke against it with faulted brilliance. He began with ostentatious support of copyright itself, declaring that he objected only to postmortem extension, and then went on at great length to attack copyright in general, making points that now form the heart of the anti-copyright case. Though modern intermediaries actually apologize for Macaulay's style, it is this that chiefly recommends him. Despite his grievous faults, he writes as gracefully and fluidly as Cicero. Nonetheless, as rhetorically pretty as it is, his famous speech begs for evisceration by any semiconscious passerby.

Starting at the edges, consider the following from Professor Boyle, writing for the *Financial Times* web site: "Thomas Macaulay, another brilliant thinker whom Mr. Helprin would doubtless think naive, made the case just as eloquently for copyrights [he means against extension: no matter] as Jefferson did for patents. . . . Would Dr. Johnson have wanted a copyright term to last more years after his death? 'Would it have once drawn him out of his bed before noon? Would it have once cheered him under a fit of the spleen? Would it have induced him to give us one more allegory, one more life of a poet, one more imitation of Juvenal? I firmly believe not. I firmly believe that a hundred years ago . . . he would very much rather have had twopence to buy a plate of shin of beef at a cook's shop underground.' Readers, by all means send a shin of beef to Mr. Helprin. Let us hope he prefers it to his current argument."[56]

A shin of beef is a very large piece, which is why no doubt Macaulay spoke of a plate of it, in cuts. Saying "Send a shin of beef," is comparable to saying, "Send a redwood" to someone building a redwood deck. We have the word *some* to buffer such inexactitude. But that's what you get when, because you are writing for an English publication, you want to get both flouncy and ruthless, using the language like a decorated cudgel. The English style of debate rewards ruthless wit, but only if it is coupled with coherent argument and is itself effective and precise. Absent that, there is very little. Rather than wit, what is apparent here is a desire to appear almost English, an embarrassing phase some insecure colonials enter never to exit. It was what, when I was a boy, we used to call "hoity-toity." People who were hoity-toity named their children Chauncey, Gaylord, and Marmaduke rather than Satchmo, Izzy, and Paisan. The names they chose were not a problem. But what was a problem was that they would pronounce hoity-toity "*hwa-tie twa-tie.*"

It is Macaulay, however, who must be addressed, and not his clumsy admirers. I do not, in fact, think him naïve, but, rather, spiteful, duplicitous, vengeful, cruel, and part of the forever enduring tragedy that those who should have the least self-doubt have the most, and those who should have the most have the least, a subject addressed with unsurpassed eloquence by William Butler Yeats, who was just an Irishman. Macaulay displays himself to greatest disadvantage not in regard to copyright, where he merely fails in logic and prediction, but in regard to his deliberately distorted treatment of the Duke of Marlborough, even in the face of evidence that Macaulay cloaked lest it impeach his case and choke off his self-indulgent and easy-flowing bile. Churchill's handling of this in *Marlborough* is a virtually airtight case against Macaulay as a judge of character and circumstances, and brings to light a suspect integrity. What else can one reasonably conclude about someone who unfairly represented Marlborough based on the misinterpretation of evidence; evidence that he knew to be false; and the evidence, contradicting his findings, of which he was aware and that he ignored?

But, character aside, in the pompous quotation pompously offered by Professor Boyle, Macaulay is wrong. Johnson, in Macaulay's presentation a kind of nineteenth-century romantic high-mindedly indifferent to money, was the one who said, "No man but a blockhead ever wrote, except for money."[57] This was because he was not only a multifaceted genius but also an intensely practical man who lived most of his life either suffering himself or witness to the suffering of others in Hogarthian poverty: "Ah, Sir, I was mad and violent. It was bitterness which they mistook for frolic. I was miserably poor, and thought to fight my way by my literature and my wit."[58] And by Boswell's account, "No royal or noble patron extended a munificent hand to give independence to the man who had conferred stability on the language of his country."[59] When finally he exited abject poverty, Johnson was certainly aware that he might not have, and that a steadier and more dependable source of income, linked directly to one's efforts and talents and available to a wider range of persons, would have been preferable to rare royal largesse or the pity of strangers.

Given that he lived so much of his life in Grub Street, where he once attended a dinner and ate behind a screen, so ashamed was he of his ragged clothing; where his friend John Hawkins wore paper cuffs, pawned the pages of his books as he wrote them, and literally sold the shirts off his back and wrote naked, in the hope but not always the success of staving off his hunger; and given that all Johnson's adult life he extended his charity to a succession of waifs that he took in and supported, how could he not have appreciated the prospect of a more stable estate for the benefit of his heirs, and for the family he might have had, had writers been better protected, and for those whom he made his family despite their misfortune and distress? Even a cursory reading of Johnson's life would suggest this. That Macaulay, whose knowledge of Johnson went so far beyond this would come to such a different conclusion is indicative of a failure of understanding that would be amplified in his more general arguments.

Unlike many who cite him, Macaulay was in favor of copyright during the author's life, a "privilege, which I should . . . be prepared to defend strenuously against any assailant."[60] It was the right of inheritance of a copyright that vexed him. Throughout his famous speech he asserts that the cost to the public finds no balance whatsoever in any benefits to the copyright holder, who, by definition in this case, is dead. This is the source of his otherwise inexplicable claim that Johnson would prefer twopence rather than (according to the terms of the bill then under consideration) an extension after his death of sixty years.

Instead of saying, like a simpleton, that nothing matters to someone after he is dead, Macaulay, who certainly was aware of man's ability to plan, project, and sacrifice, puts a sophisticated gloss on it: "We all know how faintly we are affected by the prospect of very distant advantages, even when they are advantages which we may reasonably hope that we shall ourselves enjoy. But an advantage that is to be enjoyed more than half a century after we are dead, by somebody, we know not by whom, perhaps by somebody unborn, by somebody utterly unconnected with us, is really no motive at all to action."[61]

Is this why from time immemorial and across all societies people have been so unconcerned about inheritance, and willing to relinquish the prospect? Macaulay's claim is disproved only by the structure of the society in which he lived, and those throughout almost all the world at almost all times; by the actions and motives of aristocracy; by inheritance; by concern for the extension of one's line; and by the millions who sacrificed their lives to build nations, protect tribes and ethnicities, accumulate wealth, and advance every conceivable cause and belief—all beyond the span of their natural lives. What of someone who reduces his "carbon footprint" in the belief that it will benefit people with no connection to him whatsoever, hundreds of years from now? How "faintly" is he "affected by the prospect of very distant advantages"? I cannot believe that because Macaulay had neither wife nor child he would be numb to mankind's universal concern for future generations, especially one's descendants, especially, if we are considering the term he disapproved, one's own children and grandchildren. For whatever reason, his argument is not even strong enough to be characterized as weak.

Perhaps sensing its vulnerability, he attempts to fortify his claim in yet another peculiar foray. Who would benefit if Johnson's copyright outlived him? According to Macaulay, "It would have been some bookseller, who was the assign of another bookseller, who was the grandson of a third bookseller, who had bought the copyright from Black Frank, the doctor's servant and residuary legatee."[62] This is the passage that stimulated the hissy fit about the shin of beef.

It posits four different owners in fifty-six years, a new one every fourteen years. Despite Macaulay's inexplicable declaration that, "It is . . . highly unlikely that it [copyright] will descend during sixty years or half that term [that is, thirty years] from parent to child,"[63] it seems in fact very likely that it would, and that even in the case of a man who died childless such ping-ponging would be unusual. But, take even the case of Johnson. According to Macaulay, he would have derived no benefit from the ability to pass on to someone else or others the extension of his copyright. But what about Black Frank, or Milton's impoverished granddaughter for whom Johnson had written a prologue, or any of Johnson's many "waifs"? Which would he rather have had, twopence, or the satisfaction of knowing that people he loved or wished to help would benefit from what he left behind? What if he, quite apart from benefiting his families, wanted to bequeath to a church, an orphanage, or a hospital? If the copyright were of any value, he could so direct it.

In the absence of copyright, as copyright and copyright-extension opponents so often point out—inaccurately, as we shall see—there is a diffuse and general public benefit in the potential of lower-priced editions. But even were it greater than it is in fact, by what right can anyone claim to dictate to another not only the choice of his charities, but that he can't choose at all, and must see his work spread upon the wind like dandelion seed? Perhaps Samuel Johnson thought, and desired deeply with his heart, that the best use of what he had done would be to direct the revenues from it to a children's hospital, or a library, or a poorhouse. We all make such choices in our setting of priorities and devotion to causes and principles. Who has the moral right to tell us that we cannot? Macaulay would claim that the easier availability of Johnson's works is more important than, for instance, taking a child off the streets in eighteenth-century London. Where is the justice of that claim, especially since it is possible that Johnson himself would disagree, that the work was Johnson's, and that had he owned a brewery instead of a copyright no one would have thought to interfere in his choice.

Back to Black Frank and Milton's impoverished granddaughter, the latter who, Macaulay claims, was impoverished—despite the perpetual copyright that existed in Milton's time, and had survived in a patchwork of conflicting claims and rulings well into the eighteenth century— because the rights to *Paradise Lost* had fallen into the hands of a bookseller. She would hardly have been in a better position had copyright not lasted beyond Milton's death. That despite perpetual copyright she was impoverished was due to a decision taken by one of her predecessors. If Milton's descendants chose to sell the copyright, of course they could not continue to benefit from it except from whatever use they might make of the proceeds of sale. The decision was theirs. All wealth, property, and patrimony is subject to risk. Just as any other assets that are bequeathed are subject to growth, erosion, or annihilation, so is a copyright, and so it was then.

Which leads us again to Black Frank, who also would have had a choice. Sell the copyright and make use of the proceeds—perhaps today his descendants would own hotels in the Bahamas—or keep it, which probably would have been the better bet. It is highly illogical, however, to try to prove that copyright extension is unjust because in general the performance of assets is not guaranteed.

In a misfortune that has spread to the contemporary anti-copyright enthusiasts, Macaulay, who cared little for art and was deaf to music, was also blind to economics. In what he terms "a perfect illustration of the effect of long copyright," he states that "Milton's works are the property of a single publisher. Everybody who wants them must buy them at Tonson's shop, and at Tonson's price. . . . Thousands who would gladly possess a copy of Paradise Lost, must forego that great enjoyment."[64]

Assuming that Tonson's price is "unreasonably" high, and Macaulay curiously does not state this, were it lower there still would be thousands who would not pay it. With exceptions that are most probably anomalous, the price would be set according to the demand, just as it would be during the author's life. If the bookseller/publisher elevates it disproportionately, no one will buy. Thus he will not elevate it. It will be to his advantage to set a price on the vector between, on the one hand, the highest he can charge, and, on the other, the highest volume of sales he can achieve. This is how the market works—not by design or decree, not because someone has decided that it would be best that way, but because of the nature of things. If you doubt it, visit a bookstore.

Apparently, Macaulay did: "I can buy Rasselas for sixpence; I might have had to give five shillings for it. I can buy the Dictionary, the entire genuine Dictionary, for two guineas, perhaps for less; I might have had to give five or six guineas for it."[65] He has simply made up higher prices ("I might have had to give . . . I might have had to give.") and perhaps even the second lower price ("For two guineas, perhaps for less"). These are not facts he cites but fanciful or unrepresentative illustrations leaping conveniently from his imagination to the defense of his argument. And yet, this argument, specious in 1841, has descended to his hapless present-day admirers, who make similar claims as a matter of course, such as that were Mark Twain's works still protected, schoolchildren would not be able to read them due to the prohibitive pricing. The facts are different.

For example, readily at hand on the bookshelf next to me as I write is

Henry Kissinger's *Diplomacy*, copyrighted of course, in paper, published in 1994, at 911 pages, two pounds eight ounces, and with photographs, priced at $22. *The Adams-Jefferson Letters* (the editing under copyright but the contents in the public domain) published seven years earlier, 638 pages, at two pounds three ounces, with no pictures, and assisted by a grant from the Lilly Foundation, is also available. Despite its earlier publication date and that it is only two-thirds the size of the Kissinger (anything would be), and was subsidized, it costs not 1,000 percent less (as Macaulay would have it) but the same $22.

In fiction, you can buy *Les Misérables*, plucked from the public domain, in a Modern Library binding, at 1,260 pages and two pounds nine ounces for $25.95. And you can buy (and I wish you would) my *A Soldier of the Great War*, copyrighted thank God, in trade paper with a beautiful Bellini on the cover, at 860 pages and two pounds, for $16. The Hugo is 47 percent larger and 28 percent heavier, but it is also 62 percent more expensive, not 1,000 percent less expensive. True, you can get an economy edition of *Les Misérables* for $7, but you can also get the mass market edition of *A Soldier of the Great War* for $6.

Beyond the 15 percent author's royalty on hardcover and 7.5 percent on paperbacks, copyright has little effect on book pricing. Publishers and booksellers know that other than the few people who for some reason must have a particular book, their customers have a wide choice, and will be put off by price. If only a few books were available, it might be different, but there are at any time hundreds of thousands, even millions—a choice that allows very few publishers to be either grasping or coy with the public: these impulses they save for dealings with their writers.

Neither Macaulay nor his disciples of the present confine their imprecision to such practical examples, but expand it to embrace higher things as well. Macaulay writes, and his followers frequently and thoughtlessly repeat that, "The principle of copyright is this. It is a tax on readers for the purpose of giving a bounty to writers."[66]

Words have meaning, and it is not good to be careless with them, like the official who said that a border shouldn't be a line between nations. When I was young I spent some time reading the dictionary. In so doing, I happened upon a definition of *masturbation* as "self-abuse." (As to the accuracy of this, ask Philip Roth.) It slept in my mind like a locust, until it emerged when my ninth-grade history class was asked to describe how the monks lived during the Middle Ages, and without the least bit of self-consciousness or embarrassment I volunteered that they were known for their incessant masturbation.

In *Eldred v. Ashcroft*, the banner case of the anti-copyright movement, and deservedly so, in that they lost, Mr. Justice Breyer (or a young insufficiently critical clerk mentally vacuuming from the petitioner's brief) conflates in his dissent the Constitution's copyright clause with Macaulay's description: "The clause authorizes a 'tax on readers for the purpose of giving a bounty to writers.'"[67] It does no such thing, and copyright is not a tax.

It is not a tax any more than a workman's wage or the price a merchant receives for a sale, or a fisherman for his fish, is a tax. One of the differences between a price and a tax is that the latter is compelled. And to argue that copyright entitles the holder in certain circumstances to draw upon the compulsion of the law does not make copyright a tax any more than a merchant drawing upon the compulsion of the law to deal with a shoplifter makes his price a tax. Were Macaulay speaking here in a literary sense, which he is not, he might mean a burdensome charge or an unjust requirement, but how is copyright any more a burdensome charge or unjust requirement than any other price for any other product or service? I cannot understand how a man who can write such majestic prose fails so often and so disastrously to grasp the conspicuous distinctions that separate one fairly simple word from another.

I can understand, however, that his modern imitators might fail to understand distinctions, especially when they venture into what for them are the higher regions of theory. One example they have robotically imbibed from Macaulay is the notion that, "Copyright is monopoly, and produces all the effects which the general voice of mankind attributes to monopoly."[68]

The opponents of copyright, or its extension, including Mr. Justice Stevens (or a young insufficiently critical clerk mentally vacuuming from the petitioner's brief), who, in *Eldred*, wrote of copyright's "monopoly privileges,"[69] have even less a grasp of the word *monopoly*, which is derived from the Greek *monos*, meaning single or alone, and *poolein*, meaning to sell. It has always been primarily understood, as the OED would have it, as "exclusive possession of the trade in some *commodity*," or "an exclusive privilege (conferred by the sovereign or the state) of selling some *commodity* or trading with a particular place or country." Or, figuratively, "exclusive possession, control, or exercise of something."[70]

What has Macaulay done? Well, he was speaking in Parliament, and he used a tried rhetorical trick, calling two entirely different things by the same word that in different circumstances can apply to either, and then by invisible elision transforming the one into the other as he pleases and for his own purposes. In the figurative sense of exclusive control, copyright is a monopoly, but to label it as such is meaningless, as it is no more a monopoly than the monopoly anyone exercises over his labor, or the monopoly anyone enjoys in regard to his property, or the monopoly someone might have over the sale of a watermelon he grew in his garden.

In fact, my copyright is less a monopoly than my physician's monopoly on his labor because whereas my copyright expires, the practice he may leave to his heirs or assigns (he built a practice, I wrote books) does not. The concepts, ideas, methods, and means within a copyright are free for anyone to appropriate, whereas no one is free to appropriate the labor of a laborer. My work can be excerpted at will according to the doctrine of fair use. And the law grants my work to the blind—which I approve— whereas an ophthalmologist may, and usually does, bill them, as do their landlords, the electric company, and so on, including even the welfare state, which, while exempting them from paying for my copyright (though over-looking groceries, medical care, and everything else) then proceeds to tax them in ways both creative and virtually inescapable.

And, then, no copyright results in exclusive control of any *commodity*. Books are not fungible, and, even if they were, no one has a copyright over all or even a plurality of them. Surely Macaulay, whose reputation though repeatedly undermined has nonetheless endured for almost two hundred years, could not be so obviously and transparently dishonest as to skate along such slippery ice. But he does, for shortly after his declaration that copyright is a monopoly producing all the effects of monopoly, thinking that perhaps his deception will carry (and indeed it has, for some, even so many years later), he pushes ahead full bore and asks rhetorically, "Why should we not restore the monopoly of the East India trade to the East India Company? . . . I may with equal safety challenge my honorable friend to find out any distinction between copyright and other privileges of the same kind; any reason why a monopoly of books should produce an effect directly the reverse of that which was produced by the East India Company's monopoly of tea, or by Lord Essex's monopoly of sweet wines. Thus, then, stands the case."[71]

Copyright does not create a "monopoly of books" any more than the exclusive right to sell one's pound of tea or one's watermelon creates a monopoly of tea or watermelon. The damaging effect of such a monopoly over the sale of tea would be that the commodity is controlled in its entirety and therefore so is its quality, or lack thereof, and its price. There is no monopoly of books, and never has been. Not even Barnes & Noble has a monopoly of books (yet). Who, exactly, in Macaulay's estimation, had a monopoly of books at the time he made his accusations? As a holder of copyrights, did he himself, as he implies? He could not have imagined that he did, but it would have been an interesting exercise. Think of a Barnes & Noble Superstore, or one of the great English bookstores, or FNAC in Paris, or Powell's in Portland. You enter in full expectation of an hour skimming the surface of an overwhelming treasury, but then you find—admittedly, in many languages, formats, and editions—only the works of Macaulay. Macaulay's histories, Macaulay's essays, Macaulay's speeches, Macaulay's letters. That would be a monopoly of books, a nightmare world, but hardly reality. And yet this was the world he somehow posited, and this was the condition against which he molded his grandly stated but inapplicable and immaterial argument. Thus, then, stood the case, and thus, then, it falls.

Perhaps Macaulay's best argument is his warning—drawing from examples in regard to Richardson, Boswell, and Wesley—that someone, presumably family members left in control of an author's works for a period after his death, will suppress them out of ignorance, spite, embarrassment, disagreement, or any combination of these things. His own circumstances vaguely suggest that he may uncharacteristically be close to making sense, in that he repeatedly holds up booksellers and their descendants as the villains in the piece, and his mother's father was a bookseller. Perhaps no serpent has sharper teeth than a child's embrace of a cause hostile to a parent's deepest belief, but we shall leave that to Freudian tragedians. It is a good argument, the best he offers, but although one can even reinforce it with further examples—such as Lady Burton's incineration of her husband's possibly randy papers—it can also be countered: if not fully, then at least enough to illustrate that Macaulay's remedy is disproportionate.

Because the suppression he fears goes against human nature and self-interest, its likelihood is slight. It is in fact exceedingly unlikely. Rather than people suppressing the work of their forbears, they crowd the channels of publishing with attempts to promote it, especially given that the slightest touch of fame or even, particularly these days, infamy, will be to their practical advantage. You could probably make a really fat category in the Dewey Decimal System to shelter scandalous books that people write about their scandalous ancestors, much less worshipful accounts and level-headed ones.

Further, a writer himself has this right during his lifetime and is just as likely to exercise it: that is, *unlikely* (but, in view of shame, conversion, and embarrassment by youthful indiscretions, not impossible). Presumably, however, he would rather, in regard to this right, exercise constructive influence and wisdom in delegating it. Entirely apart from any consideration of money, I would much rather have my children in charge, and in charge of subsequent delegation, of a book I might write, than simply floating it out into the hands of anyone who might distort or violate it. And, who knows, perhaps relatives who might withhold and suppress might be correct in doing so. It would have been a great loss had Boswell's eldest son, who was mortified by his father's subsidiary relationship to Johnson, been able and willing to withhold for a time the publication of the *Life* (the destruction of a manuscript and obliteration of a work, as in Richard Burton's case if one considers his papers the work they undoubtedly were, is a subject and peril unrelated to the question of copyright or copyright extension). But how fortunate if a young and hypothetical Brittany Hitler, after her father's hypothetical death and as the Nazi Party was about to pick up steam, could have suppressed *Mein Kampf*.

Not surprisingly, Macaulay closes his weak argument with bluster. In this case, both a prediction and a threat. If copyright protection were extended beyond the life of the author, he predicted, shall we say, vigorously, "Just as the absurd acts which prohibited the sale of game were virtually repealed by the poacher,"—please note that the act against which Macaulay spoke did not prohibit the sale of books—"this law will be virtually repealed by piratical booksellers." He then spends nine lines explaining that "at present the holder of copyright has the public firmly on his side," and that in regard to copyright, *nonextended*, "pass this law: and that feeling is at an end. . . . Great masses of capital will be constantly employed in violation of the law. Every art will be employed to evade legal pursuit; and the whole nation will be in on the plot."[72]

A declaration so ringing and so firm begs the question, if one were so willing to violate a copyright a year after the author's death, then why not a year before? If ten years after, why not ten years before, and so on? The public is all for authorial rights, and is firmly on the side of the author and his requirements—until his death, when, presumably, his wishes would mean nothing. The public, having honored him the day before, would no longer honor him the day after his death, because he would have been blank in regard to projecting what would follow him. This would of necessity be based on Macaulay's supposition that a deceased author, supposedly like Johnson, would not have valued extension. And it would be a rather arcane motivation for so widespread and, according to Macaulay, passionate a crime. Not only is it logically impeachable that an author would rather have some shin of beef than the extension of his rights and thus the grant of their heritability, but if such an author existed, then he could easily refuse such an extension. If he did not, then by definition he would value it, thus destroying the structure of Macaulay's rationale, mocking his indignation, and invalidating his predictions. And, vastly in the main, of course, authors do not make such refusals.

Macaulay's general prediction comes in the form of a question posed in 1841 and answered thoroughly in the more than 167 years since. "The question is whether some book as popular as Robinson Crusoe or The Pilgrim's Progress, shall be in every cottage, or whether it shall be confined to the libraries of the rich for the advantage of the great grandson of a bookseller."[73] This question is representative of Macaulay's belief, and that of his modern devotees (most of whom probably have not read him), that copyright suppresses, stunts, and retards the flowering of culture, and specifically the production and availability of books. The answer is decisive.

Not only the original but subsequent acts have been passed, their existence putting to the test Macaulay's theme of works locked up, the deleterious effects of 'monopoly,' his general argument, and the validity of his predictions, which are nothing if not embarrassing. How embarrassing? In 1825 approximately 600 titles a year were issued in England; by 1900, 6,000;[74] in 2005, 206,000.[75] And that is just England. The United States followed closely with 172,000,[76] with the number of books published just before the 1998 "infamous" Sonny Bono Copyright Extension Act almost tripling within seven years.[77] In 1998, Peru (that is, *Peru*) published three times as many books as did England in 1825.[78] What might Macaulay think of the fact that, a century and a half after he spoke, the southern half of the Korean peninsula saw the publication of 30,500 books?[79] Or that Spain, sun-drenched, primitive, bone-dry Spain, published nearly 50,000 books, 170 newspapers, and 2,000 periodicals?[80]

In 1851, the Library of Congress held 55,000 volumes, far fewer than a Barnes & Noble Superstore. Five years beforehand, it had been directed by law to receive one of each copyrighted "book, map, chart, musical composition, print, cut, or engraving." By 1992, its collection comprised more than a hundred million such items, including fifteen million books. But this is by no means the overflowing predicate to Macaulay's major subject, for the predicate would be enlarged if the Library did not shunt most works on medicine and agriculture to the national libraries established in these fields. And it would be further immensely enlarged were the Library required to keep each copyrighted work it receives, which it is not, and therefore does not, though from 1870 to 1909 it did. The scope of what is not represented may be appreciated from the fact that on an average day 31,000 items are delivered to the Library, of which it keeps on average 7,000.[81] Though it is thus impossible to determine fully the scale of what former President G.W. Bush would call Macaulay's "misunderestimation," even the figures that are the predicate's minimum might now actually be known to Macaulay, as they might be for him an embarrassment sufficiently intense to wake the dead.

Nor do these data require adjustment or division in light of population growth, economic development, or technological advantage, as the bar of copyright extension imagined by Macaulay and his modern retainers would operate uninfluenced by such changes, such as, for example, a red light will stop (or, as I live in Virginia, I must say *should* stop) a line of traffic whether it consists of two Model-Ts and a buckboard with sharecroppers and nuns on it, or a thousand Ferraris filled with Welsh supermodels and eurotrash. That is, although one cannot say with absolute certainty that copyright was either necessary to or sufficient for this expansion, or with absolute certainty that the expansion would have been either greater or lesser without copyright, one can say definitely that contrary to Macaulay's predictions and their repetition by disciples blind to fact, copyright as it strengthened did not prevent an immense efflorescence of publication such as civilization had never before experienced.

Like Marx, Macaulay has been proved wrong by reality and the long and steady development of the facts. And yet, like the Marxists, Macaulay's parrots continue to repeat every argument as if it had not been disproved by continuously evident actuality—as if facts were only dreams and dreams were facts. And they still imply that if copyright exclusivity is not overturned, the rivers of publication that have issued forth during copyright, will (paradoxically) dry up.

I apologize for not being a lawyer, except that it may allow me to comment sensibly upon the law. There is the law as it is intended, which, granted, can never be perfectly understood and would not submit to flawless interpretation even were it to have originated in one clear mind, much less in hundreds of legislative minds—which is why it is necessary to have lawyers. And there is the law of lawyers: that is, law as it was originally intended but then tortured for the rest of its life like a prisoner in the Château d'If.

To understand the perils faced by each of the laws as it exists for year after year among a million patient, bulldog-like talkers, one need only have had in college a sophomore roommate in his first philosophy course, and who, having been drawn to Bishop Berkeley, informs you that the table at which you are eating does not exist, and, when challenged to pass his hand through it, assures you that his hand does not exist, and then must be silent when informed that a hand that does not exist should be able quite easily to pass through a table that does not exist.

In a very short time he is cured of this—unless he goes to law school. If he does, he will first learn the lawyer's prayer—"God grant that I shall be superficially mauled by an alligator at the Snow White Breakfast at Disney World"—and then spend a large portion of the rest of his life arguing in excruciating detail that this or that thing must be treated as if it does not actually exist, or, if it does not in fact exist, as if it does. Supposedly to protect innocent persons from the criminal abuse of the law by its agents, the policeman is not held to account for his errors or abuse; rather, the mass murderer is set free, presumably to change the policeman's ways, but what does the policeman care, especially if he himself is lawless, corrupt, and escapes punishment? A contract is deemed unenforceable because a judge agrees with his intoxicating and bosomy clerk that the provision, "$100,000 shall be allocated for the purchase of safety equipment," does not mean that said $100,000, or any part of it, need actually be *spent* for safety equipment. Rather, these dollars have the privilege of being hypothetically corralled, not necessarily in a vault or even a separate account but solely in the exercise of a mind or two, there to be forgotten, or perhaps to be spent by Bishop Berkeley. People who enjoy a specialty power often forget that it has been granted to them by a dog that does not want to be wagged by its tail, no matter how caught up in hypotheticals the tail may have become.

The law is imperfect, we are imperfect, this is the system we have and that we must struggle forever to balance judiciously. The system allows and encourages advocates at the bar to stretch like yawning lions and propose like madmen, to say things that only the Cheshire Cat would say, and knowingly and shamelessly to take unfair advantage of gaps in the law that powerlessly admit absurdities. But it also provides judges to correct the absurdities, the unmoving text of the laws to correct the judges, the legislatures to have power over the laws themselves, some of the laws themselves to have power over the legislatures, the Constitution to be a guide for all, and, finally, the people—with various intervals of patience and procedure required of them—to have power over the Constitution itself. At times this power is exercised directly when the Constitution is amended, but mostly it is indirect, like a fleet-in-being, magically enforcing discretion, common sense, and reticence upon functionaries and practitioners who might otherwise possess inordinate power.

And no matter how much they may protest, the law is anything but the exclusive province of lawyers. The higher and more consequential it gets, the more this becomes both necessary and obvious. In fact, and thankfully, the law is no more the exclusive province of lawyers, and especially law professors, than tables are the exclusive province of Bishop Berkeley. This is important to note because of the tendency of lawyers, openly and proudly abetted by many law schools, to claims of superiority in regard to policy questions over which they have no more superior right or understanding than would a cucumber. These (questions, not cucumbers) they attempt to abduct from the public square and imprison in their seraglio awaiting a kind of involuntary sex change.

So it is with many things, not least copyright, which some lawyers have attempted to kidnap for adjudication when it is a question not of law but of policy. The slow development of the printing press over centuries was paralleled by the origination of protections for something new in the world: the ability to make many copies of a work mechanically, more or less flawlessly, cheaply, and rapidly. Such a thing had not existed before, and the new form of property at issue did not fit cleanly with the common law as it had evolved in dealing with properties of a different nature.

The difficulties of the common law in their application to copyright were ever present, and in recognition of reaction to this, copyright diverged slowly but firmly from the common law into statute law, the first great benchmark of which was the 1709 Statute of Queen Anne, "An Act for the Encouragement of Learning, by Vesting the Copies of Printed Books in the Authors or Purchasers of Such Copies."

It began:

> Whereas printers, booksellers, and other persons have of late frequently taken the liberty of printing, reprinting, and publishing . . . books and other writings, without the consent of the authors or proprietors of such books and writings, to their very great detriment and too often to the ruin of them and their families: for preventing therefore such practices for the future, and the encouragement of learned men to compose and write. . . .[82]

And with this began a divergence in English law, which is a work of geological accretion, and the cause for Madison, having written in 1785 a copyright act in the Virginia House of Delegates, and now commenting upon the constitutional provision, to write in the Federalist: "The utility of this power will scarcely be questioned [little did he know]. The copyright of authors has been solemnly adjudged in Great Britain to be a right at common law. The right to useful inventions seems with equal reason to belong to the inventors. The public good fully coincides in both cases with the claims of the individuals."[83] Joseph Story follows on with the judgment that "The copyright of authors in their works *had*, before the Revolution, been decided in Great Britain to be a common law right."[84] Even in Britain, with its immense and glacial constitution, the British Imperial Copyright Bill of 1910 "brought British copyright entirely under statutory law and consolidated and amended all previous enactments."[85]

With the founding of this country many other matters as well were just as resolutely cleaved from the common law to be made firmly a matter of statute, which is not to say that the common law no longer had a place, for the statutes were not so comprehensive as to be themselves an alternate evolution of the law, but that this place has been steadily receding as the statutory law has developed and statutory law and the regulations built upon it require adjudication. In short, statutory law trumps common law.

The copyright provision of the Constitution is beyond adjudication, and all the blather in the world cannot change the fact that it gives Congress the sole right and wide latitude in setting the term of copyright. Thus, when—in response to the Sonny Bono Act, which extended the term of copyright by twenty years—Lawrence Lessig attempted to argue the contrary in the previously cited Supreme Court case, *Eldred v. Ashcroft*, he lost by seven to two. Madam Justice Ginsburg, writing for the majority, summarized the court's view in the last paragraph of its opinion:"Beneath the facade of their inventive constitutional interpretation, petitioners forcefully urge that Congress pursued very bad policy in prescribing CTEA's [Copyright-Term Extension Act's] long terms. The wisdom of Congress's action, however, is not within our province to second guess. Satisfied that the legislation before us remains inside the domain the Constitution assigns to the First Branch, we affirm the judgment of the Court of Appeals."[86]

In a telling comment paraphrased by the *New York Times*, Professor Lessig states that "the experience was tantalizing because some of the justices who ruled against him conceded that long copyright terms were bad policy, if still constitutional."[87] One wonders about the nature of such a concession, and who made it. If it were a personal aside it would be irrelevant, and as an official pronouncement it would have no place. Since when is it the Supreme Court's role to opine upon policy? The answer might be, the court makes policy when lawyers and judges manage an end run around the political process and muddy the separation of powers. Having lost his case and turned to another cause, Mr. Lessig says,"The biggest problem progressives have had is the tendency to race to the court whenever there is a big issue. . . . Let's not think about a judicial solution, let's think about a democratic evolution."[88] On this, he and I are in full agreement, although he is fashionably late and would have undoubtedly supported the opposite—his previous—position had he prevailed. Why should law professors have to be reminded that the Constitution takes precedence over what they may or may not believe, at one moment or another, to be good policy?

About that policy, the foundations and principles of which are a matter of legislative concern, and which are the people's right to wrest from the experts, and which are unashamedly matters of open and general debate, much more can be said, beginning with the question of term. The move to elongate copyright term did not suddenly spring from the forehead of the late Sonny Bono. As tempting to snotty elitists as Sonny Bono may be as a target of ridicule—his name has lots of vowels, o's in fact; he appeared on television dressed as a caveman; he was straight man to Cher; he had a seventies haircut; he came up the hard way; he was a Republican; he ran a bar—the Act that bears his name is part of a long and dignified tradition consonant with the history of this question; and compared to his born-yesterday critics he was as reasonable, noble, and measured as Cicero, who was also, lest they forget, an Italian with lots of vowels in his name.

The anti-copyrightists who disparage the Sonny Bono Act also often exhibit a strange fixation with Disney and Microsoft. One can see why they might be agitated by Microsoft's power, ubiquitousness, and irritating influence on so much of their lives. But a mouse? Apparently they are deeply concerned with whether or not they may suborn this mouse to appear in their masterworks, or perhaps they believe that a check upon the use of Mickey Mouse by anyone who pleases is a threat to civilization. (Think of the explosion of culture, the renaissance, if only Mickey Mouse were freed from the Disney yoke.) And they are wont to merge their smoldering hatred of Disney with a populist jeremiad against the evil of large corporations (except Google) which, perhaps in the mind of someone educated by cartoons, Disney may represent in the same way that to auto workers General Motors once stood for industry. But, ironically, the Sonny Bono Act did more to right the imbalance between large combines and the little man—between huge publishing empires and lone writers; between Hollywood studios floating on money, and impoverished composers; et cetera—than ten thousand of their failed court cases and all umpteen billion of their subliterate blogs. Previously, a copyright assigned to a publisher or studio would remain there all the days of its life. Now, and thanks to Sonny Bono, if it is not a work for hire (which nothing should or need be), a licensee can keep it for only thirty-five years, after which the rights return to the author, the composer, the artist, or their heirs. This brings power to a place where previously it was absent, and checks it in the places where it tends to accumulate. How strange then that the "progressives" should term the act that brought this about outrageous, and mock the unpretentious man who achieved it.

Nor was he radical or thoughtless in regard to term. With the proliferation of written works and the growth of their importance to the life of civilization has come a long-extant and steady move toward their protection, including notably the extension of term. Prior to the Statute of Anne, when copyright had yet to become an important matter—because there were so few copies—term was, here and there, unlimited. The Statute of Anne then fixed it at twenty-eight years. In England by 1812 it would last for the life of the author, and in 1910 the Imperial Copyright Bill had extended it to a postmortem period of half a century.[89] At that time, though Greece was laggard, with protection of only fifteen years after publication, as was New Zealand, covering only the author's life, in Italy the extent was for the author's life or eighty years after publication. A similar formula, allowing for variation of the postmortem period, was long used in the United States, where the maximum length of copyright (neatly doubling the term in the Statute of Anne) was fifty-six years after publication.

The U.S. Copyright Act of 1998, extending term to a date seventy years after the author's death, merely brought American copyright
protection closer in line with the worldwide trend, something that
progressives usually applaud. Even in 1911, Austria, Germany, Japan,
and Switzerland granted thirty years postmortem, while—along with
Britain—France, Belgium, Holland, Hungary, Norway, Portugal, Russia, Sweden, and Denmark granted half a century, and Spain eighty
years. By the latter part of the twentieth century most countries had
regularized copyright term according to the Bern Formula of half a
century, and Germany had reached seventy years.[90] Thus, Sonny Bono's
rash extension was rather the rational continuation of a longstanding
evolution, bringing the United States into the company of most of the
advanced countries, many of which had had long postmortem periods
for a century or more, and some of which, like France, have far more
stringent protections of what the French perfectly and forthrightly call
droits morales.

Though even on their home turf the legalists are incompetent and
wrong, when they depart from the many pastures they expertly pollute
they are on even shakier ground, as when they make claims and accusations about hindrances to creativity, or copyright as "monopoly." They
seem unable to forgo any opportunity to wander into the ridiculous,
such as the following from the *Chronicle of* [supposedly] *Higher Education*:
"Physical property, such as real estate, is a finite resource that operates
as a zero sum [sic] game. And the laws regarding physical property treat
it as such. Intellectual works are abstract concepts and do not naturally
operate as zero sum [sic] games."[91]

This business about zero-sum games is repeated as gospel in the documents of the anti-copyright movement, notably in the Lessig ("Wow!
. . . I would have focused the attack in much the same way"[92]) wiki.[93] Of
course, property does not "operate" as a game or anything else, and intellectual works are not "concepts," but that is beside the point. This off-kilter
allusion fails to recognize the very nature of replicability that it is intended

to address. According to the logic presented, if Arthur Miller opened *Death of a Salesman* on Broadway, because it is not physical property and not a "zero-sum game," I could therefore justifiably rent a theater across the street and put on *Death of a Salesman*, charging less, because I would not have had to go through the trouble of writing it. In the same vein, nothing would be amiss were the butcher, the baker, and the candlestick maker to sleep with Queen Victoria, because Prince Albert's enjoyment would not be lessened—and, indeed in some quarters might conceivably be heightened—for the same reason that sexual pleasure, abstract in nature and wholly within the mind, is not a zero-sum game.

The inapplicability of this strain of game theory to the notion it supposedly clarifies or impeaches is stunning. Let us say someone opens a golf course. Some people pay to use it. Others sneak on to it without paying. What these solons are saying is that because the nonpayers don't spoil the enjoyment of those who do pay, no harm results. But even if the nonpayers don't tear up the fairways, and play at night so as not to crowd them, if the general rule is to sneak on and only a few people pay, very soon there will be no golf course for lack of revenue. Therein would lie the harm, both to the bankrupt golf course owners and to the general public with no more golf course. Queen Anne, with scepter and tassel, understood this quite readily three hundred years ago. Modern professors, paid to think, evidently cannot.

Just as I refer to the *Chronicle of Higher Education* (a publication that exhibits less intelligence than a Kleenex,™ see above) as the *Chronicle of* [supposedly] *Higher Education*, the anti-copyrightists frequently deride intellectual property as "so-called," because, unlike, for example, acreage or a motorcycle, it is abstract. Therefore, in their view, it cannot be property and should not be treated as such. But what about money, stocks, partnerships, futures, derivatives? What about ownership of or interest in future assets that do not yet exist, promissory notes, a business's good name or goodwill? Money, needless to say, is the crowning and mercurial abstraction of economic life. Coconuts, aircraft carriers, years of labor, compensation for bereavement, gold mines, thread, sex, trees, ice cream, islands, and horses, and sometimes nothing whatsoever, just a place holder, can all be secured and powerfully expressed in terms of money, which without any but a symbolic existence can submit to the most abstruse operations of mathematics and yet emerge as something that glows in men's minds and women's no less. Shall we nonetheless exempt money from the protections afforded property? And because by their very nature the work and product of the mind and spirit are abstract, replicable, and manipulable, shall we exempt these as well?

I remember, as a student, long ago, my shock at the frequent baseless speculations and childish inanities of certain venerable professors, a decided minority (then), who should have known more of life and had more common sense, but didn't. I speak of those who flirted with burning the libraries and starting anew, who obviously leaned toward establishing dictatorships of the enlightened (them), who believed and stated that human nature could be summarized and understood in a handful of postulates, and who in the guise of high-minded philosophy pimped for the destructive and murderous principles of totalitarianism left and right. They are still at work today, laboring to make their psychoses normative, writing immense treatises on microscopic nonsense, advocating infanticide while agonizing over the use of toilet paper. They have groups and subgroups and legions of cross-eyed devotees. They feed on the inordinate and undigested enthusiasms of youth. They disguise appeals to self-interest as pleading for the public good. They shelter ceaseless streams of absurdities beneath the indispensable arc of academic freedom. And, the ground having been so torn up and made unstable by such extremists, others, who might otherwise be sober and responsible, have taken up the subject of copyright and come to many an absurd conclusion.

But what about the Founders and Jefferson, who can hardly be thus dismissed, and whom those people who are so dismissible claim as their own?

©

In regard to copyright, the Framers were ahead of their time, moving it into statutory law in advance of virtually every other nation. Their satisfaction with a fairly short term reflects the relative novelty of such protection, and that in their time virtually no one wrote for a living. When it would become possible to do so, largely because of the country's economic expansion and copyright itself, more would be written, as we have seen, by orders of magnitude. In the eighteenth century, a lack of incentives and the slow pace and low volume of publication would have made a situation such as we have today difficult to imagine even for geniuses. Jefferson, with his lands, slaves, and offices, did not need copyright. Nor did virtually anyone else who wrote need it, as writing was largely an offshoot of being a gentleman, and not much of a living was to be made off writing anyway.

Which is not to say that they were not eager for the principle, which is why Madison wrote a copyright act for the Virginia House of Delegates, with a term of twenty-one years, and thought the principle so useful as "rarely to be questioned." Hamilton wanted the government "to encourage by premiums both honorable and lucrative the exertions of individuals . . . and to afford such other aids to those objects as may be generally designated by law."[94] This method was considered and quickly abandoned. Once rights were secured, the free market would be the most efficient judge of their value, and the entrepreneurial risk shifted from the government to the entrepreneur, without the necessity of paying for automatic back-scratchers, or the mistake of letting the transistor die on the vine. Or, what would be even more of a nightmare, the establishment of a kind of French Academy to decide the relative values and appropriate rewards for literary endeavors. Of course, we have that now, and it is called the *New York Times Book Review*, but at least it's not in the Constitution.

Understanding that, as things changed, the optimal term for copyright might also change, and that finding the optimal term either empirically or theoretically is likely an impossibility in the first place, the Founders did not specify a term, leaving that to the flexible discretion of their successors. A very long—certainly a perpetual—patent would induce a technological lethargy. Either no patent at all, or a term much shorter than twenty years, would probably make the effort of invention not worthwhile. We know that a twenty-year term protects and stimulates a continual search for the next improvement, but maximally? There is no way to tell, and the question is immaterial to copyright despite the forced arguments equating literary work with the march of technology.

Copyright is different by nature. Much of the agitation against it comes from the transient backflow of objections that the copyrighting of software stifles innovation. Unlike literary works, software is closer in every aspect to that which would require a patent. It is, after all, integral to, part of, and an extension of machines (or, perhaps more accurately, machines are extensions of it). Why is it copyrighted rather than patented? Because the time taken to examine and (subsequently) litigate would be prohibitive. The inaccurate classification is an insoluble problem, but the fallout from its difficulties should not be allowed to cloud the question of literary copyright. An entire beneficial system should not be put at risk for the sake of an ascendant but more or less substanceless machine culture that represents little more—in the nonscientific, nonclerical uses of its attributes—than busywork triumphant or entertainment pushed into omnipresence.

Perhaps the failure of copyright opponents to accomplish a clear enough delineation between patent and copyright allows them to imagine an alliance with Jefferson, who was concerned primarily with patents and machines rather than with copyrights and literary work. His well known letter to Isaac McPherson (of which most is presented below) is an example both of his focus and of the importance of making this distinction. Here we find, in the perfect fluidity and arrangement of words, great writing reminiscent of the Declaration itself:

> ... It would be curious then, if an idea, the fugitive fermentation of an individual brain, could, of natural right, be claimed in exclusive and stable property. If nature has made any one thing less susceptible than all others of exclusive property, it is the action of the thinking power called an idea, which an individual may exclusively possess as long as he keeps it to himself; but the moment it is divulged, it forces itself into the possession of everyone, and the receiver cannot dispossess himself of it. Its peculiar character, too, is that no one possess the less, because every other possess the whole of it. He who receives an idea from me, receives instruction himself without lessening mine; as he who lights his taper at mine, receives light without darkening me. That ideas should freely spread from one to another over the globe, for the moral and mutual instruction of man, and improvement of his condition, seems to have been peculiarly and benevolently designed by nature, when she made them, like fire, expansible over all space, without lessening their density in any point, and like the air in which we breathe, move, and have our physical being, incapable of confinement or exclusive appropriation. Inventions then cannot, in nature, be a subject of property. Society may give an exclusive right to the profits arising from them, as an encouragement to men to pursue ideas which may produce utility, but this may or may not be done, according to the will and the convenience of the society, without claim or complaint from anybody. Accordingly, it is a fact, as far as I am informed, that England was, until we copied her, the only country on earth which ever, by a general law, gave a legal right to the exclusive use of an idea. In some other countries it is sometimes done in a great case, and by a special and personal act, but, generally speaking, other nations have thought that these monopolies produce more embarrassment than advantage to society; and it may be observed that the nations which refuse monopolies of invention, are as fruitful as England in new and useful devices.[95]

Were Jefferson or his heirs (not necessarily synonymous with descendants) somehow to hold this under copyright (the letter was the property of Isaac McPherson), who would be so narrow of spirit as not to be delighted to pay for its use? But, that aside, assuming that he or a successor did enjoy some form of exclusivity, neither would have any right to exclusivity in regard to the ideas it expresses. One could repeat them or enlarge upon them so long as one did not copy the means of expression, either in the exact flow of its elements or in the particularities and style of its language.

And, apart from Jefferson's assessment that "Nations which refuse monopolies of inventions, are as fruitful as England in new and useful devices," which if not wholly inaccurate at the time would soon prove so—England and America, in fact, leading the world precisely as he would have thought countries that adopted such restrictions could (and did) not—there is little to contradict. Certainly he is right, and the argument is not one of principle but expediency, as is the right of patent if it is anything at all. That which a machine or a process may share with a literary work—so aptly put in the *United States Code*: "idea, procedure, process, system, method of operation, concept, principle, or discovery, regardless of the form"—is specifically exempted from the privilege of copyright, while granted to the holders of patents, which have a more profound reach into the object. Jefferson was not writing about copyright. To the extent that his views on patents might now be applied to copyright, I believe that they would be wrong, and that given subsequent developments in the economy and in technology he never would have extended his view to copyright.

A literary work is not composed of pieces of previous works, as is a machine or perhaps a chemical or manufacturing process that might depend upon the use of what analogously in a literary work would be the assembly of quotations from others. That is simply not how things are written, with rare exceptions that are not so much writing as they are editing, and the all too frequent and dishonorable crime of plagiarism.

Somewhere in between lies the internet term paper, which when not plagiarized from one source is plagiarized from many, and to be legitimate would require the abolition of both copyright and the expectation of honesty. That so many people seem to think of writing as a communal effort, an act of assemblage and additive progression as in adding storeys to a skyscraper or the laying down of railway track, points to a common misconception that though now championed by ideologues and careless dabblers has roots that stretch back several centuries and demand some explanation.

Let me begin this way. I have to confess that I have so rarely experienced triumph that I cannot claim to know it well enough to judge, but it seems to me at best a momentary joy followed instantly by sadness, and, then, of necessity, by wariness. In the few times I have been associated with a successful political tendency, I begin to part ways seconds after victory. When I was on a team, if we won I would be very quiet on the drive home. This had nothing to do with wisdom, which though I am old I still think I'm too young to claim (and certainly could not have at age fourteen), but with temperament, because, if you keep your eyes open, the light of triumph is always strong enough briefly to illuminate the darkness that lies ahead and at the end of which is death. More prosaically, victory is an imbalance of fortune that the nature of things soon begins to correct, but seldom is victory accompanied, as this would suggest it should be, by both constant vigilance and generous magnanimity.

Since the Enlightenment, we have been living in the ongoing triumph of science and reason. Their power is undeniable and their effect splendid and magnificent. The world, so much improved, could not have done without them. But like every triumph, that of science and reason, too, has been overextended. Not unexpectedly, it has wrought damage in those areas where its powers are nil, where it attempts to answer or deny questions it cannot answer, where it imposes its means and methods where they have neither effectiveness nor place.

I once served on a panel with an eminent scientist who was univer-
sally admired, and the kind of avuncular figure to whom one is eager to
give every benefit of the doubt. He was eloquent and convincing until
he claimed that human nature is a simple thing reducible to a few rules
that he then began to recite. His audience then deserted him in embarrassment, because human nature is not reducible to a few rules, as he
should have known. It is too much of a subject, too large in depth and
expanse, to submit to the kind of physical laws and relationships that
govern inanimate things.

Disparate colleagues of his have proposed, with similarly brutal reduction, that love is merely mechanical, the release of certain chemicals
that bind to certain receptors. This is what happens when you cradle
your child, behold your beloved, or mourn your lost parents, they say.
The chemical is released, and then captured. QED. Love is not only ex-
plicable, but explained, and now we can move on to the next thing. But
what they have not taken into account is why this does not happen (one
would assume) when paying a toll on the Triborough Bridge, killing a
hornet, or purchasing dish detergent. Because, they might reply, these
are not significant acts that contribute to our survival or that of our line
(proving that they have never driven across the Triborough Bridge at 5
p.m.). But what of the sacrifice and altruism, when moved by love, that
do not contribute to survival or that of a line? They say then that such
patterns are simply too deeply engraved to ignore. So that, therefore, the
mechanism operates simultaneously both rationally and irrationally, for
one end and for the other, both in contradiction of one's interests and
for their promotion. This unlikely paradox they attempt to sustain so
as to keep faith with the view that love is the chemical manifestation
of biological necessity. One wonders if anyone who can believe such a
thing has ever known real love. I think not. Which is perhaps why they
are content, forced by their own aridity, to offer such an impoverished
definition.

The paradigm can be widely applied. The philosopher and aesthetician Benedetto Croce focused his great learning and extraordinary sensibilities upon an exploration of beauty, and after five hundred dense pages of fishing for explanation and definition came back with nary a minnow. There is no satisfactory theory of beauty, just as there is no conclusive literary criticism or definitive philosophy. These things, like eschatological questions, simply will not submit even to reason in its most brilliant manifestations, for they are beyond reason, as even the most faithful children of the Enlightenment will discover when eventually they realize that a description of the instrument is not an explanation of the cause.

Which is all to say that since the Enlightenment, out of respect for the wondrous powers of science, some aspects of life have been "scientized" to harmful effect, and in some areas reason has been allowed to dominate where its strengths and benefits cannot apply: in eschatology, aesthetics, governance (which much unfortunate experimentation has shown is not a science but an art), human relations, and literature in the broadest sense.

The ancient view of literature, built upon and overbrimming with love, humanity, and risk, has been replaced by an idea-building ethos very similar to mechanization, pressing the standard modern literary work toward well phrased (or not) speculation, essay, or philosophical pirouette. The fashion in novels is to be tight, short, unambitious, carefully narrowed, intellectualized, cynical, and constructed above all to be invulnerable to the accusation that the author has transgressed the accepted norms, that he has listened to his heart. An ideal novel of this sort might be called: *Rimbaud's Macaque, a Novel of the Hypothetical Romance of Isadora Duncan and Nikolai Tesla, or, the Birds of Werbezerk,* which, to quote from the publisher's copy, is "the dark and unforgiving account of a Santa Monica professor of Jewish studies who discovers that her parents were Bavarian Nazis and practicing cannibals."

If literature is purged of its life and reduced to blocks of ideas; exposition; and something that, like science, builds narrow works of investigation into a vast structure, then of course it would be cooperative and mechanical, and why therefore would a copyright differ from a patent? But, in fact, the probability of an idea occurring simultaneously to more than one person is immensely greater than of its expression being the same. Newton and Leibniz discovered the calculus at the same time, but their revelations of this were not the same, even in the restricted language of mathematics. If, experimentally, two people were told to write a story about a Russian soldier who while fighting in Afghanistan learns that he is an orphan, it is almost certain that, although the "idea" would be the same, two different stories would result. Due to the great difference in the range of variables, the differences in congruity between, on the one hand, one idea and another, and, on the other hand, one form of expression and another, are vast, and therefore part of the sound basis of copyright.

From the *Amazonblogs* (how awkward and hideous a word) comes the following about "the fallacy of intellectual property" and the "hoarding of ideas": "The sooner we can all get past the 'idea' that anyone can own the thoughts, the words, the music, the sooner we can survive the possibly ensuing class war and get down to the business of evolving our eventual hive mind."[96] I trust that the reader need not be reminded that "the dream of the commons" and the "hive mind" are things that do not and cannot exist. Connecting people via the internet will not produce such things anymore than will connecting them via telephone, bringing them together in an auditorium, or publishing newspaper articles or letters to the editor.

These conceptions are not confined to the fringe. A letter in the venerable *Claremont Review of Books* states that, "ideas and art are inextricably intertwined [and] . . . contemporary copyright is notoriously used by owners to protect 'concepts' (that is, ideas) from unauthorized use by others."[97] To quote once again and cite § 102 of *Title 17* of the *United States Code*, "In no case does copyright protection for an original work of authorship extend to any idea, procedure, process, system, method of operation, concept, principle, or discovery, regardless of the form in which it is described, explained, illustrated, or embodied in such work."

This is the law, but even clearer are facts that exist independently of law, namely that concepts and ideas have not been repressed or stunted by copyright, and certainly not by the recent extension of copyright. Where is an example of this? How many books have been written about Pearl Harbor, the Constitution, Shakespeare, racism, education, particle physics, elephants, furniture, or veal cookery? Is the suggestion that once one is written and copyrighted the field of maneuver for pertinent concepts, ideas, or principles is somehow locked up?

The misconception stems from the dismal modern assumption that "Ideas and art are inextricably intertwined." If they are intertwined, it means that they are two different things, as something cannot be intertwined with itself. And of course, because they are different, we have a word for each. Copyright applies clearly and forcefully to one while not to the other. Also, and as a partial illumination of the structure and justification of copyright, ideas come most readily. The world is littered with the invisible corpses of not only those that luckily were stillborn but those that deserved long life and were denied it by insufficient expression and execution. (For those who think that their grandchildren are their ancestors, a note: the execution of an idea is not the same as the execution of a person.) In about 1962, I "invented" digital recording, and I'm sure that a great many other people did, too. But the laurels justly go to those who understood it better, pursued it faithfully, expressed it coherently, and realized it finally.

From another letter in the same excellent publication: "Every time an artist makes a new work, the law should assume that ninety-nine artists are waiting in the wings to make something even better. The first artist . . . should not be able to slow the ninety-nine."[98] This comports effortlessly with Lawrence Lessig's view, as reported in paraphrase by the *New York Times*, that copyright law is "too stifling of the artists who follow," and that the Sonny Bono Act "stifles creation."[99]

Where do they get the idea that copyright is a drag on artistic production? Are they suggesting that Pasternak could not write because Yeats had beaten him to the punch, that Tolstoy didn't write *War and Peace* because *Moby Dick* was copyrighted? I have published six hundred books, articles, short stories, essays, newspaper pieces, and the like. Not once in the forty-six years in which I have been engaged in this have I given a thought to someone else's copyright except when quoting a song. Literary work is not like assembling Legos,™ piling one modularized thing above another. Perhaps the cut-and-paste generation sees it that way, for which they should be rigorously held to account by—what else—copyright law. And if copyright did not exist? This would not encourage literary fecundity, but retard it. Because *Batman* is copyrighted, it means you can't write it again, or *Batman II, Batman III, Batman IV, The Return of Batman, Batman's Brother, Batman's Sister*, and so forth. You are forced instead to do what the letter-writer suggests you are prevented from doing—"making something even better": in this case, something else. This is precisely what has been done so often that even after hundreds of years of copyright and a decade of the "outrageous" Sonny Bono Act we are afloat in the richest sea of information and publication that mankind has ever known. There is so much, and it grows so fast, that the institutions tasked with tracking it cannot keep up. And upon this deep and swelling sea are a tribe of people who are convinced that, because of what they imagine to be the repressive and strangulatory effects of copyright, they are in a desert.

Perhaps many of those responsible for the three-quarters of a million postings exercised by my article in the *Times* have come up through an educational system that has addicted them to the promiscuous use of what others write, so that they think this is what writing is, and they themselves cannot write absent such reliance. Now they wish to alter the customs and laws of civilization to accommodate their failings.

Would Jefferson have been sympathetic to their arguments, their demeanor, their lack of polish? Would the author of the Declaration of

Independence have been drawn to their inability to recognize how the spark of genius actually arises, as it did so often in him? I don't think that he would have been at all agreeable to their association, much less that he was in any way their champion. More likely that upon reflection in the tranquility of Monticello, which as I write and despite the rare haze I can see in the far distance, he would have held them to be fast-talking thieves.

CHAPTER 4

THE ESPRESSO
BOOK MACHINE

*Using Machines to Hold
Machines in Check*

Not long ago, on one of those Virginia days that relieves potters of the necessity of firing their kilns, I was rowing on glassy water down the Rivanna River. Approaching a buoy where I would make a turn and head back, I looked to my left and saw, on the bank, an idiot who was mocking the ancient and unassuming motions of rowing. Evidently unfamiliar with the kind of racing shell that Eakins portrayed and that is a thing of beauty, and perhaps amused that it didn't have a motor, he was aping my motions and laughing maliciously. After all, how stupid can you be to row five miles in the heat when you might never move a muscle, eat cupcakes and pork rinds all day, smoke like a volcano, and sit in your bass boat hooked up to an oxygen bottle?

The wonders of misinterpretation flow generously from malice. Thirty years ago, based on the statement of an obviously psychopathic (and very minor) character in one of my books, a reviewer attacked me ad hominem for, he maintained, hating cities. At the time, I was living in New York, where I was born, working in the library of the New-York Historical Society on a novel, *Winter's Tale*, that is, if anything, a

748-page tribute to a city with which I was as deeply and immoderately in love as if it were a woman.

I bring this up because it bears upon the electronic culture, the machine, and the arguments that surround both. To wit, just as accusing someone of being a communist, or an anti-communist, so as to skate over the substance of his arguments is (or was) a common tactic, so in regard to anything having to do with mechanization the easiest reflex is to brand an opponent a Luddite. That is, someone who, like the early-nineteenth-century craftsmen who destroyed the powered looms threatening their way of life (and were severely repressed for doing so), rashly and irrationally fights the inevitable and the good. What most damns the Luddites in the common wisdom is that they failed to make distinctions (although they did: they did not attack machines per se, but only those that were displacing their customary industry), not even bothering with the bath water as they threw out all the babies. How stupid and pointless to object, for example, to the steam engine, the cotton gin, or the railroad.

The original progressives embraced such things as instruments of rationalism that would in tandem with their beloved techniques of social engineering make the world over for the better. Their recent heirs, however, have stopped short. A shift occurred sometime between their mocking of conservatives for objecting to water fluoridation and their own subsequent fear and suspicion of an encyclopedia's-worth of substances. In a single generation they went from an uncritical embrace of scientific culture to a supercritical rejection. They may not know it, but they have begun to swing back the other way, lured by the supposed wonders of the new digital world. It's a seesaw, feast or famine, all or nothing, up or down, on or off, never stopping in the middle, because that takes balance and skill.

Which is precisely the point. What is required, balance and careful consideration, demands in turn effort, control, and restraint. When in 2008 hundreds of children were seized by the state of Texas and removed from a Mormon faction that has more than dabbled in polygamy and child marriage, two principles were contending. The first, that society cannot allow the abuse of innocent children, and, the second, that the state must refrain whenever possible from interfering with the family, much less taking away children. To honor both principles correctly and in balance, all actions had to be considered in case-by-case determinations, which was exactly what the state failed to do.

When there is power, it must be accompanied by discrimination, control, and wariness. It is not enough simply to resist power or simply to accept it. All my life I have been involved with machines—taking them apart, putting them together, making them, repairing them. A large part of *Winter's Tale* is concerned with their role, their beauty, and their fascination. But although I embraced them in the book and have embraced them in my life, never have I surrendered to them, and nor should you.

Nature is not a machine. Rather, the machine is a part of nature, a hybrid of sorts, in full thrall to nature's laws. It has evolved with the mind of man as catalyst and intertwined itself with the landscape as if it were a natural force. The trick is not to subject man and nature to the laws of the machine but rather to control the machine according to the laws and suggestions of nature and human nature. To subscribe to this does not make one a Luddite. They, like their modern-day opposites, had no inkling of such a thing, but simply were afraid of looms. Their contemporary antitheticals are unaware that machines can exercise their own forms of tyranny, and, unaware of this, they appear not to know that it is possible to use machines to escape the tyranny of machines, although it must be done with exceeding care, like setting a backfire or using venom in medicine.

©

To understand the origins and implications of the Espresso Book Machine, first consider the protection of civil aviation from terrorism, not for the sake of the question itself, but to the extent that it is a model of production. Production in this case is the extraction of threats from a predominantly benign background. It is relevant because it illustrates how pervasive is the lust for bespoke data and customization of all sorts now that these have been made possible on a mass scale by machines with certain qualities that ape intelligence.

In the case of civil aviation, there are complementary approaches, each of which should be pursued in its fullness and bound inextricably to the others, although that rarely happens. The first is hardening and passive defense: the strengthening of cargo holds against the force of small bombs, increased fire protection, fortified cockpit doors, further redundancy in control systems, basic anti-aircraft-missile defense, and the like. The second is threat targeting: the detection of terrorists or their destructive artifacts via various methods of categorization, profiling, selective identification, and investigation, so as to stop them before their intended actions. And the third is screening: preventing any and all means of attack from penetrating an assiduously defended perimeter.

The American tendency has been to focus on the second approach, because it is cheaper and easier than the other two. It should not be surprising that we deal with mortal peril by turning to systems analysis born of the computer age and entirely reliant upon probabilities rather than upon hard-won certainties. This has become our way of life, and its advocates, drunk on the bureaucratic elixir of information-getting, believe in it as if it were religion. Which they must, for in light of its fundamental ineffectiveness continual support requires nothing less than blind faith.

To trust the strategy of allowing preapproved passengers to board aircraft, with less or no security, one would also have to believe in the impossibility or high improbability (neither of which is reasonable to expect) of either a terrorist who has no trail but does have comforting bona fides; someone with comforting bona fides who has a radical change of heart; or someone of a splendidly trustworthy nature and background, whose family is held hostage or who unwittingly carries aboard a device that will destroy his conveyance.

To trust in the effectiveness of spot checks, whether of passengers or cargo, one would have to be not only a person of faith but a player of Russian roulette, as are, if only metaphorically, the executive branch, the Congress (of the judiciary it is hard to tell), and, ultimately and most significantly, Americans themselves. Falsely comforted by cost-benefit analyses, we forgo most passive defense as too costly, and, inversely, we favor threat-targeting. What is done least, although we make a show of it, and because it is difficult and exasperating it looms large in every air passenger's mind, is screening. The excuse for incomplete screening is that the same benefits can be had more easily with "smart" targeting. But in contradiction of this a slogan from the interwar period is unfortunately apt: "The bomber will always get through."

When these points are made to officialdom it recoils into the bosom of probabilities. In the mid-nineties, it recoiled from the possibility of a revived national air defense, despite the country's many tall buildings and dense urban concentration, and the attractiveness to Islamic suicide terrorism of large cities like New York and Chicago. Now it recoils perhaps a little less, but we still lack comprehensive screening.

Almost forty years ago, I was in the Israeli army, seconded to the Air Force. I spoke imprecise but fluent and colloquial army Hebrew, and carried valid military identification and documents as well as American and Israeli passports. Hardly did I or my blonde, blue-eyed, Wellesley-educated wife resemble the Palestinian terrorists who had begun to target civil aviation, their richest prize and obsessive focus being El Al. But upon boarding an international flight at Lod, I was questioned and inspected to the extent that the heels of my army boots were prised off; my suitcase was deconstructed almost to the point of ruin; everything in it was pierced, squeezed, and eyed to death; and the Israeli army girl doing the inspection questioned me for more than half an hour about my history, views, plans, and friends. El Al combines this approach with both passive defenses and threat targeting, and although there is no absolute guarantee of safety, it has been for decades at one and the same time the most desirable target for terrorists and the one they have been unable to hit.

We can't institute such thorough measures in this country because of the size and throughput of our commercial air networks. True enough, but we can take enough trouble and spend enough of the greatest cumulative wealth of any country in the history of mankind to make an almost totally impervious barrier, the price of which would be the acceptance of hard work and expense rather than evading it via the supposedly magic channels of data processing.

This would demand, however, not merely extra care and expenditure but an adjustment of prevailing attitudes sufficient to be a retreat to an earlier time in which machines and industrial processes worked according to general applicability rather than a tailored approach, which was left to craftsmen like tailors. Machines were generally comprehensive and indiscriminate. The cotton gin goes through all the cotton and blindly removes the seeds: it does not identify them. Nor does it miss them. Its action would be exactly the same if the cotton were infested with seeds or had not a single one. In fact, its action would be the same if it were combing through polyester or wool. The combine does not seek out and identify an ear of corn, it takes in everything and because of their characteristics the ears of corn are blindly stopped by its selective filter. Even something so apparently able to "scribe" contours as an apple- or potato-peeling machine of the nineteenth century accounts for variation only by the constant application of a single pressure following the shape of the apple as unconsciously as a wheel takes a dip in the road.

In regard to this characteristic of manufacturing processes and the action and design of machines, we are now between eras. Day by day, machine methods are revised and the preponderance of one approach shifts to the other. The household thermostat no longer depends upon the expansion or contraction of a coiled wire that tilts a mercury-phial switch, but reads the temperature exactly and issues a digital command. Though temperature, like time, is analog, it may be expressed numerically, and the modern thermostat not only measures more precisely but acts or refrains from action in a process of complex decision making.

Moving from analog to digital, from the general, unmodulated application of force to its controlled and targeted application—as in precision-guided munitions in contrast to a blind artillery barrage, or in individually targeted advertising in contrast to roadside billboards—we are adjusting the processes of industrialization to bring them more in line with those of the *pre*-industrial era. This has always been the motivating factor in the design of machines such as the Jacquard loom (which can do what the most skillful weaver can do), or the sewing machine, or the Cuisinart.™ We build mechanisms either to do what we are incapable of doing—flying, communicating across the seas, shattering mountains, lifting 100-foot trees—or to relieve us of what we can do. The machines of the first category have far outperformed those of the second, until now, when we are approaching a kind of critical mass that will usher-in the eventual predominance of mechanization's new phase.

The combination of miniaturization, striking advances in materials science, and exponentially improving information storage and processing will allow things never thought feasible even in the most hopeful blushes of the machine age. The theme newly made possible is particularization, the goal of the federal bureaucrat who wants to stop a hijacking not by making it unachievable for anyone but by finding the hijacker, just as it is the goal of the bureaucrat overseeing a container port, who would forgo inspection of each container for the presence of nuclear weapons, in favor of finding out by investigation who might put a nuclear weapon in a container and in which container he might put it.

Explanatory analogies are abundant, such as, for example, a method of shaving that (unlike a razor blade, which runs along an entire front without making distinctions) would select and cut each hair. To Ptolemy this might have seemed as impossible as it might have to Francis Bacon or even to Einstein, although probably any one of them could have drawn a good map to the end result, identifying in terms of its simplest elements that which, though missing, if present would allow the "miracle" in question to occur—a miracle that is now only a matter of time. Strong nano-structures, nano-gearing, subminiature power storage, and the progress of information-processing compression must lead to such things: perhaps a thousand nano-lawn mowers applied to the face, each one chopping one hair shaft at a time, close to the surface, after gripping it like a logging machine, and then returning to base as a magnet is swept over them, the machines thus retrieved and simultaneously recharged by induction. Or perhaps, and for this you may pray without embarrassment, there will be cancer excision cell by cell, and patrols within the body to detect pathological irregularities in more or less real time.

The possibilities are so many that they call for a new Jules Verne to write about their wondrous application; a new H.G. Wells to view them with a more jaundiced eye; and new Huxleys and Orwells to warn darkly of their carelessly or maliciously cultivated potential. But along the way, during the transition, many conveniences will arise, not so miraculous even if hailed as such, but, even if short of miracles, clear departures that will be the cause of great changes. Take, for one example, tailoring.

A most interesting and disappointing phenomenon that one must witness day after day is the belief of so many people in their own importance. Fly across the country or overseas and in almost any seat is someone who is convinced that what he does and who he is makes him superior to everyone around him. The construction worker looks down upon the Harvard professor, who looks down upon him in return. The sculptor thinks middle managers are no better than ants, and middle managers think the sculptor a pathetic fool. The combinations are endless. Once, a powerful financier, knowing that my mother was an actress and my father was in the film industry, turned to me at a dinner as if to share a presumed superiority, and began to demean the intelligence of people in show business. "Can you imagine," he asked, expressing his contempt, "an *actor!*"

Had I the presence of mind at that moment, which I did not, my answer would have been, "Why don't *you* imagine *yourself* on a stage in front of a thousand people poised to hear a pin drop and about to spend the next three hours closely and critically observing as you play Hamlet. Or Willy Loman. If you have the chance to do either you might instead jump the Grand Canyon on a motorcycle, because it's easier." Other people always are less worthy, contribute less, and have it easier than we do, we think, as part of our human nature. We take things so much for granted—such as clothing, which we wear every day and usually possess in great abundance—with little regard to the skills required and the difficulties in making it.

In the nineteenth century, my grandmother was a seamstress who, in kerosene and gas light, made shirtwaists. When I was young, she tried to teach me how to sew, and ever since I have had great respect for tailors. There are competent tailors and there are great tailors, not to mention designers and pattern cutters, even if so many people in so many other lines of work fail to understand, from ignorance and lack of sympathy, the intensely difficult requirements made upon such people, and the nature of their skills. This ancient profession now is figuratively in the curve of the wave. You can still see it, and it is still breathing air, but it is nonetheless soon to go under, subsumed in the change that will roll through almost all things.

For, not long from now, most clothing will be bespoke, not by tailors and seamstresses but by machines. A person who wants to be clothed will submit to a scan that will sense and then store his measurements in a digital pudding of algorithms and solid geometry. Overlying algorithms will adjust, if necessary, for the big dinner he had the night before, or the ten pounds he hopes to lose in the summer. Then he will choose the clothing he wants, specifying variations in cut, material, color, fasteners, or placement of buttons. And somewhere, perhaps in Hong Kong, Russia, or the room next door, a machine will lay out the fabric, laser-cut the patterns into the material, and then baste, sew, knit, hem, or stitch the cloth, quickly making a garment that previously would have cost a great deal more and taken many times longer to complete.

We have already entered the new paradigm that will bring us such things, and it can only strengthen. It will work upon almost anything manufactured, including the scribed objects that since the beginning of time have required hand and eye. The first things to have fallen—a long time ago—were those that early invited industrialization because of their easy replicability: sugar cubes, bricks, pig iron, stamped parts. Then came the things that required the complicated, if blind, direction of precise machines: filling and capping bottles, baling and tying hay, weaving patterns into cloth. The last stage will be machines that seem almost to think, that will build a house, make a custom-tailored suit, or travel through your colon to scout out and snip polyps that it will give to another machine to deliver to yet another machine for diagnosis.

Printing and publishing fit into this hierarchy very near the bottom, because their essence and utility from day one have been derived from the quality of replicability. The printing press is a masterwork of the old paradigm, and to rationalize the old paradigm economically it was necessary to have large print runs, and, thus, centralization, and following from that an immense and ponderous distribution network. If, however, it were possible to dispense with large print runs, neither centralization nor the trucks and rail cars for transport would be required, nor warehouses in which to store books in the downtime during fluctuation in demand, nor the large bookstores, inventory, and personnel with which to move stock. All of this apparatus and trouble is now rapidly becoming vestigial, and as in most great shifts in industrialization, and so often too in presidential nominating contests, the front-runners early in the competition, that which and those who seem inevitable, are often replaced by a compromise candidate or someone or something that appears to have come out of the blue.

In the case of books and publishing, for decades the front-runner as heir apparent to the printing press was the computer screen, whether (and at first) on the desktop, laptop, e-book, or i-book. A whole book—indeed, a whole library—can be sent over copper, fiber-optic, or the air, and at its destination manipulated, reproduced, searched, displayed, and stored with ease and speed heretofore unheard of. But there has been so much understandable resistance to this that the old ways, long vulnerable to replacement, are still with us.

As often happens with new technologies, digital technology being a rich example, its stewards become so intoxicated with the adventure they are living that they forget that mechanism must adjust to man rather than vice versa. Much of the alienation and failure of the electronic age is due to the fact that its enthusiasts lack education in the humanities, and, like Soviet planners, value the design they have come to worship over the people they claim to serve. They tend to overlook and ignore human needs and preferences, which seldom run parallel to the powers and tendencies of machines, because in their careless mania they have been easily educated out of them, never having been well educated in them.

Thus it was widely assumed—and it may yet happen—that books would be replaced by the magnificently efficient digibook, which can accomplish miracles, if you allow that miracles are manifested in quantities rather than qualities. Although I am sometimes accused of being a kind of anti-Christ ignorant of and hostile to technology, this is hardly the case. I have had a lifelong interest in technology, and in physics half-theoretical, half-empirical, and entirely amateur. Starting a long time ago with my parents, I have made my family suffer through sincere disquisitions on horsepower, electrical engineering, thermodynamics, and much else. As an undergraduate, I took Professor Bode's course on communications theory and thus heard directly from a recently retired director of the Bell Labs what, had I been a courageous investor rather than an investment chicken, I could have parlayed over the last forty years into perhaps a billion dollars.

Not born to be rich, by 1981 I had nonetheless begun to use a PC that required for its operation the absorption of several hundred pages of protocols and the placement of very large floppy disks in the freezer to fix frequent crashes. Combining this relatively early and intense experience with Professor Bode's clear picture of where the field could lead, I went to my publisher, William Jovanovich, with a proposal. He hardly fit into the publishing industry, which frequently had its long knives out for him. They said he was rash, and they were right, but the reason they didn't like him was that he embodied what they, lacking it, had come to detest. He was brilliant, courageous, far-seeing, daring, and deep. Unlike many of his shallow counterparts, he was aware that mortality gives to our lives, no matter how glorious, a signature in a minor key. That gave him perspective, gravitas, and wit. Not that he didn't enjoy being a tycoon (he did), but while some of his fellow publishing chairmen and CEOs of the period were fattening in the Hamptons, parading in the main dining room of the Four Seasons, or—and this is neither fabrication nor exaggeration—snorting cocaine and dressing in women's underwear and pig masks during fornication with Key West prostitutes, William Jovanovich, whom these pompous, glossy, corrupt, fly-by-night fakes thought somehow beyond the pale, was carefully reading through many volumes of Hazlitt. In today's world, I suppose, reading Hazlitt does not bode well.

Because I knew him to be unburdened by either fear or conformity, I presented to him, in 1983 or 1984, my proposal for the following. It would be approximately 8½ by 11 inches, about ⅓-inch thick, bound in leather in some shade of brown (which, in my long-lasting view is the only appropriate color for leather), like the portfolio that my parents had recently presented to me, that I showed him, and that as I write now sits on my desk to my left. When opened it would reveal two 8½ x 11 screens, textured as much as the art of glassmaking could transform frosting into the feel of paper. To a near-sighted person it would look like an open book—the pages off-white or cream, the print black, illustrations in four colors, no glare, no flicker, no hum, and very high resolution. Eventually, as it was perfected, pages would be turned by placing your fingers on them and doing almost exactly what you do with a real book. The pressure and direction of a sweep of the hand would be read and obeyed. You could also turn pages by commanding it verbally to do so. You could tell it to search for a particular word or phrase, or assemble, for instance, all mentions of feldspar, the guillotine, or Easter Island. You could make a concordance or ask for a dictionary definition or a citation from another work, and these would appear.

Inside would be not merely one book but dozens, or scores. You could replace them by plugging and unplugging modules the size of Chiclets.™ Eventually, you would have access to the contents of the entire Library of Congress—*by radio*. And, you could tell it to take a letter, to read it back to you, to correct the spelling, and to file it in your computer at home and print out multiple copies. I confess that interconnectivity, the real gold ring, did not occur to me, and in this I bow to its well known inventor, my classmate, that spritely lummox, Al Gore. (Since he left college, no one has spoken to him, as no one has been able to interrupt him.) My quite limited concept, as presented above, would not have taken the kind of big bite out of things that could have changed them fundamentally.

Jovanovich was, to say the least, a very perspicacious man. His conclusion at the time was that something important was lacking, and that, regardless of whatever was absent, we were simply not ready for this. He was of course quite right in view of capabilities then (and those readily accessible even now) and the probable reception (again, then and now). What was lacking? Five hundred years of habit, tradition, and affection; the tactile feel of real paper; the weight and density of many pages; the difficulties that, conquered, instill pride; the smell of ink and new paper; the variations in texture and color; the inalterability of the printed page; the sense that it was there and although it might vanish in fire or flood, it would not vanish because of a lightning strike half a mile away, excessive humidity, a magnet, or a malfunction in one of a million lines of computer code. That is, what was, although peripheral to the substance of the text, the independent nature of a book in which the writing does not simply vanish into thin air.

That was what was missing, and, therefore, the industry would stay fundamentally the same for time unspecified. I was discouraged, but he was right on the mark. The thesis would prevail because the antithesis was insufficiently compelling or developed. But, as in historical processes and other forms of the dialectic, the existence of even an insufficiently compelling antithesis is often a nagging pressure that presages the movement of mountains. It is something that can be neither forgotten nor ignored as it glows persistently in the mind. For at every weakening of the dominant trend, every setback, every pause, it will be there as a ready alternative.

With the advances of the last quarter of a century, the powers of this particular antithesis have grown. It is like an army in former times that has approached a walled city and begins its siege, filling the plain, its campfires burning like fireflies, its pots boiling, its ranks swelling. The two forces are very strong, and the pressure is great. This has produced, in compromise, a synthesis of the two currents, now present like a tiny trickle that becomes a spectacular flood. It has an interesting but in some ways unfortunate name. It is called the Espresso Book Machine.

Unfortunately the name of the book machine is reminiscent of the espresso bar, without which, evidently, the modern bookstore cannot exist, which doesn't say much for the naked appeal of books. The name is, however, perfectly appropriate in view of the machine's attribute of making up an individual order.

Although in its initial stages it is probably as immature as a late-nineteenth-century typewriter, it is nonetheless a synthesis of the slow, unwieldy, and inflexible book; and the complicated, vulnerable, and off-putting devices that have failed to replace the book. About half the size of a small Fiat, it takes digitized books from the internet or elsewhere and prints, binds, and covers them automatically. According to various press reports, it can turn out a three-hundred-page book with the characteristics of a trade paperback, including a four-color cover, at a cost of three dollars and in less than five minutes.

Invented by Jeff Marsh and developed, with the help of the Alfred P. Sloan Foundation, by a team under the leadership of former Random House chief Jason Epstein, it has printed thousands of books at test locations including the World Bank in Washington, the New York Public Library, and the Bibliotheca Alexandrina in Egypt. Blackwell, in England, plans to put them in each of its sixty bookshops. Scores of thousands of books in the public domain are available in digitized form, primarily from university libraries, and hundreds of thousands of more recently published works are easily convertible from the publishers' and printers' electronic databases to a uniform format suitable for the machine.

Once it is shaken out, this extraordinary device will relieve the publisher of the need to deal with or pay for printing, warehousing, shipping, order processing, remaindering, and, most significantly, returns. Returns—worse than mere excess inventory, because they require shipping, receiving, and refunding before settling down as dead weight—are the great sorrow of publishing. Whether they are the vast numbers of unsold copies of a "big" book upon which a publisher has gambled unsuccessfully, or the cumulative lesser returns of books from which less is expected and of which fewer are printed, they are an immense, suffocating, incapacitating burden on the industry.

Were publishers to switch to distribution via the Espresso Book Machine or its like, they could increase their profitability almost unimaginably. They would still be indispensable for screening, editing, layout, design, advertising, and publicity—a combination of validation and presentation that has always been their chief role and will remain so despite the hopes and dreams of many in regard to self-publishing. Publishers will still come under the murderous assault of authors accusing them of insufficiently promoting their books, and, as always, the levels of advertising and publicity will function primarily as protection for the advance—the fullness of one a direct variable of the fullness of the other. Sales forces will remain, as books will still fight for display space in bookstores and college professors will still require flattery and romance as if they were doctors in the sights and pay of drug companies.

The bookstores, however, needing to display only a single copy of each work, will either be much smaller (due to shallower shelving) or have many times the number of titles for inspection than they would otherwise be able to carry. They will no longer need to invest in or handle inventory, their major expense. Some titles in high demand, or at least expected high demand, would have to be stacked as always, having come from traditional presses or via the Espresso Book Machine churning them out during closing hours. The machine would have very little inefficient downtime, for bookstores would run it, or, more likely, them, all night long.

With no need to invest in inventory, a bookstore would be able to afford improved machines that will inevitably be able to produce books indistinguishable from books as they are now—in all sizes, with hard covers, with every type of paper, full-color illustrations, and whatever else may be required. The distance between this and what the first machine can already do is short and only a matter of accretion and rearrangement rather than adaptation to elemental changes. Not so many years from now, you will be able to go into a bookstore (or order online, as is now common) and have any kind of book printed for you expressly in every sense of the word.

Pricing will evolve from the cost of materials for the book itself, the costs associated with purchasing, running, and monitoring the machines, and whatever overhead the bookstore will have to recoup. The publisher will no doubt set a base price, but the bookstore will vary it, as is done now, according to its own strategies. If the store is spare and the management efficient, the books will cost less, and if the store offers acrobats and elephants, books will cost more, depending in both cases upon the levels of fixed overhead and the success in moving volume.

Overall, however, books will go down in cost, enabling publishers to take risks, offer more, and perhaps reverse their drift toward the protective reflex of catering to the lowest common denominator. Obscure and out-of-print books will awaken from the dead, suddenly available, a wonderful thing for their authors, their audience (even if it is limited), and culture in general, which is always stronger and healthier if it offers safe harbor and the opportunity of expression to authors and their works that, ill fitting to the times, may sleep long but then emerge in a different world to enjoy a second chance. For those who have been weaned away from paper and ink and are wedded to the electronic interface, the flood of availability will be the same, though the ability to manipulate, search, hold, *and copy* text will be far greater. But for those who prefer the old form, it will have been freed of its present constraints and cured of its perilous dilemmas, in a synthesis of the best of both worlds.

But as alluring as is the promise of a print-on-demand publishing system, it will never be a paradise. With more or less universal printing on demand, publishers will not need to give advances except to popular authors to lock them in. The more obscure and less commercially promising books will earn royalties as they are sold, changing the system whereby the profits from the whales subsidized the bets made by the publishers on the development of the minnows. And the publishers, not having advanced to the minnows, will not need to protect an investment as they do nowadays with advertising and publicity. This, needless to say, will not be ideal for many.

Even if authors' revenues would decrease per book as the price of books declined (or perhaps not, as the elimination of middle-men would and should allow an increase in royalty, although no such increase followed the savings realized when writers became their own linotypists), the decline might be made up in greater volume. Whatever the economic consequences, copyright need not be degraded. Although copyright's opponents argue the burdens and impracticability of keeping track of payments due, in the fast and fluid world in which they live and of which they want more without limit, their concern is suspect given that cell phone companies track calls to the second, the location from which they are made, and exactly to whom, and then bill with apparently no trouble at all. My family's cell phone statement for October of 2007 contained 4,881 pieces of discrete information logged without apparent effort as we circulated around the country. Yearly, this is a rate of 58,572 discrete figures. The cell phone companies have not yet complained of the complexity of billing me in a process far more daunting than any that copyright opponents commonly claim to be too complex to work, such as the tracing of rights holders or the accounting and division of atomized licensing fees as a result of electronic distribution (I believe this is done routinely by the Copyright Clearance Center.) The power of the technology, in fact, borders on the absurd. Let us say that you write a letter to your sweetheart in Mozambique and send it by Gmail.™ If you happen to mention sponges, she will see, alongside the text, advertisements for sponges, books on sponges, Greek sponge-fishing holidays (vastly overrated), and various sponge exposés.

This power neatly solves the problem of orphan works. These are the copyrighted works, with no apparent claimant, that copyright critics claim are withheld from civilization by the inherent injustice and unworkability of copyright law. But due to the new means of storage, transmission, and tracking, they can easily be kept in print, and the cost of doing so would be virtually nil. If an obscure book (or otherwise) can be found online, it can also have an assigned home—a publisher, or perhaps the copyright holder directly—who can license it to each user much in the way Google charges each time its "AdWords" appear, Apple charges by the song, and phone companies by the second. In the absence of a claimant, a notice could be posted on a universal copyright internet notice board. After a reasonable time and no response, a potential user or publisher could be granted permission to use or publish, with royalties held in escrow for yet another period, until they were claimed. And if they were not claimed, they could be directed to a fund of some sort, or revert to the payer. These simple steps would make orphan works available and protect the copyright holders at the same time.

Why is it that the internet-dizzy anti-copyrightists, proud of their technical savvy, have spent so much energy complaining about orphan works rather than thinking up a system that should have been for them a simple reflex of their mouse fingers? It is because the resistance to paying for copyrighted material, although often characterized as arising from a supposed technical burden or principled concern for the public interest, arises rather from exactly the same segment of the brain that is dominant in shoplifters. And the Espresso Book Machine or any other wonderful devices, syntheses, compromises, or solutions will not stop the assault on copyright, because, among other things, those carrying it out are on automatic and are sustained by motivations that are skew to the point.

And although they say what they want is ease of access, the revivification of dormant works, and a reduction in costs, the opponents of copyright view these mainly as useful auxiliaries to their argument, the heart of which is that they want to abolish all forms of intellectual property. What they really want is evident not only in the occasional direct admission ("Seems we need to lay off on copyright laws as it [sic] is starting to slow growth in the U.S."[100]; "I am at the point that I simply see no justification for copyright anymore."[101]) but in both the underlying justifications and general direction of their movement.

©

Given that things like the Espresso Book Machine will go far in providing the benefits that supposedly would ensue with an absence or further restriction of copyright, what then is the driving force behind such a passionate movement? Of course, greed helps to make ideologues, but it does not make them entirely. There is to be sure a diffuse, watered-down echo of Marxist and other utopian objections to the idea of property, which thrives among the privileged in their various and comfortable la-la lands and then for some enlarges fearsomely when they are graduated and meet the shock of an entry-level job, but this is not sufficient by itself to explain an obsession with copyright rather than a general reaction and a general assault. Nor can envy or nihilism completely explain the impulse. Many things are involved, among which, very importantly, is academic orthodoxy: not politics of any sort as they now thoroughly intrude upon a university both unwilling and unable to resist their commanding influence, but the academic modus operandi, which is in itself valuable, necessary, and good, assuming it does not, like the scientific method, overreach like Germans seeking *Lebensraum* and force itself into places where for various reasons it does not belong.

Whence the collaborative impulse and worship of collective effort that has so completely saturated American education? Marxism and the like simply do not have the power to sustain it. Rather, it may come from a perversion of legitimate academic practices. One encounters in Arabic education something called the *Isnad*, or chain, in this case a chain of authorities. It is the formulaic recitation of a line of citations so long that whatever you say will contradict at least some of what you present as your authority for saying it.

This kind of thing is hardly confined to Arabia. In a short article I read recently the following sentence jumped out at me like an electrocuted cat: "To grasp fully what he is up to, one must re-read Aristotle, Thucydides, Plato, and Xenophon [Isn't that a type of headlight?] and then re-read them again alongside the related chapters."[102] What would you do in the afternoon? It was not, as far as I can tell without rereading Xenophon, a witticism, as it should have been. It does illustrate the world of intellectual tangle—the endless Möbius belt—in which every thread of the cloth is borrowed from another, every pick-up stick touched by twenty others, and no observation fresh from the mind of an observer left unencumbered lest it corrupt the spirit of complication. Those who operate this way both worship and detest those who don't. The primary texts to which they are devoted are not derivative as are theirs, which should give them a hint, and perhaps does, which may account for a lot. Theirs is the prisoner's envy for his fellow prisoners who charge electrified wire while he himself is afraid to run out an open and unguarded gate.

In the more sclerotic academic circles, where everything must be supported, even that which theoretically cannot be, a multiplicity of footnotes is godliness, and to be cited in them is bliss. The German tradition of scholarship suffers exquisitely from this, as does Jewish scholarship, always on the defensive, and (necessarily, with no alternative) English and American law. And of course a history without complete sourcing is valueless other than as a literary work, even if written by a participant (assuming it goes even an inch beyond his own story).

Students therefore are taught to support their assertions with crushing citations. Well and good, unless it is mainly the deadening hand of "authority" in both senses of the word, and unless it becomes a substitute for thinking, risk, labor, and originality. It often does, especially when, in a metaphysics reminiscent of Thomas Nast's cartoon of Tammany characters standing in a circle directing blame at the person to the left, the blind cite the blind, the careless cite the careless, the ignorant cite the ignorant, the biased the biased, and so on.

At risk of straying too far, I must relate the story of how a long time ago a great friend and I, alighting from a freight train in northern Virginia, proceeded to Crystal City, where we insolently skated in our shoes across an empty ice rink while a Zamboni machine was grooming it, leading to our detention by a security guard with the physique of a whale. As we were led into the guard station, my friend (somehow a government attorney) appointed me his attorney, and I appointed him mine. During interrogation, I referred all inquiries to him, and he referred all inquiries to me, in the most polite, respectful, and legalistic way. This is exactly what too often passes for scholarship and authorship.

If authorship is simply an echo chamber, which for many it is, then copyright is of course a terrible hindrance and should be gutted for the good of all. But that it is an echo chamber is the choice and view of those who recoil from independent thought. As in the worst of medieval scholasticism, they dare not venture beyond the rim of received authority lest they fall off the edge of the earth. To help those who cannot face the terror of doing something independently, the electronic age has provided WEbook,™ which, according to the *Washington Post*, "by adopting the growing crowd-sourcing model ["Crowd-sourcing" was invented by sheep.] . . . hopes to help frustrated writers realize their potential. . . . Members can help one another overcome writer's block" (if you have writer's block you should heed it as you would heed a cobra), and the company has an employee who (Tolstoy would have appreciated this) "makes the final call in disagreements between writers or helps moderate brainstorming sessions."[103]

Such stunning mental dependency was often evident in the voluminous reaction to my single editorial piece, and may have been inspired there from the top down, by the leader of the movement, Lawrence Lessig, who is also and not coincidentally a passionate advocate of "remix," or, in my terminology, Legos.™ Taking a work that someone else has made, chopping it up, and rearranging it, perhaps adding or subtracting elements according to whim, is a favored "art" form of a generation weaned on push-button alternate endings and Microsoft's "cut and paste." Lessig writes, "Helprin barely cites anyone. . . . Helprin doesn't bother with what others have written. . . . Now between . . . pure remix . . . and Helprin's . . . pure Helprin . . . which is more respectful of authorship?"[104] It's one thing to learn from others, but another to copy them. In another context, he is what old-fashioned people might call careless about aesthetic standards and the integrity of a work, when he writes: "How better to revive a 30-year-old series than by enlisting armies of kids to make content interesting again?"[105] That might be an interesting project for *Star Wars*, the thirty-year-old series to which he refers, but not for *War and Peace, Dubliners,* or *A River Runs Through It.* One is allowed to do it, in fact, with *War and Peace* but not with *A River Runs Through It,* because the latter is protected by copyright. When its copyright expires, *A River Runs Through It* could be "remixed" into a transvestite musical with dolphins. That might be a lot of fun, but perhaps it wouldn't have been so much fun for Norman Maclean and those, strangers and otherwise, who hold him dear. Which is, of course, one of the many arguments for extending copyright.

If I am to understand it correctly, part of the view of, and common to, the movement I oppose is the idea that one can respect and/or actually achieve authorship by rearranging the works of others. And how do the others achieve authorship? By melding and rearranging the works of other others. But authorship is something entirely different. It is an adventure of sorts, a dangerous and risky thing that in its essence must depart from authority and is based not upon a compilation of previous works but on observation and what follows ineffably in the mind and heart of the observer. Since the beginnings of civilization this has distinguished almost everything worthwhile that has ever been written. It is not following the "remixing" mole into his suffocating tunnel, but, rather, standing on the cliff's edge above the sea, in the sun and the open air, on your own. There is no machine that can change this.

CHAPTER 5

PROPERTY AS A COEFFICIENT
OF LIBERTY

Property Is Not Antithetical to Virtue

At age fourteen, on a cheap three-speed Robin Hood bicycle that my father inexplicably (to me) provided as a replacement for a magnificent English touring cycle, the color of a Weimaraner, that I had left to rust in the rain, I set out on a trip across most of the country. A great deal happened in those months: I was not many miles away from Ernest Hemingway on a sunny July morning in Idaho at the instant of his death; in the lobby of an office building in Arizona, Barry Goldwater informed me that I was not permitted to carry the hunting knife that hung from my belt; and with what now seems like a remarkably small number of other visitors to Zion National Park, I listened to a park ranger's radio as the Berlin Wall crisis unfolded. In regard to copyright, property, and decency, the pertinent incident occurred in a field in Iowa.

As a child roaming sparsely inhabited land along the Hudson in a paradise that is now carpeted with condominia and conference centers, I had gotten into the habit of eating the fruit, berries, or other crops that in various seasons would easily come to hand, whether in the wild or at the edge of fields or gardens. Never did it occur to me that these apples, peaches, pears, corn, tomatoes, berries, watercress, and grapes were anything but a gift of nature and the common property of mankind.

No longer exactly a child, I halted my bike by the side of a cornfield on a hot day in Iowa to drink from my canteen. I was at the edge of thousands of acres. You couldn't see the end of it, and the stalks, as dense as a Vietnamese bamboo forest, were heavy with young corn, probably animal corn. I helped myself to an ear, and, after shucking it, began to eat. Then appeared the farmer, as if from nowhere, as irate as Al Sharpton. Still eating, I wondered why he was agitated. Forty-eight years ago, it went roughly like this:

"Where'd you get that corn?" he asked, throat tight.

I didn't lie, and say that I had bought it at Gristedes on Lexington Avenue, but instead made a kind of hitchhiker's gesture, pointing backward with my thumb at the thick green front of corn stalks. I wasn't able to say anything anyway, as my mouth was full.

"That's my corn. You have no right to take it. You stole it from me."

"What?" I said. "One ear of corn?" After all, he knew and I knew that there were thousands of acres of corn, and probably tens or scores or hundreds of millions of ears of corn, and that neither he nor anyone else could possibly have missed just one. Had he not seen me, he would not have known of my expropriation or been affected by it. All this was said by the simple phrase I had uttered, with the unspoken addendum, which I felt, that he was greedy and a little crazy to care about just one ear of corn, and that, although I knew he would never give it, in my view he owed me an apology.

"No," he said, taking in all arguments at once, "it doesn't matter whether you took one ear or all the corn, you have no right to do so, you've stolen from me, and you're a thief. I struggle to pay for this land, I plow it, I pay for the fertilizer and seed, and I work to cultivate and to harvest. I take the risk, I spend the time, the land is mine, the corn is mine. Who are you? What did you do?"

My presumption that because I was from New York I could outdebate an Iowa farmer was beginning to go the way of all flesh. "There's no sign," I said, stupidly, beginning to fear that he was right, but, at fourteen, making a stand anyway.

"Do you mean to say that without a sign you have no way of knowing that this is not your field and this is not your corn? Did you think, 'Oh, this must be the corn I planted when I was passing through here last spring. Otherwise there'd be a sign telling me that it isn't'?"

"It's just one ear of corn," I insisted.

"Are you starving?" he asked. "You look pretty well fed to me."

"No."

"If you were, then you might have to steal someone's corn, but at least you'd know that you had no choice—having asked for some in the first place, having tried to plant your own, having looked for work, having suffered until you were pushed. None of these things applies to you."

"I'll pay you," I said, in one of my lowest moments. By now, I was ashamed.

"No you won't. It doesn't work that way. When a thief is caught it doesn't change things if he offers to pay. 'Sorry I robbed your bank. Here's the money. See you later.' Think of what the world would be like if that were true."

"You want me to throw it back?" I asked sheepishly, holding up the ear of corn as if it were a fish.

"And then get out of here."

"Do you own the side of the road?" I asked, voice cracking in defeat.

"Yes, I do."

The rest of the day, bicycling toward Nebraska and a night camping on grasslands beneath a sky miraculously heavy with stars, I thought of rejoinders. I would not—even after the fact—let him do that to *me*. The problem was that I had not a single argument better than his. My pride was shattered, I had no excuse, I had been totally in the wrong and had had neither the presence of mind nor the good grace to recognize and admit it. It didn't matter that he had thousands of acres of corn, and, perhaps like Van Gogh, would not have missed a single ear. It didn't matter that taking the corn was easy, and except by chance would have been undetectable. I stole from him. That's what mattered. And if I had been not a single kid passing through, but one of hundreds of thousands who stayed put and habitually raided his fields—simply because they could—then not only would it have been wrong, it would have been hurtful and destructive.

The farmer was right to have shamed me. Once I had made sense of it, and by the time we got to Nebraska and were camped under the sky as I had never before seen it, I felt freedom and enjoyment far superior to the corrosive delight of getting something for nothing.

Having been initially instructed in why most takings of property are unjust, I passed into adulthood nonetheless with an almost unconscious residual bias against property. (That's part of what you get from living on the Upper West Side of Manhattan, in the same way that a fish gets water when it opens its mouth). It took decades, actually, for me to understand the positive—and, for a democracy, indispensable—effects of property, and to grasp in full the theoretical proposition that property is the guarantor of liberty. Though hardly as elegant as the word *guarantor*, the word *coefficient* is perhaps more precise.

According to the *Shorter Oxford English Dictionary*,[106] the adjectival meaning of coefficient is "Co-operating to produce a result." As a noun, it is "a multiplier that measures some property of a particular substance, *for which it is constant.*" In regard to the relation of property to liberty, *coefficient* is thus a good predicate. This requires further explanation.

To begin, where would copyright, patent, and trademark be obviously unnecessary? Only in an entirely centrally directed economy, whether "perfect" socialism, communism, "democratic centralism," or whatever it might be called. There, for example, drug firms would not need to own the rights to their discoveries, because to raise capital they would not need to promise a return, having obtained their capitalization by decree. (How this would work in comparison to the predatory capitalist model may be illustrated by comparing the number and qualities of drugs developed in the Soviet Bloc and China with those originating in the West.) Writers and composers would draw equal salaries from their cooperatives, or, as in the USSR, "unions." As inventions would be produced only in the factories directed to do so by the central planning authority, with no possibility of competition, patents and trademarks would be unnecessary.

Is it significant that the only conditions in which such protections would not be required, or would be ill fitting at the least, and perhaps harmful, are those in the target end-states of Marxism? Of course it is, as this is the ethos from which the anti-copyright movement emerges. The theses they rely upon are sensible in their minds because they have already decided—even if not formally or consciously—against property, competition, and the free market. This is the foundation upon which their movement rests. Their arguments are mainly a subspecies of the greater and more consequential battle between those who favor a world that is planned, controlled, decided, entirely cooperative, and conducive of predetermined outcomes, and those who favor and tolerate market-based systems that admit and honor chance, competition, unexpected developments, peril, and reward. It is very easy to dispense with the structures and protections of the market economy, of which copyright is one, if you are willing to dispense with the market economy itself.

Rather than defending free markets—which would swell this short chapter into a large book that has already been written many times and well—I will try, with a discursiveness I cannot suppress, to address the favorite and particular arguments the opponents of copyright bring to the fore in making their case, and which draw, apparently without consideration, upon assumptions in regard to property, liberty, and time.

While teaching at the University of Iowa thirty years ago, I went to a summer barbecue at the farm of novelist Vance Bourjaily, and his wife, Tina. It was an eventful evening. The Carvers were there, minus Ray, who had just run off. Tina came up the hill riding one and leading another of two magnificent horses, as white as clouds, as if in a giant Rosa Bonheur painting, and invited one of the guests to accompany her in taking them bareback to a higher pasture. As he mounted, a few puppies new to the farm nipped at the horses' pasterns, and quickly drove them into a frenzy. Though at first the horses went rampant they soon were sprawled in the dust like war horses felled in battle, their legs windmilling in a tangle, in the midst of which was the lady of the farm, who would have been killed had not her riding companion pulled the animals away by their halters. Nonetheless, she was severely injured, and lay for a while in a coma. Apart from that, and enough angst, loneliness, bitterness, and heartbreak to fill the pond across which, before the dinner that due to the accident was never consumed, there had been swimming races, the most notable thing and the reason (if not sufficient justification) for telling this story, was Vance Bourjaily's extraordinary control of his sheep.

On the next hillside, they looked like a mobile lake of whipped cream. From the perch of his writing cabin across the valley, where we were, he could stand with a trumpet and direct them as precisely as if they were at the end of a mechanical arm. One blast, and they would go here, two and they would go there, some tootles and they would run up the hill, a high note and they would stop short (not being a sheep, I don't remember the actual code, and am approximating). From the way they moved you would think they were Republicans or Democrats in a presidential election year. All of which is to say that, because taking refuge in words embraced by partisans who willingly glide over faults and contradictions is harmful both to one's integrity and the public discourse in general, I am uncomfortable about using the word *liberty*.

It is one of those words that has been freighted so heavily that it has almost lost its meaning, although not as much as *freedom, fairness,* or *diversity*. Lest anyone jump like sheep to Vance Bourjaily's horn, the scope of the word must be limited. It comes from the French *liberté*, a carrier of more freight perhaps than even the English word, and the Latin *liber*, meaning free: that is, unencumbered; without external controls or the internalization of external controls; not being subject to captivity or a will other than one's own; and, untrammeled by binding requirements.

Nothing is entirely free, not even an electron (hardly an electron) or an atom floating in the inaccurately named vacuum of space. Everything that exists is subject to the pull or constraint of something else. Even God, in almost every theology, is bound by certain of His own consistencies. Freedom, and, therefore, liberty, cannot be absolute but only a matter of degree, and the liberty here endorsed is the condition in which one finds oneself when decisions of governance are made with a constant prejudice against compulsion and *dirigisme* rather than with persistent affection for them.

Even in the most nightmarish prisons, freedom exists in the interstices: not merely because of the impracticability of absolute control, but because it is not in the nature of man completely to ignore natural rights. (By the same token, though conversely, anarchists are marvelously organized thanks these days to their seduction by the internet, of which they are one of many classes of enthusiastic slave.)

The balance of liberty, and the nature of predilections for and against it, is legible in many forms, one of which is the level of taxation. While a small number of tax protestors believes that taxation completely lacks justification, another small number believes that, property being unjustifiable (or at least immoral), taxes should, in one manifestation or another, be all consuming and vacuum up every form of property or possession as soon as it comes into being, as in their view property is a kind of redistributive grant or loan from the collective. In between these rims of the bell curve lies most opinion. Liberals and conservatives alike recognize that taxes are necessary for the operations of government. What distinguishes one from the other is that conservatives are always wanting and willing to put a cap on the levels of taxation, whereas liberals, believing that we are very far from the appropriate level of state intervention, generally are not.

Whereas liberals find it cruel and inexplicable that someone would want to set limits before every mouth is fed and every cry comforted, conservatives find it deeply alarming that anyone can fail to recognize the danger of pressing ahead in the absence of limits. In my lifetime I have seen effective tax rates (the marginal rates were of course higher) of 88 percent.[107] Although the argument that this extinguishes incentive is not quite true—we are configured to suck at the marrow of even the smallest bone—it cannot fail to degrade incentive. But it accomplishes far more and far worse: it extinguishes liberty. It does not do so absolutely. But because its effects are more than just material, it can be a sin on a much higher plane.

Granted, the argument is often presented solely in material terms. Cyril makes a hundred thousand a year, Irving ten thousand. One kind of justice dictates that Cyril be allowed to keep the fruits of his labor, talent, or luck, but another dictates that it is a great deal more than unseemly if some children of God suffer or die for lack of material goods, while others, created equally and of similar worth, luxuriate in excess. Thus, Cyril is compelled to give to Irving. In such an argument, cars, roast turkeys, antibiotics, and things such as roof repairs are often the elements of an ethical equation. But this is more than a material question.

For if Cyril is required to surrender half his income to the state, which will presumably attempt to benefit Irving, he is, therefore, laboring for the state during half his working life. Every January through June, he must hold his metaphysical breath as the product of his labor, no matter how hard or brilliant his work, vanishes from his control. Someone else, someone who, like an Egyptian bureaucrat, dreams of rooms full of seals, stamps, and ribbons, with a thousand people camping meekly at the door, will decide how to use it and what to do with it, which means that this someone else, even if in the person of the state, has appropriated his time. If you spend twelve hours digging potatoes, you find it unnatural and tyrannical to go home, as you may from January through

June, with an empty bucket. The counter to this is that except for the sake of theoretical illustration, the bucket will be half full. But the answer to that is that if it takes twelve hours to fill your bucket and at the end of twelve hours you go home with half a bucketful, you have spent six hours digging potatoes at the end of which the bucket is empty. And the response to this is usually, more or less, that, "It's for a good cause." It may be, but even good causes must have limits, without which they become tyrannies.

A kindly slave master who does not visit upon his slaves the particular atrocities normally associated with the ownership of human beings is still fundamentally indecent. For, no matter how beneficent he is, he presumes that the labor of his slaves belongs to him, that its product should lie within his power of disposition, that he is the owner of their time and their concentration, that whatever they make is rightfully his, to be distributed to them according to his lights.

It is no different if rather than with a plantation owner in a Panama hat the power of decision rests with ten million innocent bureaucrats each laboring so far beneath the horizon of moral alacrity that none can see the illegitimate effects of their compulsory power. Illegitimate, that is, mainly insofar as it exceeds the common agreement known as the social contract, about which many arguments of property and liberty rage like thunderstorms in the Hudson Highlands. These arguments are, unsurprisingly, an essential characteristic of democracy. We are individuals but we are not alone, and the tension of the two truths creates a perpetual dispute as natural as the tides. My purpose here is not to argue for the ideal limit in each of various circumstances (in war, for example, it would obviously be different from what it would be in peace) but rather to illustrate that property is directly related to liberty, that its existence influences more than the material, that its suppression results in the suppression of liberty, and that therefore property cannot but be one of the elemental guarantors of liberty.

As such, property cannot and should not be taken lightly, as a buzz word or a trumpet blast at Vance Bourjaily's sheep, as something that, undeserving of more than superficial considerations confers a kind of moral superiority upon whoever is "noble" enough to dismiss it. In my experience I have found that most people who think they are above property are usually swimming in it. My father was once uncomfortably on a yacht when the owner's wife turned to her husband and asked, "Michael, are we communists?" Such are the vapors of Long Island Sound acting upon a brain the size of a Gummy Bear,™ but the trophy wife was not straying far from the dictate of polite society, that property, ownership, profit, riches, exclusivity of possession, are forms of selfishness. One is warmly received when promoting this common conceit, and viewed with suspicion when contradicting it. It is the root of the argument against copyright, and its pedigree is as ancient as envy. But you never need be ashamed to claim what is rightfully yours—not merely as a pragmatic compromise with reality, or the expediency made necessary by an imperfect system of economy, but as a just principle morally superior to its opposite.

Before my satellite television system was destroyed by a discerning lightning bolt, I saw a series of commercials touting TIAA-CREF, the mammoth (at one time more than $400 billion) pension fund for "those in the academic, medical, cultural and research fields," whom it distinguishes with its motto of, "For the greater good." You may remember TIAA-CREF's former president, Thomas Jones ("Now the time has come when the pigs are going to die. . . ."),[108] serving the greater good as a leader of the armed group escorting the president of Cornell to a news conference in which he gave them the store (they had the guns), but that is almost irrelevant to the fact that certain classes of people presume that because they work "for the greater good" they are more deserving than others.

I cannot recall a time absent the received wisdom that the public sector is superior to the private, or that the work of nonprofit organizations is higher than that of private industry. Since I was seven, I have been exhorted to cast aside the temptation of selfishness and work "for the public good," because such work is on a morally higher plane.

Jefferson would beg to differ. He understood that the individual farmer or craftsman, and his family—who worked and defended their land, their forge, or their mill, and the right to their labor, their profit, and their property—were, not least in being the object of the state's aim to foster the general welfare, the bulwark of society and free republican government. He did not share with those who now wrongly expropriate him a contempt for what they would call the bourgeoisie. "The small landowners," he wrote to Madison, "are the most precious part of the state."[109] Jefferson understood as a result of experience, observation, study, and wisdom that when they worked for themselves they were cumulatively serving the greater good with more potency, efficiency, and justice than that of any other agency or from any other motive.

Actions must be judged by their effect, by the motivation of the actor, and by the conditions in which they occur. The order of importance assigned to these criteria changes with the circumstances. For instance, conditions become critically important when comparing a Sunday spent picking up litter in the park, with the saving of one's patrol by throwing oneself on a hand grenade. In comparing in this country and in this time what people do for the most part, the prime consideration must be effect, with conditions next, and motivation a distant third, especially since motivation is so often misrepresented, self-serving, and ultimately irrelevant.

What is the difference then, in effect, between surgeons who operate in nonprofit or in for-profit hospitals? If the tumor is removed or the hernia repaired, the patient will be able to note the difference only in the bill. If he is charged less in the nonprofit hospital, it is because he or someone else is paying indirectly. Taxpayers must pay more to make up for the nonprofit's tax exemption and privilege of receiving deductible contributions. They pay for the direct government grants to the hospital. They offset the lesser amounts paid by those who contribute and receive a deduction. And, while footing the bill for services provided to the tax-exempt nonprofit hospital, they also carry its share of taxes that would have been devoted to more general local expenditures. The non-profit is accorded these privileges and enjoys a special position because it produces benefits such as curing pneumonia.

The for-profit hospital also cures pneumonia, but is not afforded similar status because it *may* be profitable, which is seen as somehow less than admirable and puts it in a different category literally and legally. How does it dispose of its profits? It returns them to the shareholders who funded it, just as the nonprofit hospital returns money (theoreti-cally, and certainly not consistently) in the form of lower prices, to the community that funded it through tax privileges and direct grants. As in the case of the for-profit hospital, as the day follows the night, every-thing is paid for and someone pays for it, just as the internet did not fall from the internet tree but was paid for by taxpayer dollars apportioned to the military research that the progressive warriors of the internet might fashionably reject as unnecessary, immoral, and distasteful. The benefits and returns are highly variable, complex, and hard to predict, and they are never distributed evenly and seldom equitably. And yet of the two hospitals, one is held higher in public esteem for its sup-posed purity. If the indigent are treated in both, as is usually the case and usually by law; if in both the charges are more or less the same for the nonindigent; and if in both the quality of care is more or less the same, what is the purpose of the distinction? Should the answer be that the nonprofit treats more of the poor, that is because in a multiplicity of ways, as explained above, it is compensated for doing so. What, then, elevates it to a higher moral plane?

Consider a hypothetical lawyer with the hypothetical "Charlottes-ville Housing Alliance," a nonprofit public service organization. On Tues-day last, he secured for his pro bono client access to an apartment from which she was wrongfully excluded because of her race, national origin, religion, or—more likely—because she was a Hollywood screenwriter.

Without the lawyer's representation, she would not have been able to exercise her legitimate rights. In righting this wrong, he has served the public generally and his client specifically. Of this he is proud and for this, and because it is"nonprofit," his organization is accorded the special privilege of being tax-exempt: federal, state, and local. As TIAA-CREF might say in its ads, he is working for the greater good.

But what of the contractor who actually built the apartment? Without his work and risk of capital and labor, the client would have no apartment and the public in general would have less expectation of a reasonably priced housing market. To say that he serves the greater good less than the lawyer is logically unsupportable. He is not afforded the same recognition and privileges because he works for profit. What is his profit? The difference between revenues and expenses (including taxes, fees, and officially extorted proffers); that is, what he takes home is profit. What does the lawyer take home? The difference between revenues (from contributions, grants, possibly even fees) and expenses (not including, of course, taxes and proffers). What then is the difference? The contractor can potentially make large amounts of money, whereas the lawyer mythologically cannot. In fact, nonprofit compensation is often on a level with that elsewhere, but on the other hand the lawyer has not risked capital and his employer is insulated from taxes, which makes the lawyer's prospects brighter and more assured. The effect of what each has done is the same: both have been necessary, and neither sufficient, in providing the apartment. The contractor has not invented buildings, and is only applying previous principles; and by the same token the lawyer has neither made nor caused to be made new law, and is only applying the law that exists.

They are working more or less equally in the public interest, they suffer and enjoy different but in the end roughly balanced risks and rewards, and neither deserves to be held in higher esteem than the other or granted special status and privileges. And, yet, one is. Kings, politicians and their underlings, and all those whose faculties are amplified and actions are generalized merely by their position, often fall victim to an invidious presumption. The lawyer in this case, standing in for many others who also think this way, may believe that because of what he does he is nobler than most. He isn't.

My fate after unsuccessfully seeking a glimpse of Faye Dunaway was to spend a year reading Melville with Professor Alfred. I am glad of it, and glad as well that Professor Alfred was generously supported by Harvard for, among other things, teaching Melville to me. Harvard exists, in part, to do just that. Having accumulated an endowment of $40 billion, it can certainly afford to do so. And during all its long life of almost four hundred years it has been free of taxes. Not even the Queen of England is free of taxes anymore.

Why is it, however, that Harvard, the job of which, partly anyway, is (or was) to teach its inmates Melville, pays no tax, whereas Melville's publisher—who, just as Harvard paid Professor Alfred, paid Melville—did have to pay, and now of course would also have to pay? One produces *Moby Dick*, and pays tax. The other teaches it, and does not. One is for profit and the other is not, but Harvard is richer and its professors and chiefs are paid as well as or better than their opposite numbers in publishing, and the money potentially distributed to the shareholders of a publisher is probably no greater than the various benefits received by the affiliates of a university, minus the costs borne by various segments of society in compensation for and to foot the privileges of a tax-exempt organization.

Though effects, conditions, and even motivations—if not self-advertisement—are comparable, a bias exists for the nonprofit nonetheless, of honor accorded, support granted, and privileges awarded. In many cases, nonprofit institutions, which need not respond to market forces and often lose touch with what people actually want, serve the general interest less well and less efficiently than profit-making entities that must, if they are not to vanish, heed the dictates of the public. It is not necessary to penalize the worthy nonprofit, which often would not be able to function within the market, and would therefore leave a need unfilled. Rather, it is necessary to point out the disparity in treatment that does penalize profit-making activity that can serve the public equally well or at times better. For just as needs might go unfulfilled were nonprofits driven from the field by taxation, they do go unfilfilled when profit-based enterprises *are* driven from the field by taxation.

The prejudice that wrongly favors one type of endeavor over another which can be equally or more virtuous and often responds more precisely to the public interest, shares a common ancestor with a disdain for property, a hostility that overlooks not merely the necessity of property but its function as a prop of liberty. As Shakespeare had Shylock say both perceptively and justly:

> You take my house when you do take the prop
> That doth sustain my house. You take my life
> When you do take the means whereby I live.[110]

It is true that compared to our higher nature property is base, but as we are creatures of the material world our base imperfections require a material structure so that our spirit may be free. Too ready and too careless a seizure of property—whether by eminent domain, taxation, "progressive legislation," or simple theft—impinges not merely upon well established and utilitarian rights, but is a partial taking of life itself.

We are hardly familiar with the maxims of Louis IX, the Pious, who prayed like a dervish and wore a hair shirt, but it was he who wrote, in strikingly Chinese style for a medieval French king: "If a poor man has a quarrel with a rich man, support the poor rather than the rich—*at least until the truth can be ascertained.*"[111]

This makes sense in light of the probable advantages a surfeit of resources might bring to the rich man, and it is why one of the common suggestions for tort reform, that the loser bear all the costs, is fundamentally unjust. Very few would dare sue or defend when faced with an adversary possessing great financial resources. Such a "reform" would mean that the powerful would be virtually unaccountable and the ordinary citizen would look upon the justice system as something so dangerous as to be even more forbidding to his interests than it is already. A bias for the poor is commendable where appropriate, as a compensating weight in an imbalanced world. But even in the thirteenth century, when animal skins were hung in the heights and on the walls of the cathedrals of Europe, Louis knew enough to state, "at least until the truth can be ascertained." That is, compensatory bias as an instrument of justice cannot live beyond the facts, and must be subject to continuous and searching consideration. If it becomes merely habitual, it becomes an instrument of injustice. If it is a matter of rote, of formula, and, worse, of self-satisfaction—a means to preen and glow for the public—it becomes insufferable, not least because the judgment of who is rich and who is poor is entirely relative.

I once returned to my apartment in Cambridge, pedaling ten miles home early in the morning after my night shift. Passing through the Brattle Street neighborhood, I saw a group of young men and women my age walking from a van, with surfboards on its roof rack, into one of the mansions there. They were sunburnt and relaxed, and everything about them said money—their brand-new vehicle, their fashionable beach clothes, their hair, their languid gait. Though I was working two jobs in Boston's hottest summer ever, I had neither envy nor a quarrel, until I saw a bumper sticker on their van that said, "Eat the Rich." These were the predecessors of the Creative Commons movement, which suffers the illusion that if ownership is abolished, everything will be free, when the opposite is true; and thinks that in opposition to copyright it is the ally of the little man, even as it fights the battle in behalf of the great combines and business powers of the imminent future.

Anyone who blithely recommends expropriation as a means of "economic justice" should first divest himself of most of what he has and give it to those who have less—and there are certain to be those who have less and are greatly afflicted for it. We tend to look up rather than at ourselves when surrendering to such passions of righteousness. The assault on copyright is a species of this, based on the infantile presumption that a feeling of justice and indignation gives one a right to the work, property, and time (those are very often significantly equivalent) of others, and that this, whether harbored at the ready or expressed in action, is noble and fair.

It is neither. It is, rather, a cowardly self-indulgence and a depredation of the public interest as much as it is destructive to the interest of the individual, for in truth these are in many respects one and the same: that is, the public interest is served when the rights of the individual come first rather than vice versa. When individual rights are pre-eminent, everyone is served. When they are not, the only thing that is served is an abstraction. Whereas community can be only an idea, concept, construct, or fiction, the individual actually exists in flesh and blood. One can claim to love the collective or the community, but it is the sterile, sick love of one who can love nothing, or, rather, no one. Love that is not echoed in a human heart is apt to petrify into tyranny, and so often in history a devotion to the abstraction of man has been a blind for hideous oppression.

Property is to be defended proudly rather than disavowed with shame. Even if for some it is only a matter of luck or birth, for the vast majority it is the store of sacrifice, time, effort, and even, sometimes, love. It is, despite the privileged inexperience of some who do not understand, an all-too-accurate index of liberty and life. To trifle with it is to trifle with someone's existence, and as anyone who tries will find out, this is not so easy. Nor has it ever been. Nor should it ever be.

CHAPTER 6

CONVERGENCE

Wait As Long As You Want, It Will Not Come

A long time ago, and for a mercifully short while, I was a graduate student in England. Absolutely alone when I arrived and not knowing a single person in the British Isles, my circle of acquaintances soon became quite different from what it had been at home, and included eventually a famous English lord who began what appeared to have been the tentative process of introducing me to a secret rite. I despise secret rites. And because I left the country before I progressed very far in my introduction, and didn't find out enough to betray it, I have no hesitation about discussing it.

The secret societies of which we know are by definition not entirely secret. Some tend to silliness, like the Secret Service, so many of whose members are enough taken with being secret agents that they carry themselves as conspicuously as orangutans in the Louvre. (*Looking* alert is not the same as *being* alert.) Some societies are secret but only mildly so, like the Masons, who put Masonic decals on their cars and wear Masonic jewelry. Of course, no one knows precisely what they are up to, perhaps even including them. The smaller an organization the better chance it has of achieving real secrecy, though Yale's Skull and Bones is famous precisely because it is supposed to be secret. Harvard has two similarly elite groups, the Signet Society and the Porcellian, which, because they operate in the open, are virtually unknown. The secret is that in challenging everyone to find it out, secrecy transforms itself into publicity.

But not always. Some secrets are kept successfully. Within the notoriously open American intelligence apparatus, for example, are inner chambers entirely opaque to the public, and historians have unwittingly passed over at least some covert initiatives (of this I am sure) because the prime movers and their operators have been discreet unto death. Thus perhaps with the rite to which I was so briefly introduced that its secret remains safe.

Whatever it was, it centered, honest to Betsy, on the Egyptian god Thoth (as in "path the spthegetti thoth"), whose Hellenistic name was, obviously, Hermes Trismegistus. When the dentally challenged peer (teeth apart, he could give ex tempore orations in Latin) who introduced me to this first told me about it, I thought he was mocking me. But he wasn't. Though it could have been, for all I know, nothing more than a kind of "I-hate-girls" club for barmy English aristocrats, Hermeticism does have a long, impressive, and secretive history, which, to my wonder, I was assigned to study. At first blush it seemed much like the standard run-of-the-mill Eastern mystical cults of antiquity, to which, as a Jew, I have a profound and inbred aversion. Just for starters, I can't stand incense. Though inexact and self-contradictory—if you have mystery, you need neither precision nor consistency—its major themes were that everything in the universe is actually only one thing, that divisions (such as between various fields of study and endeavor) are therefore illusory and destined to dissolve, and that by a process of development that is half a conscious inquiry and half a subconscious, mystical tide (see above, the "dream of the commons"), man will ultimately unify his disparate understandings, obtain knowledge of the unity, achieve immortality, and go on actually to become a god.

That is why, in my sleepy college town in the heat of a Southern summer, a former astronaut making a guest appearance at a science camp for children told them, "You are an infinite being with infinite possibilities with the ability to do anything."[112] No, my dear astronaut. As wonderful as life is, our beings are limited, as are our possibilities, and we do not have the ability to do anything. Perhaps he was exaggerating so as to make a point, but even if so, the exaggeration is both familiar and telling.

Quite familiar, in fact, most of this, the standard stuff of hubris and heresy, all of which would appear to be contradicted by the record of history and confounded by the constancy of human nature—that is, the human nature not of theory but of actuality. Nonetheless, these beliefs cannot be written off merely as impractical. They have run through the ages in an unbroken thread, flourishing remarkably in the Renaissance, in a trail that led through alchemy to modern scientific inquiry, to the Age of Reason, and to the magician John Dee of Mortlake, a Hermeticist whose navigational formulae are part of the reason I am writing this in English rather than Spanish.

And they run right down the center aisle of the electronic culture, for the quarrel runs deeper than copyright, deeper than what can be addressed in law, deeper than politics, deeper than a fight over property no matter how inextricably property is woven into the fabric of liberty. It is a dispute over the nature of things, and, therefore, what the world is to become. The argument is as old as man and perhaps a matter of inherited temperament, but it can be argued nonetheless. Of late we have seen its intensification fueled not as much by the vapid advances of technology but by a fervent embrace of these things that is far out of proportion to the rewards obsessive engagement can offer.

This surrender, in which people have become obsequious to machines, comes not merely from mistakes in judgment but from the absence of civilization's counterweights, which otherwise might illuminate the dangers, stand in the stead of false promises, and provide alternate satisfactions. Weakened by war, neglect, cowardice, hostility, impatience, and time, these counterweights previously were the stabilizing and calming structures that checked all-consuming enthusiasms. In the decline of ethics, knowledge, and civility, and the wilting of restraint and deliberation, much has been carried too far.

It begins, as is often the case, with elites freed of the normally astringent necessities such as the struggle to make a living, surviving war and other forms of violence, and the need carefully to husband resources. Thus untethered in a world of gas, they propagate and accept peculiar doctrines without limit. At prestigious institutions, celebrated professors opine that newborns, being almost insensible, have a lesser right to life than, say, a celebrated professor at a prestigious institution, and that, therefore, their murder should be "understood" or even accepted as a right of the parent. Social theorists who have spent the last half century relentlessly attacking marriage have suddenly reversed course with the advent of legalized homosexual union. Formerly passionate defenders of free speech now propose and accept that the government, of which they are normally skeptical, regulate political speech, especially prior to elections. (They say they are regulating money, but as the size of the population precludes any but the most local candidates from going door-to-door, advocacy depends directly and as a matter of its life and death upon money. To say, I'm not controlling political expression, I'm just regulating money, is the same as saying, I'm not preventing you from speaking, I'm just forbidding you to open your mouth.)

I cite these few examples not from satisfaction in deploring them, for deploring, like heavy drinking, renders one powerless and sick not long after, but as an introduction to some of the notions that long ago arose in overprivileged asylums and are now joyfully inhaled from Santa Monica to Somerville. Serious and enthralled, some people liken the internet to the divine, and neither I nor they are making a metaphor. In the scientific equivalent of the medieval church's indulgences, they promise the cheap, ill-thought-out, and unsubstantiated science-fiction chestnut of immortality via the transference of human memory into a mechanism. As I recall, we are now about three or four years past the point where this was to have been possible. They held, and perhaps some still do hold, the naïve and tragic belief that newly technology-intensive weaponry can win traditional wars in ancient and dusty places against people who are even crazier than are we.

Such things find quick adoption in the public mind given the general feeling that to keep pace with the machines and remain adequate in an era of inhuman speed, all decisions must be instantaneous. Those who rush forward to lap at the first trickles of what is new even have a name. They are called "early adapters," a rather grandiose term for someone who buys a new cell phone and molds his life to all the petty and useless things it does—witness the coyly misspelled, ungrammatical messages that have neither the wit of telegram language nor the information content of a lichee nut.

Take the new way of making an appointment. Instead of, "Shall we have dinner on Monday?" "Okay, what about Sakura, one-thirty?" "Dinner at one-thirty? In the morning? "I like to eat late." "Okay, see you then," which takes place in nine seconds and one phone call, the text-messaging approach would take at least four messages, each typed in even more time than required by the entire voice transaction, over a period of hours or days, "from my BlackBerry." Excuse me? From your BlackBerry? I don't think the purpose of this declaration is to explain the brevity of your message, as you could probably type *War and Peace* with one thumb tied behind your BMW. I think its purpose is an ad from BlackBerry to let me know that you have a BlackBerry. May your BlackBerry rot in hell.

Why must something—perfectly handled by the telephone, an instrument invented among other reasons to replace the telegraph—be forced through a less efficient, hideously overcomplicated procedure, and with great fanfare? This is what is done by the "early adapters," the long sheep-lines of vacuous fanatics who must have the latest device upon which to watch "The Sayings of Zsa Zsa Gabor" (a historical figure) as they keep in constant touch with forty friends whom they have never met, and do their homework during ten minutes of otherwise unendurable captivity in a bus or a ski gondola, when they might otherwise have had to look blankly out the window and, despite the spooling by of Manhattan, or a hundred-mile view, suffer the equivalent of sensory deprivation.

My mother, I suppose, was an early adapter when she began making toast in an electric toaster rather than in the oven, but I don't think she waited in line all night to buy a toaster, or would have given herself or even accepted a title for doing so—Early toaster? *Avante-tostée?* And I wonder what my father, whose first automobile, at the beginning of the last century, was actually a horse, would think about the PDA-calendar entries that advertisements present as typical:

11:00 a.m.	Power Point Presentation for Putin and Brad Pitt.
12:00 p.m.	Sushi with Jason
2:00 p.m.	Help Jennifer Move Into Loft
4:00 p.m.	Drinks with Albert Einstein at Sphere
6:00 p.m.	Sushi with Kaitlin and One-Armed Jack
8:00 p.m.	Indonesian Film Festival, Bring Skateboard and Hitler Puppet

Not so long ago, it would have been impossible to find people with lives like this: that is, poseurs of fashion with brains the size of cocktail onions. Now, it isn't. When the Apple iPhone™ was introduced in June of 2007, not a few stores that carried it in the Washington area hired police to control mobs in the hundreds as, giddy and ferocious from waiting twenty hours in the sun or rain, they surged toward the ecstasy of consummating their transactions. According to the *Washington Post*, "Some said they expected the phone to change their lives. Others said they just wanted bragging rights." One "triumphantly held up his two iPhones to the cheers of the crowds behind him," while another likened it "to a massive 'paradigm shift' or 'gestalt effect'," and "after 15 hours of waiting in 90 percent humidity and bouts of rain, iPhone *hopefuls* [italics supplied] . . . exchanged e-mail addresses to swap their iPhone experiences."[113]

The faith of people in such things—a faith that will leave them empty and aching—is but one vulgarization of the longstanding fallacy that by his own powers man not only can improve his condition, which he certainly can, and must, but that he can bring it to perfection, lifting himself not merely up but to a divine state. The biblical story of Babel is about just that, although the builders of the tower were more modest than their descendants in that they did not fancy that they could equal God, but only wanted to make a name for themselves by visiting Him. And thus their punishment, to be separated by different tongues, was far less severe than the punishment of watching one's own soul exsanguinate into the arid dust of modernity. For modernity, ceaselessly mercurial, is nothing more than obsolescence yet to occur. To put one's faith in or devote one's attentions to it is to chase after a vapor.

One of the latest manifestations of this universal hubris is the theory, recently revised by a pack of intellectuals intoxicated with their own powers and the money they and their associates were breathing-in during the internet boom, of *convergence*. This theory is not actually a theory but a kind of jelly donut of many manic expectations—of an all-explanatory unified field theory in physics; of the notion that the sexes will merge into one; of the quest for a single instrument embodying all convenience technologies (except, presumably, the shower); of the desire for a world government, beloved of the Left despite the fact that it would be the empire they as anti-imperialists have always detested, and detested by the Right despite the Right's indelible soft spot for the nineteenth-century world in British red. The idea of convergence has done its job quietly and efficiently in re-aiming the common wisdom about a great many things, but it is all wrong.

©

I do not have the ancient and delicate volumes I consulted in the Bodleian Library after appearing in my robes and kneeling to an oath never to keep an open flame within its precincts, so I cannot attest to whether in the Hermetic oeuvre one actually finds the word *convergence*, but there is no question that the two go hand in hand. Despite its definite air of absurdity and even lunacy, Hermeticism includes expressions of elemental human tendencies, temptations, and truths. Though you may abandon it as I did even before taking it up, it comes back at you with a vengeance from various points of the philosophical compass.

To wit, Teilhard de Chardin. Ordained as a Jesuit priest in France in 1911, he was a heroic stretcher bearer in the trenches of the Great War, lived in inhospitable deserts, jungles, and stranded captivity in China during the Second World War, and contributed notably to the great enterprise of science. Science, which requires many hands, painstaking and time-consuming comparisons and eliminations, expensive machinery, and the blessings and money of government and institutions, has now—partly by its very nature and partly by refusal of opportunity, the pressures of modern social organization, and lack of courage—been collectivized. The spark of individual genius is no longer as free as the rough waters of the sea, having been confined to channels, canals, sluices, pipes, and corked bottles. There are brilliant ants, and wise ants, chief ants, and even Feynman-type ants, but the light of the blazing, burning, magnificent ants like Newton, Galileo, and Einstein is now muted beneath layers of communal gauze and collaborative discipline, like the light of a firefly so deep in the grass that it will never find a mate.

This was not quite the case at the time of Teilhard. He was freer than that, and he wrote not, as is commonly and incorrectly stated, to reconcile science and religion, but, rather, simply to find the truth. That truth, greater than any human accomplishment, would by definition easily encompass both reason and revelation. To my mind, Teilhard's major accomplishment was to confound the hapless nihilism based on the misapplication of the idea of entropy (if all things merely decline and energy levels drop, then what we know or dream is nothing more than a candle burning down) with an exposition of how elemental physical forces are conducive to aggregation and, thus, higher form. One cannot rely upon entropy as a *philosophical* precept and at the same time accept the evidence of evolution, and few who would reject the evidence of evolution would be content with entropy as a philosophical precept. That is to say that the evidence of evolution—planetary, biological, systemic in any form—points to a progression toward a higher state and suggests the presence of a motivating and organizing force even if it be only an inexplicable coincidence of natural laws. And if evolution is merely a metaphor for creation, the light ahead is still the same.

But Teilhard went much further, arguing that in the agglomeration of various elements into things more and more complex, able, and sentient, there is a pattern of convergence, that the various phenomena on their upward courses have not developed and are not developing along independent lines but are aimed at the same point: in short, that everything that rises must converge. Even in separate evolutionary careers marked by analogy rather than a common origin (such as those of winged birds and winged insects) elemental forces dictate convergence in both form and function. Teilhard's vision of concordant physical and spiritual evolution meeting at a single point, which by any name is God, is the deeper background of the contemporary fascination with the idea of convergence.

Rather than simply surrendering to this concept, one may ask a number of questions. Are the indications of what some may take as impending convergence only an anomaly, and unsuited to the general implications attributed to them? Are they the product of careless observation and definition? And is there a fault in the notion of convergence even in its highest and most elegant formulation?

Convergence (movement toward or terminating in the same point) is neither *coalescence* (things growing together), *concaulescence* (the coalescence of separate axes), *concurrence* (running together), nor *conglomera-*

tion (forming into a more or less rounded mass). The forces and trends of human life are always coming together or moving apart. Even as they run askew they are, in relation to each other, variably closer or more distant. That is the nature of things, but to imagine that now they are all running closer, or, more portentously, that they are on a path of convergence in which all things will be explained by the same explanation, is to invest the normal patterns of existence with inflated significance.

If we choose to work and shop around-the-clock with no customary rest or truce, if we must be accessible at all times rather than risk losing the slightest opportunity, and if our teachers scoff at dividing their subject matter into history, literature, and science, and wade instead into an amorphous "interdisciplinary" bouillabaisse that relieves them of the responsibility of knowing what they are talking about, it is not because we are at the brink of some great convergence, it is because we lack the discipline, focus, and clarity required to make refusals, maintain divisions, and uphold distinctions. It is not surprising that some would attempt to dress this grave failure in a metaphysical gloss until it appears a success.

Generation after generation, given the right circumstances, tries to square its circle, imagining itself about to answer the eternal questions it can never come even close to answering. An independent offshoot of this is the scientific arrogance that, feeding off man's deference to the most powerful tool he has yet devised, imagines our ability to run the world according to scientific principles, a supposedly benevolent dictatorship of the boffins. But though nature is identifiable by the simplicity and elegance of its laws, to which all natural phenomena readily conform, humanity is different. It is a hive of countless and surprising variables, and it cannot be understood, much less managed, according to scientific principles. When such principles are applied to it the product is often misery and death. As the history of half the world in the previous century shows, even when so discreet and systemic a thing as an economy is directed according to "scientific principle" (which is only that thing that some fallible someone says it is), it ends in dismal failure. Humanity requires for its understanding and governance not science but art, and when this is forgotten—as in the case of Samuel Johnson's natural philosopher who, having electrified a bottle, thinks that the problems of war and peace are inconsequential—the result is always the coercion of irrational mankind by frustrated and indignant masters.

We are at the beginning of a new millennium, and though the numerology of millenarianism has even less significance in regard to events or conditions than the positions of the stars and planets have in regard to destiny or mood, the power of coordinated belief, mass suggestion, and mass illusion is demonstrably accountable (as it was during the last millennial shift) for the feeling that we are at the verge of some final resolution. Even in Marxism, "contradiction" will cause a "fall" after a "struggle," and the denouement, as in most religions, will be the convergence of previously disparate elements in harmony, in "a new heaven and a new earth."

Not only do we who live now want this as much as ever it has been wanted, the generation born after the war has long been convinced that it *deserves* it. Our fathers returned from a struggle of mythical proportions, and their victory was absolute. In the War of Independence we achieved self-determination but did not destroy England. After the Civil War we emerged as a single nation that nonetheless was half-vanquished. And in the First World War we came to terms with an opponent that we failed to crush and did not reconfigure. But in the Second World War our armies destroyed and occupied enemy countries more powerful and threatening than any we had ever faced. We leveled them, conquering every inch. In a famous photograph, Churchill struggles gamely through the ruins of the Chancellery in Berlin. It was done, complete, more than Wagnerian. It made the *Iliad* look like very small potatoes. And yet, these were our fathers, one generation removed. They told us that we were smarter than they were, that we would stand on their shoulders, that they had fought for us (it was true), and that we would outshine them.

Having been deprived of this glorious vision by history and circumstance, many of us then went on to hallucinate it. Drugs probably helped, as did a surfeit of material things, and the degradation of the educational system. This generation and those descended from it have abused and discredited the past and convinced themselves of their capacity to repair and remake the world—not according to the principles that preceding generations have proved with blood, patience, and genius, but in contradiction of them, by their own set of newly made laws, hardly a single one of which is not precisely what will lead to the suffering and destruction that they do not know, having been lifted beyond such things by the sense and sacrifice of their elders. This and the following generations, by and large, that have done more than any others to cut the ancient sinews that have kept us whole and alive; these generations, characterless, spendthrift, and vain, that have lost the capacity of embarrassment; these generations that have desecrated history, buried the word, murdered tranquility, and done about as much as can be done to turn the world into a cartoon, are sure that they are on to something big: convergence, consilience, theories of everything, immortality, perfection.

Are they really. There is no question mark at the end of the previous sentence, because it is not a question but a dismissal. Take for example the hopeful meows about immortality. Like good Hermeticists, some who speculate on such things really have latched on to the notion that immortality is just around the corner. No matter that the world of life is like a river that disappears mysteriously over a fall, and that of all the billions who have come before, and of all the billions alive today moving inexorably toward the edge, not a single one has failed and not a single one will fail to go over it. Now it has actually become fashionable here and there to comfort oneself with the hope that this death will be defeated by a machine very like the one in which resides the miracle of the spreadsheet.

But between expectant lips and this particular cup are distances so vast that you had better take a good look around while you can, for even if in a far-distant time everything in one's memory can be preserved or transferred to some medium of storage, it is not the sum of these things that makes the soul, but how they are integrated and with what speed, depth, bravery, and unpredictable wit. It wasn't what Raphael knew, but that things of beauty flew off his hand. All the great worlds of information packed into the Library of Congress do not, in their totality, begin to make a life. Nor would merely linking them create consciousness, the essence of which remains an utter and absolute mystery. No mechanism for cradling the soul will ever be found better than the one we have been given, and if something eventually comes close, that which will be left out will be that which looms largest.

The illusion of the perfectibility of man is based on ignorance of his splendidly complex nature, which is weighted and counterweighted already so delicately and brilliantly that amending it would be far more profitless a thing than, say, rewriting Shakespeare for the better, or adding a backbeat to a Verdi aria. And even the BlackBerry-less and benighted medievals (who had real berries) knew that immortality was one of the elements not only of heaven but of hell. Thus Paolo and Francesca and their eternal kiss. For every tick there is a tock, for every triumph a defeat. This is the balance of human nature, and it cannot be countermanded.

Yet we persist in thinking it can. Often, as with Daedalus and Icarus, the effort to countermand is a matter of degree, of pace, adjustment, lack of patience, and lack of humility, because our designs too quickly run out of control. Stalin, Hitler, Mussolini, Mao, and their hundreds of millions of followers were convinced of a dream of perfection that they would bring first to their countries and then to the world. But one need not be a psychotic in control of a nation to suffer the same delusion. A friend of mine in college, a protégé of Marcuse, told me that he wanted to burn down, quite literally, the world's greatest library and replace everything therein (which is to say nearly all recorded human knowledge) with the contents of his battered spiral notebook. According to him, this would become the basis of a new and just order. Needless to say, he wouldn't let me see what he had written, perhaps because I existed on too low a plane. He wouldn't have burned down anything, for he was in fact a kindly intellectual, but many terrible notions were circulating among kindly intellectuals at the time.

The electric flow of hubris is such that in all eras it touches all classes and types. Now it is endemic, if only because the belief that man can be a god runs parallel, though illogically, with the decision that there is no God. In the absence of God, all nature is merely accident. Amidst all the accident there is only one purposefulness other than instinct, that of man. Standing thus above the randomness of the rest of the universe, he is no longer a piece of work (no will having worked upon him) but the ultimate and decisive power, alone above all else, the sole possessor of volition. It is hardly a new theme, though rationalism and the triumph of science have pushed it farther than in other ages. Previously, the conflict was between monotheism and idolatry. Now it is between any kind of theism and worship of the self. It is not a coincidence that in this era narcissism has inflated to the point of flattening many aspects of character. Hardly unique or surprising is the horribly cute pretension exemplified, for example, in a cookbook entitled *How To Be A Domestic Goddess*, dedicated to "John, Goddess-Maker."[114] This found sufficient resonance to be echoed. Seven years later you could read magazine articles such as, "The Easy Way To Be A Domestic Goddess," with a picture of a woman aglow like Diana (courtesy of a bodice of electric lightbulbs), with the secret of how to become divine simply to "Wrap an odd-shaped gift."[115] Such things are not serious, but, like Freudian slips, they betray what is underneath. And in the bankrupt and bankrupting quest to escape history, mortality, and human nature, the necessary illusions are furthered with unprecedented power by the electronic culture and its informal system of belief. There, the world is made into a kind of shrunken head, a tame thing with neither wind nor storm; a playhouse where it is possible for those who share in the illusion to imagine that they are in charge; a closed system in which the word *virtual* is applied to that which is not virtual, and the masters are masters of nothing, not even a puff of real smoke.

Someone who is understandably if not forgivably centered in such a way upon himself can easily misinterpret any course of events as part of a planned or evolving harmony favorable to his destiny or opinions. Lack of humility comes from insufficient attention to how the world really works. The illustration of this has been one of the cornerstones of literature from its earliest beginnings, and in regard to it there is a lesson of history at every turn. Consider the dialectical placement of statements by three of what Churchill called "English worthies"—in this case Conservative politicians in the National Government of the late thirties. Mussolini said of them, "These, after all, are the tired sons of a long line of rich men, and they will lose their empire." (He was right, of course, but it didn't do him terribly much good.)

First, the thesis, from Sir Samuel Hoare, then home secretary, in March of 1939. He saw a "golden age" about to dawn, when "five men in Europe, the three dictators and the prime ministers of England and France," would converge (not his word), and "in an incredibly short time transform the whole history of the world."[116] The antithesis came on the very same day, when (according to his memorandum) Lord Halifax told Ribbentrop that "Experience of all history went to show that the pressure of facts was sometimes more powerful than the will of men: and if once war should start in Central Europe, it was quite impossible to say where it might not end, or who might not become involved."[117] And, finally, the synthesis, in Neville Chamberlain's speech to the Commons, of September 3, 1939: "Everything that I have hoped for, everything that I have believed in during my public life, has crashed into ruins."[118] So much for the golden age.

The optimism and confidence of the fin de siècle a hundred years ago became the First World War; the Second World War; the Holocaust; the Cold War and its attendant, costly, proxy wars; and a century as much, or more, of alienation, misery, and death, as of progress and the alleviation of suffering. Churchill was able to make an exception to the rule of blindness in the age of appeasement only because he had been an optimist prior to the Great War, and had bitterly learned the lesson he went on to teach—not that one policy or another is always right, but that throughout history grandiose expectations are almost always confounded and overturned in tragedy.

Thomas Hardy knew not only that fate deals severely with what he called "the Pride of Life," but how. In "The Convergence of the Twain (Lines on the loss of the *Titanic*)," he wrote:

> And as the smart ship grew
> In stature, grace, and hue,
> In shadowy silent distance grew the Iceberg too.
> Alien they seemed to be:
> No mortal eye could see
> The intimate welding of their later history,
> Or sign that they were bent
> By paths coincident
> On being anon twin halves of one August event,
> Till the Spinner of the Years
> Said "Now!" And each one hears,
> And consummation comes, and jars two hemispheres.[119]

Teilhard de Chardin's recognizably Hermetic concept that salvation comes through the development and convergence of human capabilities with the divine is a doctrine with a dark side that he chose optimistically and faithfully to ignore, a side that Yeats (he of balancing this life with this death) expresses with customary and disconcerting beauty:

There all the barrel-hoops are knit,
There all the serpent-tails are bit,
There all the gyres converge in one,
There all the planets drop in the Sun.[120]

That something is very wrong with the notion of convergence in even its most elevated formulation is supported by its most eloquent critique. In "Everything That Rises Must Converge," a simple and profound short story by Flannery O'Connor, a mother and son travel on a city bus in the newly integrated South. The mother clings to the old ways and is clearly wrong in doing so, but, in practice, she is kind and good. The son is the apostle of progress and justice, but in practice he is smug and cruel. He represents pride in achievement, faith in emerging perfection, reason, justice, the linear concept of history. She—humility, tradition, conservation, circularity, continuity, mercy, and forgiveness.

It is no coincidence that in the interplay between the two in the context of their individual struggles he finds that his actions have assured "his entry into the world of guilt and sorrow." And it isn't a coincidence that the title of the story, which Flannery O'Connor wrote to address the great French philosopher, is from Teilhard, for it is a velvet demolition of his belief that mankind can evolve to perfection.

If salvation is a function of perfectibility, what does this imply about the lame, the weak, the befuddled, and the oppressed? Are they by implication less beloved of God? In one spare short story, mortally ill Flannery O'Connor, with the Southern and the Celtic knowledge of hubris and defeat running naturally in her blood, checkmated Teilhard's great erudition, multiple volumes, and splendid dreams. This she did with the same kind of totally unexpected, breathtaking power of the Maid of Orleans, or Anne Frank. She, who would never know temporal glory, or be rewarded in this world, who died without husband or children, who suffered and had no sway, she knew the simple truth that salvation is ultimately a matter of grace. That is, when all is said and done, man is simply unable to construct the higher parts of his destiny, and must know this to survive even the simpler challenges that he is expected to meet.

At least since the Enlightenment, man has modeled himself and his society upon the machine. Slowly shorn of his knowledge of and feel for nature and human nature, he has been brought over to the principles (and, often, the mere effects) of speed, efficiency, economy, and emotional detachment: doing the most with least; just-in-time inventory; lack of feeling; absence of commitment; neutrality of conscience; all the techniques common to a business, an organization, a mechanical contrivance, or a modernist novel. But neither nature nor man are machines, and, treated as machines, they sicken.

Convergence is not a fact on the horizon but a contrivance of human vanity. It will not come from a hand-held toy, an electronic network no matter how powerful, or a machine that sits on a desk. It will not come by virtue of universal or near-universal agreement or by virtue of the new. Wait as long as you wish, it will not come.

CHAPTER 7

PARTHIAN SHOT

Calling Barbarism for What It Is

If it is to be honorable, a military objective must be not merely to check or destroy an enemy's forces, but to do so while sparing innocents and noncombatants as much as is practicable. Unfortunately, most of the time this is not possible on a scale sufficient to redeem the terrible necessities of war. And when it is impossible, no victory can be unalloyed. Even in the heart of the Nazi war machine (that is, Germany) were children as innocent as angels, who when caught in the immense crossfire deprived an otherwise clear-cut and morally urgent victory of any pretense to perfection.

Intellectual argument, unsaddled with the finality of death, is unsaddled with the laws of tragedy. Once an opponent's attack is gutted, one may look upon his formations in disarray and pull from them perfectly alive everything worthy of preservation. Doing so, however, is no more magnanimous than carrying off the Sabine women, but rather another blow, in that what was once dear to the enemy may then cleave to the other camp.

What is useful and good in the arguments and justifications that the previous pages have opposed? Though they are confusedly coy about it, the critics of copyright and legionnaires of the machine would severely cripple or scuttle the system for the sake of universal access, which they term *open*. Their presumption is that copyright is a bar, and much of their motivation stems from indignation that it is therefore an impediment—even a fatal impediment—to an obvious public good.

But why must widespread or even universal access, which is unquestionably good, be "open"? That is, what makes the licensing of and payment for works not in the public domain, and apart from fair use, a bar to universality of access sufficient to change the quality of universality? Nothing, of course. Universal access needs no more to be free of licensing and payment than a transportation system, to be comprehensive and excellent, or a communications system, to be all pervasive, must be free of charge. One pays for access to the internet. One pays for hardware and (presumably) for software. One pays for telephones and PDAs. One pays for advertising on the internet—with money if one is an advertiser and with time and distraction if one is an internet user. None of these things is free. To facilitate fluidity of information, why must "content" be free? Why must one seek not to pay for music or television shows that come over one's iPhone, with no such effort in regard to the instrument itself or the substantial and continuing user fees? If paying for the means and instrumentation of universal access is not a barrier to universal access, paying for the substance cannot therefore be more of a barrier, for, as discussed previously, the reasonable charges can be tracked, tallied, and managed as conveniently as are cell phone charges.

The availability of information is not and will not be restrained by the copyright system any more than it is or will be restrained by the delivery systems that make it possible. To focus on copyright as the impediment is a false argument, and to imply that those who would uphold and strengthen it are opponents of universal and ready access is a false argument as well, as there is no inherent contradiction between the two. Like most, I am looking forward to the promised fluidity of information. I don't know of anyone who opposes such a thing, useful and beguiling as it is.

Although at present its effect is chiefly a rise in economic productivity and a surge in frivolous entertainment, the phenomenon is in its infancy, and the synergy and ferment that can result from a new world of almost effortless appositions and cross-fertilizations may be of unchartable value. How could one fail to be enthusiastic about the transformation of every home, every seat on every commuter train, and every park bench, into a full-fledged branch of the greatest libraries in the world? Ignoring for a moment the coincident if not directly related decline in reading that is both obvious and documented, there are wonderful aspects to the transformation as well as drawbacks and dangers, and no reason that it cannot be implemented ethically and intelligently. Most certainly copyright does not stand in its way.

As we have seen, some are fervently convinced that it does, and their strong advocacy has moved public perception, pulling it in their direction partially because the opposition to their advocacy has been largely confined to immensely rich and impersonal corporate bodies with which it is nearly impossible to be sympathetic, and that are not agile enough to have created armies of blogging-ants steeped in self-righteous anger. These armies may be disreputable, but, like the graffiti that extend the limits of acceptability merely by their brazen appearance, they are influential.

Normally I don't deal with foundations. My last grants, hangovers from the habits of the academy, arrived long ago. But in the months preceding the writing of this book, a foundation offered very generously and from the blue to underwrite the production of another book on an entirely different subject. I had to decline, but soon thereafter asked if they might underwrite this one. Their judgment was that they would not back such extreme and controversial positions as you have just read. This reaction, from a group of accomplished people whose resumes could choke a hippopotamus, made me doubt my sanity and discernment, until I reflected that the extreme position I advocate is a defense of the copyright system that has been with us, in one form or another, for three hundred years; an extreme position largely endorsed by the Supreme Court, the Congress, and the Founders, as well as the governments and peoples of most of the countries of the world. Although of course I do not think so, my stance may be not entirely correct, it may be the weaker of the two positions, it may even be wrong, but it cannot be extreme.

What magic has given the young coalition protesting this venerable system its sudden force? They have grounds only to be concerned with copyright's efficiency relative to the processes and machines that have temporarily outrun it, something that can be easily corrected by the application of these very machines and processes to bring it up to their speed. You would think that this would obviate the necessity for their activism, let alone its groundswell. But it hasn't.

I understood why, when I realized that when I think of them I cannot help but think of California. They are everywhere, from Boise to Trondheim, Barcelona, and back, but whenever they come up an image appears before me associatively of palm trees, strip malls, golden hills that reel under searingly blue skies, and surfboards strapped to purple Volkswagens driven by skinny boys with nineteenth-century French facial hair. I asked myself why I invariably associate the tormentors of copyright with these pictures. Is it because, when I lived in California in the late sixties it seemed so much like another planet, cut off from the history and culture of the East (not just the East Coast, but Europe and everything else all the way to China)? Is it because so many there have taken the opportunity to wipe civilization's slate until it is squeaky clean, and that after they have done this there is in fact nothing on the slate? That in such a gorgeous place there is a contagious mental vacuum as deadly and dangerous as a black hole? That it is, as I used to call it, beauty and the abyss?

Actually not. It was much simpler than that, it was just the recurring image of the surfboards. A surfer is a skilled rider who achieves his transit and momentum through no force of his own—which in this case would be argument—but by opportunistically taking advantage of a wave. The wave here, like the tremendous waves that in some seasons strike the north coast of Oahu, is the technology that has washed almost without resistance over much of modern life.

The changes that have come in train make the destruction of the copyright system not only feasible but easy. The argument has not created the capability, the capability has created the argument. It was the same in Macaulay's time, though on a lesser scale, when he protested, in his way, in reaction to the advent of mass printing techniques and an expansion in the reach and transmissibility of information analogous to that which we are now experiencing.

Flush with money and power, the keepers and users of the new machines and processes (whether giant corporations like Google portraying themselves as selflessly centralizing information within their control, or individuals high on their ability to summon information and images from all over the world without effort or, they may think, price) fund, organize, and carry out attacks upon the old system. Is it not ironic that their motto is rage against the machine, when in fact they rage in behalf of the machine? And is it not ironic that those who protest against what they misidentify as the monopoly of copyright are aiding the centralization of information by Google, which may become the most powerful monopoly the world has ever seen? It is, and they are, despite the fact that their battle cry is, "Down with monopoly."

They are now entering a particularly aggressive phase, suing holders of copyright for the temerity of asserting their rights under law. As one violator who is suing Universal Music Publishing Group for "abusing copyright law" puts it: "I don't like being made to feel afraid, and I don't like being bullied." Or as a couple who make their living by pirating copyrighted images states: "They think we are just some country bumpkins they can push around. This is our livelihood, and we stick up for ourselves." These kinds of people are aided, abetted, and stimulated by groups such as Public Knowledge, Public Citizen, and the Electronic

Frontier Foundation. With the exception of Public Citizen, in these organs the power of Silicon Valley is grafted onto a "progressive" outlook by means of what progressives used to love to call (though perhaps not anymore) interlocking directorates. In regard to companies that take action against the piracy of their copyrights, a representative of Public Knowledge says: "They like to accuse their customers, the music fans and TV fans out there, of not respecting the law, but I don't think *they* respect the law."[121] (If your customers don't pay, but, rather, shoplift, they are no more your customers than your burglar is your guest.)

As even a cursory observation of politicians confirms, power makes people particularly vulnerable to the fault of human nature that tells them that if something can be done it should be done; that if there is a desire it should be fulfilled; that if there is a hunger it should be satisfied; that if there is an opportunity it should be taken. The powers in this case are the gifts of modern life, the sheer capabilities of the new technologies, and, not least, the money and success that have concentrated in the hands of the owners and directors of the new systems and machines.

The theater in which they maneuver has until now been primarily that of litigation, where they are met by corporations with interests in intellectual property. But they are both fresher and smarter than the old corporations struggling to suck air out of the previous paradigm, and their next move will almost certainly be to expand the battle to Congress, where, after defeat in the courts, they now realize the power of decision rests. They have more than enough money to buy off Congress, which as everyone knows can be had for a song, but there they will be met by an almost equal power more experienced in lobbying and cajoling. There, however, the corporate defenders of copyright (distinguishable from the corporate attackers of copyright by very little except that they are accidentally on the right side) will begin to run out of options. And there they will appear embarrassingly sclerotic, and may well lose.

They will have won in the courts, yes, and they probably will tie in lobbying and bribing Congress—which would ordinarily be enough for them to claim victory, for to be victorious the opponents of copyright have the added burden of altering the status quo. But the opponents may sweep in from the flank and catch the old guard unaware with a decisive stroke. What is the flank? Where is the vulnerability that the defenders have not taken sufficiently into account, much less fortified, as they deploy their lawyers and lobbyists? What will move the stalemate?

Congress has the ultimate power of decision, and the ultimate power over Congress is not influence or money but public opinion. The Left, the Right, and everyone in between look at Congress and they see the surface action in ordinary circumstances—money, influence, party interest. True, this is how it works, and it is how the wise and cynical alike (assuming they are not the same) will tell you that it works. But, no matter how worldly wise, cynical, and sure they may be, when public opinion coalesces, see how they run.

How often supremely confident politicians and their handlers are dethroned by this sometimes wonderful and sometimes terrible flood, and of the two sides in the question at issue, the only one working the currents, the winds, and the waves of public sentiment is the one that knows well how to ride a wave, because it has ridden one to where it is and is intoxicated with the thrill of being there.

With their agility, overflowing capital, and huge audiences, the new industries—Google alone—can shift public opinion and succeed in crippling or destroying copyright, which by its very nature is fragile and dependent upon the kind of outlying political consensus that in the modern age can rapidly be shifted by a patient and devoted minority able to gnaw like a rat. This would radically alter the culture as we have known it. The standard counter to a concern of this nature is that cultures, language, art, and anything anyone can think of to supplement the list, evolve; and that deploring the factual trajectory of things makes one reactionary, a dinosaur, rigid, unimaginative, impotent, a fascist, and a chipmunk. But one need not be a Nazi brontosaurus to question the trajectories of one's time if indeed one's time produces people who think their grandchildren are their ancestors. I return to this example out of continuing astonishment, but it is accurately representative. At a rest stop in Maryland not long ago, I heard a high school girl ask her father where they were "now" (perhaps she was related to Yogi Berra). When told "Maryland," she asked, "Is that in New Jersey?"

Nor need one be senescent to note that the middle ground has been continually pressed to the extremes, so that on one edge of what is published we have, from Edna Moisture, professor of gender studies at California State University at Uponga:

> To clarify the fascistic class burst of intra-pseudo-transgenderism, one must accept that the other is the object of the actor, and the actor is an apodeictic imagination of the object. In my *Transgender and Back: Male to Female; Female to Male—A Study of Possibly Unnecessary Surgery*, I attempt to deconstruct the false question of pointlessness in an effort to struggle against the suppressed value distinctions representational as palliatives of detrimentally invisible self-reliance in the mimesis of faux postcolonial *dependencia*. The extrapositional question is whether Ognitz is correct in her paradigmatic dissection of Eric the Red and Barbara Bush (boldly displacing Caesar and Daffy Duck) as ideal typologicals of the penis theory of the Berkeley rejectionists; cf. Ognitz's monumental (but flawed) *On Apodeictic Self-Identical Being*. p. 3, 217.

And on the other edge, from the immensely popular John Geisha, whose books are to airports what kudzu is to the banks of the Tallahatchie:

> The boy sat on the swing. He saw a dog. Here, dog, he said. Come here. The dog saw the boy. I can not come to you, boy, the dog said. I am looking at a crime. Oh, said the boy. What do you see? The dog said, I see Walter Cronkite. He has a machete. He is hitting a milkman. He is hitting a milkman with it. The milkman is yelling. The milkman is yelling stop! Oh, the boy said. I will call a police man. The dog was glad.

What used to be the center has been drawn toward such painfully idiotic extremes ever more steadily as the extremes move from strength to strength and the center quietly atrophies. As anyone in publishing can tell you, the last thirty years (strangely, since I published my first novel) have seen a Spenglerian decline. The diminished ranks of those literary readers that remain have swollen with people who read for political gratification, flattery, titillation, or to be au courant and conform properly and efficiently to what they are "supposed" to think. These are the fragile souls who buy a book with an eye to what the other people in line and the clerk who checks them out will think; the narcissists who use literature as a mirror in which to gaze lovingly at themselves or their narrowly defined brethren instead of as a window through which to see the world; and "movement" people who, like self-basting chickens, read to propagandize themselves. Their minds may run in terribly stiff gutters, but they are miraculously ductile when commanded by the supposed authorities they embrace. If you are, let us suppose, a Waponyite, how many books on Waponyism do you need to read past your orgasmic conversion? Why not read a history of France instead, or go on a picnic?

In recent decades the decline of voluntary reading has been Gibbonesque: 18 percent among college graduates in the twenty years ending in 2002, according to their self-reporting, which probably flatters them more than would the facts. Only 45 percent of college freshmen and 33 percent of college seniors read of their own volition. People fifteen to twenty-four—yet another wave of the televisioned American family— spend two-and-a-half hours a day in front of the television (which is always on) and seven minutes in voluntary reading. And when students in grades seven through twelve are reading, 35 percent of them are watching television, listening to music, playing video games, e-mailing, surfing the internet, or picking their feet in Poughkeepsie. Perhaps not surprisingly, according to the definition of the U.S. Department of Education's National Center for Education Statistics, in 2003 only 13 percent of all adults and 31 percent of college graduates were proficient in reading prose, the latter representing a 23 percent decline since 1992.[122]

I provide these statistics because they quantify what is obvious even to skeptics, who will anyway say that when people were more literate we had slavery and child labor, and women couldn't vote. In 1960? It is quite true that when I was a child other children got polio and now they don't, but this improvement is not a function of the decline in literacy. When faced with the accusation that the machines and new practices of information/entertainment are to a large extent stupefying the culture, their exponents (particularly those who are making money hand over foot) protest that they are in fact enriching it. Apparently, of the hundred chief benefits to humanity, the digital revolution is responsible for a thousand. The force that drove the tobacco companies to claim for at least half a century that smoking is good for health was not the ignorance they now rush to claim but the dollar about which they still don't want to speak. To assert that the atomization of attention spans, the degradation of concentration, the triumph of the image over the word, the rise of multitasking, the surge of easy plagiarism, the destabilization of citation, and, of course, the various forms of assault upon the independent voice and the incentive to create, are an enrichment is to attempt the same sort of absurd maneuver Adolf Eichmann tried when he brazenly claimed to have expedited the acceptance of hundreds of thousands of Jews into heaven.

Much of this stuff—these games, images, the shakier tools of research as opposed to those that are useful, and the floods of ill-informed and rushed communication—dances around the heart of the matter, which is the ability closely and objectively to analyze and thoroughly understand essential and important texts. My household is bombarded by catalogs that offer material implements that one company characterizes as "tools for serious readers." That is, special chairs, stands, tablets, blotters, racks, lights, bookcases, pens, diaries, pads, clips, and much else that, apparently, frivolous readers do not need. You might buy all these things and sit surrounded by them like an astronaut surrounded by buttons and screens in a space capsule. But, to read, all you need is a book. If you want to take notes or write your own book all you need is a pencil or a pen and some paper. The rest will make you neither a better reader nor a better writer. The attributes necessary for this are not cultivated by specially colored inks and stands for custom-made cards, or knapsacks with pictures of Gerard Manley Hopkins, or clocks that tell you what time it is in Nairobi, but by something entirely immaterial and materially unreachable, in the mind and in the soul. If you rely upon accessories, electronic and otherwise, you will starve that which you are supposedly nourishing. Indeed, if you rely on them excessively, they will replace you in yourself.

Better to follow Churchill's admonition, "I am all for your using machines, but do not let them use you,"[123] because the only tools that will work for the close, careful, and informed analysis of a complex text (even the text of your life) are, in fact, invisible. They are in some ways much harder and in some ways much easier to use than something that comes in a box and is supposed to make the work attendant to literacy unnecessary. This is so, because the benefits come from the effort itself rather than from trying to outwit it. Which begs the question, why would we move in this direction with the enthusiasm of the newly converted and entranced?

The countries of the West and those of systematic Asia are variously subject to fallacies of equipment. Man has made his way up with tools, and the more advanced and mechanized his society the more faith he puts in them. In the seventies, I took up climbing. I was never much good, but I was a superb equipment handler. Had I not actually climbed, I would have been what we used to call "an equipment weenie." Maybe I *was* an equipment weenie. More recently and more appropriately to my age, I've taken up fly fishing. Looking back at my climbing days, I recognized the danger and decided to avoid weeniedom as much as possible. You can see investment bankers and the like clanking down to the stream as heavily laden with equipment as if Orvis made Sammy

Davis Jr.'s gold chains. Were they to slip on the mossy rocks over which their felt-soled British waders are supposed to take them without incident, they would sleep with the fishes after being pulled under by their thirty-thousand-dollars'-worth of clothing and tackle. They are often so heavily accoutered that they may not be able to tell that they're outdoors (if they can actually get out the door). Although my Yeatsian dream of cutting a switch and using it and thread to best the guys from Goldman Sachs has proved impractical, I did buy the cheapest and most incomplete set of equipment that works, and it feels better that way. The equipment is responsible to me, not vice versa. I don't have to give it a thought, and instead can concentrate on the elusive fish. Nor was it necessary to float a bond issue.

This is not surprising to me, in that I've always run fastest in my oldest shoes. At the Rivanna Rowing Club in Albemarle County is a man who has won first place in his age group at the Head of the Charles Regatta five or six times. The racing shell in which he triumphed was worn and unfancy. Surrounded by glistening gel-coated sharks with Ferrari-like rigging, his boat looked unimpressive. But with him in it, no one in his class could catch him. Perhaps he might have gained a few more seconds had he had a boat three times as expensive as the one he had, and perhaps not. More likely, the relaxed feel of his battered shell and the opportunity to focus not on it but on the race itself afforded him more than just a few extra seconds of speed. And in reading, writing, and understanding the world in its richness and truth, equipment is of far less moment than it is in a rowing race, though the conventional wisdom is evolving as if the opposite were true.

We move in this false direction because we accumulate materials and power for their own sake and as a result of impulse rather than thought. The new machines and new processes bring at least the illusion of exactly the kind of powers for which people hunger as if for opium. And yet the accumulation of things or power is one of the most efficient destroyers of happiness, running close on the heels of poverty, disease, and death. We look back with perhaps the greatest affection at those times in our lives when often we had the least, times of a certain austerity when the story was authentic and love and beauty apparent, clear, and accessible. Not the deprivation that weakens and kills, and not austerity imposed purely by circumstance or from above (although it is possible to make use of these in the same way) but the austerity of our own will, in which life can be made richer and its colors deepened by refusing that which dilutes and obscures it. Choosing to be always connected, to do a thousand things at once, to have "everything" available instantly, to skip at great speed from subject to subject and person to person, is to model oneself after a machine, to take on its attributes and, by necessity, to leave behind many of the qualities of being human. Electronic loneliness is truly insidious, because it seems like its opposite. The new "connectedness," though it may appear to be a broad snowfield welcoming one ahead, is rather a paper-thin crust over a black crevasse.

Whereas the ability to gather and manipulate information has increased by orders of magnitude, the effect on the ability to synthesize and integrate it has been nil. The new oceans of fact and data thus overload the unaltered talents of synthesis, distorting or, in some cases, breaking them. Thus overwhelmed by the machine, many have turned to it for relief. It only gets them in deeper. If the machine is uncomfortable with certain of the old ways, they clear them from its path, and in so doing they serve its cause and promote its implacable progress.

Although bluntly and petulantly insisting upon an unfettered right to property that is not one's own appears closely correlated with this servitude, such a metastasized sense of entitlement has multiple causes. There is the common illusion, one of the chief tools in appealing for votes, that wealth arises without effort or risk, and one is entitled to it mainly by having been born. One votes in that case for the candidate who promises to divide up the self-generating pie equally, and if someone complains that his labor is unjustly appropriated his petition is filed and neglected under greed in regard to ill-gotten gains. This sense of entitlement is long suffused into the American bone, but as wealth does not in fact come from a fountain, every material entitlement enjoyed by one person is an obligation suffered by another: an almost mathematical truth that the pridefully "generous" must of necessity ignore.

As the movement against copyright is notably youthful, it is perhaps unsurprising that a sense of entitlement drives it. A young person, having spent most years of his life with others providing for him rather than the other way around, easily mistakes this for the natural order, and may, when it begins to fall away, become incensed and try heroically to "restore" it via various forms of protest. Many, living within the university, a privileged semi-socialist anomaly sustained from without by the wealth of the market economy it disdains, think not only that living thusly should be the mandated state of the world, but that it is.

And, then, the deeply held belief that the work of the intellect and spirit cannot in any way but obscenely be treated as property may come from more than half a century of intensive, pattern-forming education in this premise as actuality. Previous generations paid far more often for what current generations now call "content." Movies, vaudeville, theater, news, and music were until relatively recently not available for "free" on radio and television. Even as radio and television took hold in the formative period from the late twenties through the early sixties, the proportion of overall news and entertainment for which one had to pay directly was greater than now in a "free media" universe.

New generations progressively more and more media saturated have been more and more habituated to pay via their toleration of constant interruption and intrusion, and in the generally higher prices that cover the high costs of ubiquitous advertising. That, rather than targeted dollars, is the currency extracted from them. The habit has been inbred until it is their instinct, leading them en masse to believe that paying directly is a repugnant scam equivalent to forcing someone to pay for the air he breathes. Indeed, "content" is so pervasive for someone bathed in a world of continuous multiple inputs that it must seem very much like air. Thus, breathing in and breathing out as nature intended may explain, for example, why in this country it is estimated that 21 percent of all software in use is pirated.[124] It cannot be merely greed or opportunism that generates theft on such a massive scale that its adherents and sympathizers want to recalibrate law and the norms of civilization to accommodate it. It must be ever more intense, rapid, and destructive acculturation.

Among other things, as intemperate revolutions often do, without adjustment this revolution will destroy the dream it advocates. By insistence upon unhindered access without regard for rights and incentives that have been carefully balanced over centuries, the hurried new order will diminish the substance over which it demands sovereignty. It will have its access, but, as time passes, to less and less, and eventually perhaps to almost nothing, the means having grossly overpowered the ends. The past may be brilliantly cataloged and made accessible as never before, but at the cost of making the culture of the present relatively barren. Though it may never be entirely extinguished, it can be made as eerily quiet as if without the beat of a single heart.

We can turn the whole world into the most wonderful museum imaginable, overcoming problems of time, space, and distribution that only recently were considered insoluble. Culture, though, is not something to which you can buy a ticket, even the miraculous ticket now on its way. It is not something to be viewed in a museum, read on a page, bought, owned, or possessed in any form. To believe that it can be is a mistake in more than just nomenclature on the part of "consumers" of culture, which is a thing that cannot be consumed. What they mistake for culture is in fact its product. Culture is the activity, atmosphere, surroundings, knowledge, conditions, understandings, assumptions, predilections, accidents, necessities, and events that create the things you can buy a ticket to see, or take home in a canvas bag silk-screened with a picture of Jane Austen. Culture is to what is widely mistaken for culture as fishing is to fish. As such, it cannot be appropriated, and, if it is to stay alive, it cannot be handled with a summary upending of the rather delicate mechanisms—copyright being one—that over the centuries have evolved to sustain it.

Recently, in the horse country west of Washington, D.C., a stable of thoroughbreds made the news. Obviously, their owner had gone to some trouble to obtain them. Stables of thoroughbreds don't simply appear. But then, either because he lost some capacity within himself or just fell out of love, he decided—and it was in fact a decision on one level or another and not just neglect—not to feed them. Taking care of horses costs money, requires diligence, and courts trouble. In the end, he no longer paid out, so he had his money and he had his thoroughbreds, but their skin was stretched tight over their bones, they were covered with sores and wounds from fighting each other for the stubble in their paddocks, their legs were like fragile reeds, and they moved slowly and painfully as if close to death. Perhaps when the owner first withheld their feed and he had the delight of both money and beautiful horses he imagined that he could do anything, that they would remain beautiful, that his wilfulness would exact no price. But, of course, it did.

Hardly am I saying that there isn't good in the new forms or bad in the old, but that a mindless embrace of either leads to the acceptance of anything whatsoever in one and the rejection without merit of the other. This tendency, in part the product of embittered and joyful partisanship, undermines the belief that judgments and standards are necessary. In the case of the rush to faith in the machine, and by putting trust merely in what is new or next, it nurtures the view that truth cannot exist independently of fashion or consensus, and that truth is therefore malleable and defined purely or primarily by power.

In this regard, the quick and dirty mobilization made possible by the internet, if applied to the workings of political decision, would result in a choice as wrong as the Romans made when they abandoned the Republic. Were Ross Perot's now seemingly ancient proposal for instant electronic referenda to be realized, as it now so easily could be, it would threaten the republican form of government and its essential moderating mechanisms, which rely upon time, consideration, and the principles and conscience of each elected representative, to filter out frenzies, crazes, and panics. We are rapidly building a nation in which, intoxicated, we will have no chance to regret in the morning what, intoxicated, we did the night before.

The subjects of my criticism will protest that they do judge soberly and that they are not pushed to their opinions by the quick-rising squalls of mass enthusiasm or drawn to them by the sudden and giddy powers they now exercise. But the evidence does not support them. Their newly acquired powers have made them careless and coarse, and, in their enjoyment and anticipation of what they have and what they wish for, they now appear like all those whom power corrupts.

Though they are only masters of the surface, if that, they expect to master the universe, and masters of the universe need never compromise. What a pity, because to some extent the very powers that desensitize them can be applied to heal the wounds they have made. It is necessary to go into the new world, as we shall, but to keep faith with the humanity and achievements of the old. Above all, this demands a reversal of the process in which people have begun to model themselves according to the virtues and behaviors of machines. But perhaps this is too much to expect. Revolutions are characteristically violent. They arise from hope, and, with few exceptions, go on to destruction. And never have revolutionaries drunk on revolution been the best judges and guides of mankind, even though they never fail to think they are, and readily present themselves as such.

The revolutionaries of copyright are simply a subset of the machine revolution, and though in mien they are the diluted shadows of their predecessors, they are spiritually much the same. For the rights of authorship that have developed over time and as the world has changed are part of and an achievement of civilization. An assault upon them is an attack on one narrow front against civilization itself, and is accomplished by civilization's malcontents—who would destroy it without consideration as they accumulate intoxicating powers; who would destroy it out of self-indulgent grievance; who would politely destroy it by radical amendment; who would destroy it capriciously; or who are simply caught in the tide of others.

Perhaps the whole of modern times can be said to be a flirtation with force, regimentation, stress, and power, subjecting frail human bodies and emotions to the limits and strains appropriate to steel, ceramic, engines, and blast furnaces. It need not be so. It should not be so, if only because, to cite Montaigne, "Nature always gives us happier laws than those we give ourselves."[125]

The new, digital barbarism is, in its language, comportment, thoughtlessness, and obeisance to force and power, very much like the old. And like the old, and every form of tyranny, hard or soft, it is most vulnerable to a bright light shone upon it. To call it for what it is, to examine it while paying no heed to its rich bribes and powerful coercions, to contrast it to what it presumes to replace, is to begin the long fight against it.

Very clearly, the choice is between the preeminence of the individual or of the collective, of improvisation or of routine, of the soul or of the machine. It is a choice that perhaps you have already made, without knowing it. Or perhaps it has been made for you. But it is always possible to opt in or out, because your affirmations are your own, the court of judgment your mind and heart. These are free, and you are the sovereign, always. Choose.

NOTES

1. C. P. Cavafy, "Expecting the Barbarians," in *The Complete Poems of Cavafy*, ed. & trans. Rae Dalven (New York: Harcourt Brace, 1961), p. 18.
2. Charles de Gaulle, *The Army of the Future* (Philadelphia: Lippincott, 1934), p. 109.
3. Mark Helprin, "© Inequity," in *Claremont Review of Books*, Summer 2007. Previously published as "A Great Idea Lasts Forever. Shouldn't Its Copyright?" (title supplied by the editors), *New York Times*, Op-Ed, May 20, 2007. The texts of the two pieces are similar except for some stylistic changes made by the *Times* and an example or two that ran in the *Claremont Review of Books* and not the *Times*. The piece was syndicated by the *Times* in the *International Herald Tribune* and other places where the editors exercised their prerogative of changing the title, and may have made editorial changes to the text without the author's knowledge.
4. Winston S. Churchill, *Marlborough: His Life and Times, Book One* (Chicago: University of Chicago Press, 2002), p. 571.
5. Should Authors Hold Copyrights Forever?" *gawker.com/news/ask-an-expert*, May 24, 2007.
6. Robert Harley, First Earl of Oxford, *Portland Papers, Report of the Royal Historical Manuscripts Commission*, IV. p. 625.
7. *Statistical Abstract of the United States, 2001*, Washington, D.C., Tables 1137, 1139, 1140. *Statistical Abstract of the United States, 2008*, Washington, D.C., Tables 1107, 1109, 1096, 1111, 990.
8. Matthew Humphries, "Piracy of Books on the Increase," *geek.com*, July 3, 2008.
9. Edward McCoyd, quoted in Matthew Humphries, "Piracy of Books on the Increase." *geek.com*, July 3, 2008.
10. James Boyle, "Smarter than Jefferson?" in *Financial Times, ft.com*, May 21, 2007.
11. "Copyright Without End, Amen," in *The Wired Campus, Chronicle of Higher Education, chronicle.com*, May 21, 2007.
12. "Arguing for Infinite Copyright . . . Using Copied Ideas and a Near-Total Misunderstanding of Property," Section 1, *Techdirt, techdirt.com*, May 21, 2007.
13. Posting No. 12 in reply to Mike Nizza, "To the Editor: Please See Wiki," *The Lede, thelede.blogs, nytimes.com*, May 21, 2007.
14. Posting 3:41 in "Oh no you didn't," *Voice of Reason, missnemesis.blogspot.com*, May 24, 2007.

15. Comment by "Peep," in Matthew Yglesias, "Copyright Forever," *Atlantic Online, atlantic.com*, May 21, 2007.

16. Barry Posen, "Command of the Commons," *International Security*, Summer 2003, p. 5.

17. Captain James H. Patton Jr., USN (Ret), "Dominance," *Proceedings of the United States Naval Institute*, June 2008.

18. Hon. Robert F. Gates, Secretary of Defense, Speech at Maxwell AFB, Alabama, April 21, 2008.

19. *Webster's Third New International Dictionary.*

20. Letter to the author from Edwin Frank, *The New York Review of Books*, May 21, 2007.

21. "New Home for History Faculty," in "University News," *Oxford Today*, Vol. 20, No. 1, Michaelmas 2007, p. 9.

22. John C. Briggs, "Statecraft and Wordcraft," *Claremont Review of Books*, Summer 2007, page 31.

23. Frank Ahrens, "An Egghead With Bold Threads," *Washington Post*, July 14, 2008.

24. "Copyright Without End, Amen," in *The Wired Campus; Chronicle of Higher Education*, *chronicle.com*, May 21, 2007.

25. Courtois et al., *The Black Book of Communism* (Cambridge: Harvard University Press, 1999), p.151: caption, plate 10.

26. "Against Perpetual Copyright," Section 1,*Lawrence Lessig Wiki, wiki.lessig.org*, May 24, 2007.

27. Mike Nizza, "To the Editor: Please See Wiki," *The Lede, thelede.blogs, nytimes.com*, May 21, 2007.

28. Siva Vaidhyanathan, "Write Your Own Response To Mark Helprin's Perpetual Copyright Op-Ed," *sivacracy.net*, May 21, 2007.

29. Mike Nizza, "To the Editor: Please See Wiki," *thelede.blogs, nytimes.com*, May 21, 2007.

30. Boyle, "Smarter than Jefferson?"

31. "Against Perpetual Copyright," Section 4, *Lawrence Lessig Wiki, wiki.lessig.org*, May 24, 2007.

32. "Arguing for Infinite Copyright," Section 20, *techdirt.com*, May 21, 2007.

33. Comment by "Anon," in Matthew Yglesias, "Copyright Forever," *Atlantic Online, atlantic.com*, May 21, 2007.

34. Lynne Jolitz, in Mike Nizza, "To the Editor: Please See Wiki," *The Lede, thelede.blogs, nytimes.com*, May 21, 2007.

35. William Barber, in "I Wrote It. Is It Mine For All Time?" *nytimes.com*, May 20, 2007.

36. "Against Perpetual Copyright," Section 3, *Lawrence Lessig Wiki, wiki.lessig.org*, May 24, 2007.

37. "Arguing for Infinite Copyright," Section 27, *techdirt.com*, May 21, 2007.

38. "Bridging the Intellectual Property Divide," in BC, *Blogcritics Magazine, blogcritics.org*, May 22, 2007.

39. "On the Helprin Reply: Wow," in *Lessig Blog, lessig.org*, May 31, 2007.

40. Boyle, "Smarter than Jefferson?"

41. Mark Draughn, "Eternal Copyright," in *windypundit.com*, May 27, 2007.

42. "Arguing for Infinite Copyright," Section 12, *techdirt.com*, May 21, 2007.

43. John Betjeman, "Reproof Deserved, or, After the Lecture," in *Collected Poems* (Boston: Houghton Mifflin, 1971), p.358.

44. Rev. Michael David Knowles, "Macaulay, Thomas Babington," in *Encyclopaedia Britannica*, 15th ed.

45. Thomas Babington Macaulay, Speech in the House of Commons, February 5, 1841, Hansard, 3d Series, Vol. LVI, pp. 344–357, in *Speeches by the Rt. Hon. Thomas Babington Macaulay, M. P.,* Vol 1, (New York: C.B. Norton, 1853), p. 390.

46. "Arguing for Infinite Copyright," Section 2, *techdirt.com,* May 21, 2007.

47. "Arguing for Infinite Copyright," Section 25, *techdirt.com,* May 21, 2007.

48. "Arguing for Infinite Copyright," *techdirt.com,* May 21, 2007.

49. "Arguing for Infinite Copyright," Section 10, *techdirt.com,* May 21, 2007.

50. Comment by "Constantine," in Matthew Yglesias, "Copyright Forever," *Atlantic Online, the atlantic.com,* May 21, 2007.

51. "Arguing for Infinite Copyright," Section 36, *techdirt.com,* May 21, 2007.

52. "Arguing for Infinite Copyright," *techdirt.com,* May 21, 2007.

53. C. P. Cavafy, "The Inkwell," in *The Complete Poems of Cavafy,* p. 191.

54. Howard Daniel, *Hieronymus Bosch* (New York: Hyperion, 1947).

55. Marlborough's Letter to Godolphin, August 30, 1703, in Winston S. Churchill, *Marlborough: His Life and Times, Book One,* p. 683.

56. Boyle, "Smarter than Jefferson?"

57. Samuel Johnson, as quoted in James Boswell, *The Life of Samuel Johnson,* ed. Christopher Hibbert (London: Penguin), p. 209.

58. Samuel Johnson, as quoted in Boswell, *The Life of Samuel Johnson,* p. 47.

59. Boswell, *The Life of Samuel Johnson,* p. 82.

60. Thomas Babington Macaulay, Speech in the House of Commons, February 5, 1841, Hansard, 3d Series, Vol. LVI, pp. 344–357, in *Speeches by the Rt. Hon. Thomas Babington Macaulay, M.P.,* Vol 1, p.389.

61. Ibid., pp. 392, 393.

62. Ibid., p. 393.

63. Ibid., p. 395.

64. Ibid., p. 397.

65. Ibid., p. 394.

66. Ibid., p. 394.

67. Supreme Court of the United States, No. 01–618, Eric Eldred, et al., Petitioners v. John D. Ashcroft, Attorney General, January 15, 2003, Breyer, J., dissenting, IIA.

68. Boswell, *The Life of Samuel Johnson,* p. 391.

69. Supreme Court of the United States, No. 01–618, Eric Eldred, et al., Petitioners v. John D. Ashcroft, Attorney General, January 15, 2003, Stevens, J., dissenting, VII.

70. *The Shorter Oxford English Dictionary,* 3rd ed., revised, see under "Monopoly" (English language italics supplied.)

71. Thomas Babington Macaulay, Speech in the House of Commons, February 5, 1841, Hansard, 3rd series, Vol. LVI, pp. 344–357, in *Speeches by the Rt. Hon. Thomas Babington Macaulay, M.P.,* Vol 1, p. 392.

72. Ibid., p. 402.

73. Ibid.

74. *Encyclopaedia Britannica,* 15th ed., see under "Publishing, History of."

75. Jeffrey Goldfarb, "Bookish Britain Overtakes America as Top Publisher," *Reuters,* May 10, 2006.

76. Ibid.

77. "Book Production, Number of Titles by UDC Classes, Total, United States,1996," *Unesco Institute of Statistics, stats.uis.unesco.org,* and Jeffrey Goldfarb, "Bookish Britain Overtakes America as Top Publisher."

78. "Book Production, Number of Titles by UDC Classes, Total, Peru, 1998," *Unesco Institute of Statistics, stats.uis.unesco.org.*

79. "Book Production, Number of Titles by UDC Classes, Total, Republic of Korea 1996," *Unesco Institute of Statistics, stats.uis.unesco.org.*

80. "Spain: Communications and Media," *Europa World Yearbook,* Vol. II, London, 1998, p. 3, 109.

81. For all figures relating to the Library of Congress, see "The Collections," in *Jefferson's Legacy, A Brief History of the Library of Congress, loc.gov/loc/legacy,* August 24, 2007.

82. "An Act for the Encouragement of Learning, by Vesting the Copies of Printed Books in the Author's or Purchasers of Such Copies," 8 Anne, c. 19 (1709); in Philip B. Kurland, and Ralph Lerner, eds., *The Founders' Constitution,* Vol. 3 (Chicago: University of Chicago Press, 2000), p. 36.

83. Publius (James Madison); in *The Federalist Papers,* No. XLIII, edited and with an introduction by Isaac Kramnick (London: Penguin, 1987), p. 279.

84. Joseph Story, *Commentaries on the Constitution of the United States,* Vol. 3: §§ 1147–50, (Boston: Hillard, Gray, 1833), italics supplied.

85. *The Encyclopaedia Britannica,* 11th ed., see under "Copyright."

86. Supreme Court of the United States, No. 01–618, Eric Eldred, et al., Petitioners v. John D. Ashcroft, Attorney General, January 15, 2003, Ginsburg, J., writing for the majority.

87. Noam Cohen, "Taking the Copyright Fight Into a New Arena," *New York Times, nytimes. com,* July 2, 2007.

88. Ibid.

89. *The Encyclopaedia Britannica,* 11th ed., see under "Copyright."

90. *The Encyclopaedia Britannica,* 15th ed., see under "Copyright Law."

91. "Copyright Without End, Amen," in "The Wired Campus," *Chronicle of Higher Education, chronicle.com,* May 21, 2007.

92. "On the Helprin Reply: Wow," in *Lessig Blog, lessig.org,* May 31, 2007.

93. "Against Perpetual Copyright," Section 5.2; *The Lawrence Lessig Wiki, wiki.lessig.org,* May 24, 2007.

94. Alexander Hamilton, "Report on Manufactures, Dec. 5, 1791," in Harold C. Syrett, *The Papers of Alexander Hamilton,* Vol. 10 (New York: Columbia University Press, 1961–1979), p. 338.

95. Thomas Jefferson; Letter to Isaac McPherson, August 13, 1813, in *The Writings of Thomas Jefferson,* Vol. 13, edited by Andrew A. Lipscomb and Albert E. Bergh (Washington: Thomas Jefferson Memorial Foundation, 1905), p. 333.

96. Jason Kirk, "Coldplay and the Fallacy of Intellectual Property," in *Chord Strike, Amazonblogs,* June 19, 2008.

97. Letters in response to "© Inequity" (*Claremont Review of Books,* Summer 2007), in *Claremont Review of Books,* Fall 2007.

98. Ibid.

99. Cohen, "Taking the Copyright Fight Into a New Arena."

100. "Arguing for Infinite Copyright," Section 40, *techdirt.com*, May 21, 2007.

101. "Arguing for Infinite Copyright" Section 53, *techdirt.com*, May 21, 2007.

102. Paul A.Rahe, "The Great and the Good," *Claremont Review of Books*, Summer 2008, p.37.

103. Kim Hart, "Bethesda Start-Up Makes Writing a Little Less Lonely," *Washington Post*, April 14, 2008.

104. "On the Helprin reply: Wow," *Lessig Blog, lessig.org*, May 31, 2007.

105. Lessig, Lawrence; "Lucasfilm's Phantom Menace," *Washington Post*, July 12, 2007, p. A23.

106. *The Shorter Oxford English Dictionary*, 3rd ed, revised, italics supplied.

107. *Historical Statistics of the United States, Part 2*; Bureau of the Census, Washington, 1975, Series Y 412–439, "Individual Income Tax Liability and Effective Rates for Selected Income Groups: 1913 to 1970, p. 1, 111.

108. "Campus Journal; Evolution of a Protestor: From Gun to Governing," *New York Times*, April 7, 1993.

109. Thomas Jefferson to James Madison, October 28, 1785; in Julian P. Boyd, ed.; *The Papers of Thomas Jefferson*, Vol. 8 (Princeton: Princeton University Press, 1950), p. 681.

110. Shakespeare, *The Merchant of Venice* (Baltimore: Pelican, 1959), IV.1.373.

111. Alistair Horne, *La Belle France* (New York: Hyperion, 2006), p. 53, italics supplied.

112. John Henderson, "Students Get Crash Course in Sciences at UVa Camp," *Daily Progress* (Charlottesville), July 19, 2008.

113. Kim Hart and Sabrina Valle, "Hype Meets Reality At iPhone's Debut," *Washington Post*, June 30, 2007.

114. Nigella Lawson, *How to Be a Domestic Goddess* (New York: Hyperion, 2001).

115. "The Easy Way to Be a Domestic Goddess," *Women's Health*, June 2008, p. 162.

116. Address of Sir Samuel Hoare, March 10, 1939, in Alfred Havighurst, *Britain in Transition, The Twentieth Century* (Chicago: University of Chicago Press, 1985), p. 276.

117. Lord Halifax's Memorandum of March 10, 1938; in Alfred Havighurst, *Britain in Transition, The Twentieth Century*, p. 272.

118. Prime Minister Neville Chamberlain in the House of Commons, September 3, 1939; in Alfred Havighurst, *Britain in Transition, The Twentieth Century*, p. 284.

119. Thomas Hardy, "The Convergence of the Twain (Lines on the loss of the *Titanic*)," in G. M. Young, ed., *Selected Poems of Thomas Hardy* (London: Macmillan, 1968), p. 44.

120. William Butler Yeats, "There," in *The Collected Poems of William Butler Yeats: Definitive Edition With the Author's Final Revisions* (New York: Macmillan, 1956), p. 284.

121. Catherine Rampell, "Standing Up To Takedown Notices," *Washington Post*, October 19, 2007.

122. National Endowment for the Arts; *To Read or Not To Read, A Question of National Consequence*, Research Report No. 47, Washington, D.C., 2007, pp. 1–20.

123. Martin Gilbert, *Winston S. Churchill, Volume VIII, 'Never Despair'* (Boston: Houghton Mifflin, 1988), p. 1, 170.

124. Associated Press, "Small Business in the Cross Hairs of Software Industry," *Daily Progress* (Charlottesvlle), November 26, 2007, p. 1.

125. Michel de Montaigne, "Of Experience," in *Selected Essays*, ed. & trans. Donald M. Frame (Princeton: Princeton University Press, 1943), p. 293.

INDEX